RECEIVED
26 AUG 2011
FROM RBLC

D1395444

AMERICAN ILLUSTRATION 3

AMERICAN ILLUSTRATION 3

Edited by Edward Booth-Clibborn

The third annual of American editorial, book, advertising, poster, unpublished work, film animation, and promotional art

American Illustration, Inc.
67 Irving Place
New York, New York 10003

Managing Editor: Lita Telerico

Captions and artwork in this book have been supplied by the entrants.

If you are a practicing illustrator, artist, or student and would like to submit work to the next annual competition write to:
American Illustration, Inc.
67 Irving Place
New York, New York 10003
(212) 460-5558

Distributed in the United State of America and Canada by
Harry N. Abrams, Inc.
100 Fifth Avenue
New York, New York 10011
ISBN 0-8109-1821-8

Distributed in the United Kingdom by:
Columbus Books
24 Elmfield Road
Bromley Kent, England

Book trade inquiries for the rest of the world:
Fleet Books
100 Park Avenue
New York, New York 10017

Printed and bound in Japan by Toppan Printing Company

Paper: 128 GSM matte coated

Display Type: Clarendon Bold

Text Type: Caslon

Typesetting and Mechanicals: The Seven Graphic Arts

CONTENTS

THE JURY

Bob Ciano
ART DIRECTOR, *LIFE*, NEW YORK
Bob Ciano studied design with Alexei Brodovitch. He has been working for 18 years and has had 13 jobs.

Patrick JB Flynn
ART DIRECTOR, *THE PROGRESSIVE*, MADISON
Patrick Flynn is Art Director for *The Progressive*. He also has an art and design studio in Madison. Formerly he has been a publication designer for Steve Phillips Design Ltd. and Art Director for *The New York Times*, *The Runner* magazine, and Minneapolis' *Metropolis Weekly*.

Judy Garlan
ART DIRECTOR, *THE ATLANTIC MONTHLY*, BOSTON
Judy Garlan has been at *The Atlantic Monthly* since 1981. Previously she art directed other magazines including *Art News* and *Cue* and served as a special design consultant for *Time*. She recently co-authored a children's cookbook and a humor book. Ms. Garlan has received recognition and awards from International Editorial Design, AIGA, the Society of Publication Designers, the Society of Illustrators, Graphis, and the Art Directors Club of New York which presented her with last year's gold medal for editorial art and illustration.

Steven Heller
ART DIRECTOR, *THE NEW YORK TIMES BOOK REVIEW*, NEW YORK
Steven Heller is the Art Director of *The New York Times Book Review*. Formerly he was Art Director of *The New York Times Op-Ed* page and *Evergreen Review*. He writes frequently on graphic arts and illustration for *Graphis*, *Print*, and *Upper & Lower Case*. He has written and edited numerous books including *Artists' Christmas Cards*, *Man Bites Man: Two Decades of Satiric Art*, *The Empire State Building Book*, *WarHeads*, *Art Against War*, *The Art of Satire*, and *The Art of New York*. With Seymour Chwast he packages books under the imprint *Push Pin Editions*.

Elton Robinson
ART DIRECTOR, *THE LAMP*, NEW YORK
Elton Robinson is Art Director of *The Lamp*. He has a BS in industrial design from the University of Michigan and a MFA from Yale. His work has appeared in *Horizon*, *Art in America*, *Holiday*, *Fortune*, *People*, *Life*, and other publications for Exxon Corporation.

Fred Woodward
ART DIRECTOR, *TEXAS MONTHLY*, AUSTIN
Prior to joining *Texas Monthly*, Fred Woodward was Art Director for *Memphis*, *D Magazine*, and the *Dallas Times Herald's* Sunday magazine, *Westward*. His work has won recognition from the Art Directors Club of New York, the Dallas Society of Visual Communications, the Type Directors Club, the Society of Illustrators, *European Illustration*, *Communication Arts*, *Graphis*, *Print*, *Folio*, *AIGA Graphic Design USA*, *Idea*, and *Creativity*. He is a frequent lecturer at various universities and professional organizations.

INTRODUCTION

Three years ago, when we first started publishing American Illustration, I was very much aware of the influence on American illustrative art of a number of émigré European illustrators who, at that time, had come to live and work in America.

Now, I'm glad to say, and I know my jury was glad to see, the true spirit of American and Canadian illustration is beginning to emerge. And what a joy it is to behold. Looking through this third annual of *American Illustration*® I'm sure you'll see work which will excite you, startle you, surprise you and even shock you, whether you're employed in the media or simply an interested watcher on the sidelines. What you'll also see is, I believe, what I might describe as some of the most dynamic art of its kind: the colloquial art of today created by people whose senses are constantly alive to the life that's around them and the world they live in. For that's what commercial illustration is, when it's practiced at its highest level.

And that, I think you'll agree, is what we have here: the highest level of commercial art.

But what is the true spirit of American illustration, and how can it be fostered?

For me, truly great illustration contains an element which, I fear, is still missing from the work in *American Illustration*®: the element of self.

To me it seems that, in far too many colleges across the States, students are being actively discouraged from developing the element of self. Instead—and as if to fulfill some dreadful idea that success as an illustrator is only measurable by the number of dollars you can amass—young people are being encouraged to produce a mass of pastiche. Indeed, far from many American illustrators being able to express the sensation of being an ape, they could only ape the image of an ape. And then only in some style which someone else seems to have deemed "American."

What's important in any art form—whether it be 'fine' or 'commercial'—is that the artist somehow finds his or her own sense of self to bring to the project. That, at its most fundamental level, is what makes one artist great and the others merely good. It's the difference between a perceptive eye and an eye for pastiche.

For my part, I sincerely hope that, encouraged by the encouragement we have given those students whose work we have published this year, both students and teachers throughout the country will go further towards the development of self. America is such a colorful tapestry I believe there must be brilliant threads within it which, given the space to stretch their limits, will produce bright, fresh images, true to the spirit of America. Then, perhaps, we will see a flowering of illustration which is true to that spirit.

In the meantime, enjoy this third annual of *American Illustration*®. It includes some fine work by Americans and Canadians and it also contains some good work by Europeans, although because of the new committee ruling it is limited to only those Europeans who are residents of the U.S.

Next year we hope *American Illustration*® will have developed yet more, so that its contents truly reflect the spirit of its name.

EDWARD BOOTH–CLIBBORN

Editorial

This section includes illustrations for newspapers and their supplements, consumer, trade and technical magazines, and periodicals

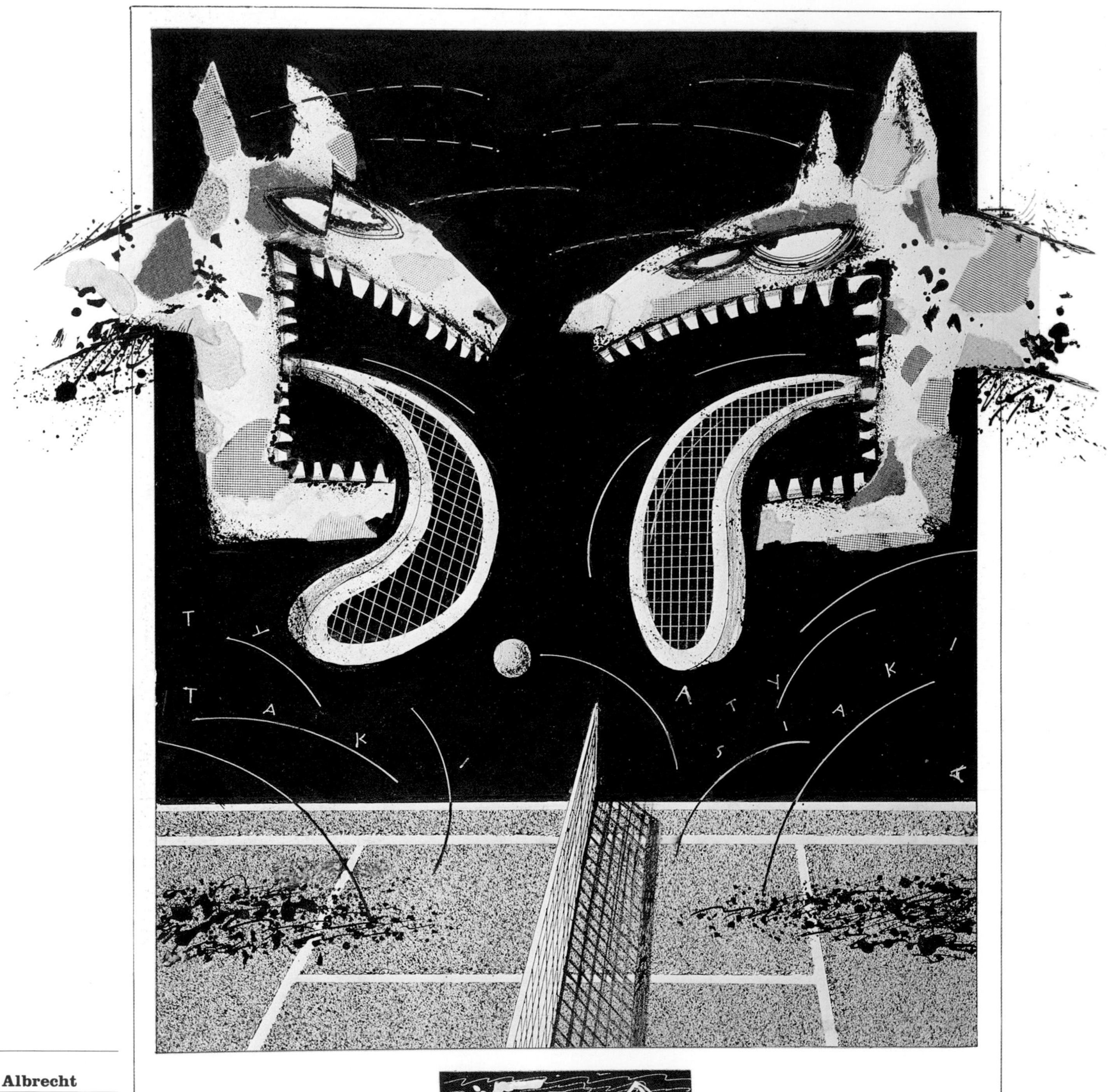

10

ARTIST
Maciek Albrecht

ART DIRECTOR
Andrea DaRif

PUBLICATION
Racquet Quarterly

PUBLISHER
Heather & Pine International Inc.

ILLUSTRATION ENTITLED "FEAR," AN ART PORTFOLIO IN *RACQUET QUARTERLY,* SPRING 1984.

Ink

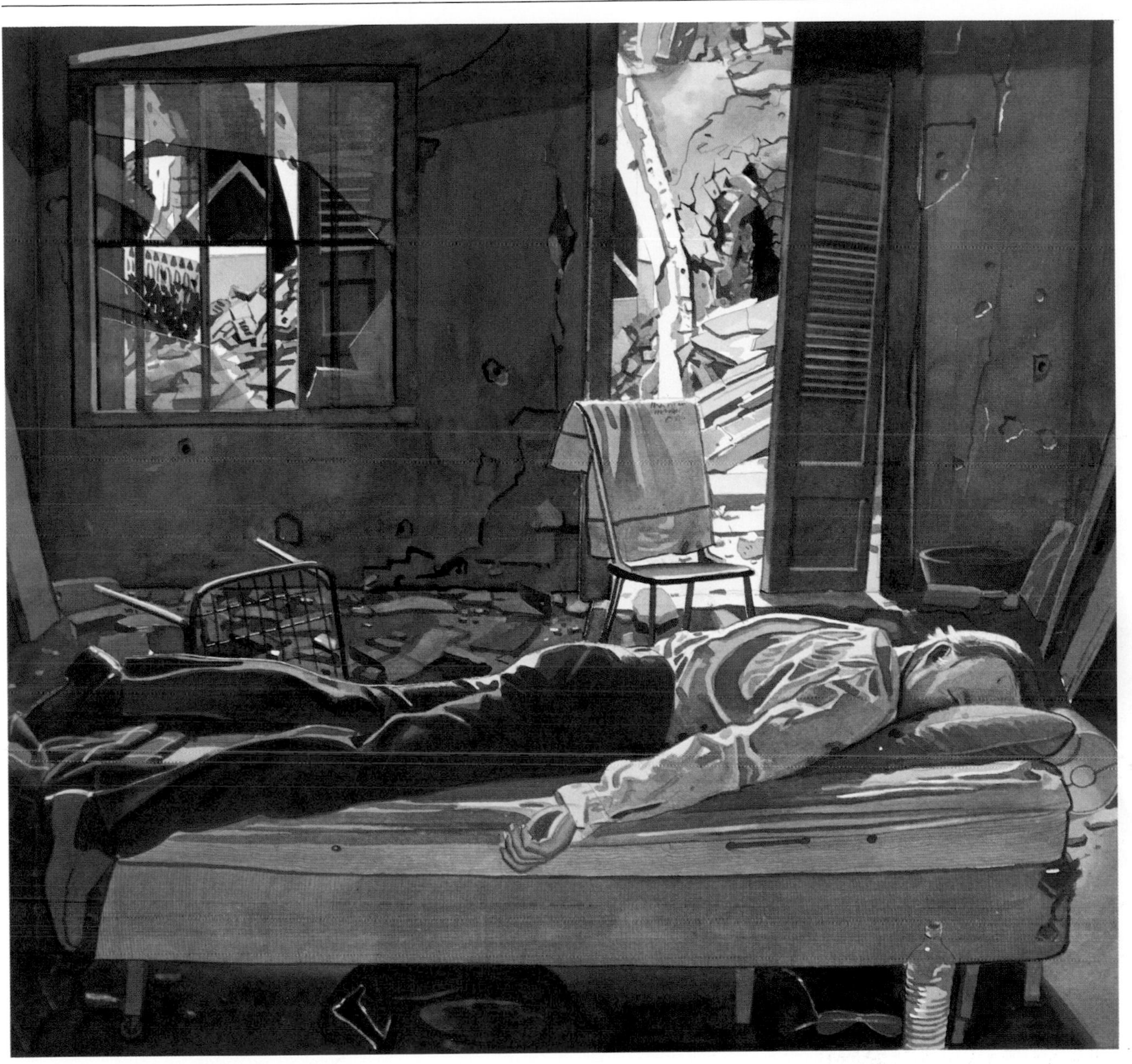

11

ARTIST
Julian Allen

DESIGNER
Jolene Cuyler

ART DIRECTOR
Louis Fishauf

PUBLICATION
Saturday Night

PUBLISHER
Saturday Night Publishing

ILLUSTRATION FOR AN ARTICLE ENTITLED "JOURNEY INTO FEAR" BY TIM KOTCHEFF IN *SATURDAY NIGHT*, FEBRUARY 1984.

Watercolor

12

ARTIST
Julian Allen

DESIGNER
April Silver

ART DIRECTOR
April Silver

PUBLICATION
Esquire

PUBLISHER
Esquire Associates

ILLUSTRATION FOR AN ARTICLE ENTITLED "THE EMIGRÉ" BY ELIZABETH HARDWICK IN *ESQUIRE*, DECEMBER 1983.

Watercolor

13

ARTIST
Julian Allen

DESIGNER
Robert Priest

ART DIRECTOR
Robert Priest

PUBLICATION
Esquire

PUBLISHER
Esquire Associates

ILLUSTRATION FOR AN ARTICLE ENTITLED "LOOKING FOR HEMINGWAY" BY GAY TALESE IN *ESQUIRE*, JUNE 1983.

Alkyd

14

ARTIST
Terry Allen

DESIGNER
Fred Woodward

ART DIRECTOR
Fred Woodward

PUBLICATION
Texas Monthly

PUBLISHER
Texas Monthly, Inc.

ILLUSTRATION FOR AN ARTICLE ENTITLED "TAKING OVER" BY NICHOLAS LEMANN IN *TEXAS MONTHLY*, OCTOBER 1983.

Airbrush and ink

15

ARTIST
Thomas B. Allen

ART DIRECTOR
Sanae Yamasaki

PUBLICATION
People Weekly

PUBLISHER
Time Inc.

ONE OF A SERIES OF ILLUSTRATIONS ABOUT A CYSTIC FIBROSIS VICTIM ENTITLED "THIS IS HOW A CHILD DIES" IN *PEOPLE WEEKLY,* OCTOBER 1983.

Watercolor

16

ARTIST
Thomas B. Allen

ART DIRECTOR
Harvey Grut

PUBLICATION
Sports Illustrated

PUBLISHER
Time Inc.

ILLUSTRATION DEPICTING A GOLDEN GLOVES BOXING DEATH FOR AN ARTICLE ENTITLED "AN ENCOUNTER TO LAST AN ETERNITY" BY FRANK DEFORD IN *SPORTS ILLUSTRATED*, APRIL 1983.

Sepia ink and watercolor

17

ARTIST
Marshall Arisman

DESIGNERS
Fred Woodward/David Kampa

ART DIRECTOR
Fred Woodward

PUBLICATION
Texas Monthly

PUBLISHER
Texas Monthly, Inc.

ILLUSTRATION SHOWING THE ARTIST'S INTERPRETATION OF THE TERM "WESTERN ART" IN *TEXAS MONTHLY,* OCTOBER 1983.

Oil on canvas

18

ARTIST
Marshall Arisman

DESIGNER
Ronn Campisi

ART DIRECTOR
Ronn Campisi

PUBLICATION
The Boston Globe Magazine

PUBLISHER
Globe Newspaper Co.

COVER ILLUSTRATION FOR A FEATURE ENTITLED "WAR GAMING" BY FRED KAPLAN FOR *THE BOSTON GLOBE MAGAZINE*, SEPTEMBER 1983.

Oil

19

ARTIST
Marshall Arisman

ART DIRECTOR
Gary Sluzewski

PUBLICATION
Cleveland Magazine

PUBLISHER
Cleveland Magazine Co.

ILLUSTRATION FOR A NON-FICTION PIECE ENTITLED "MAD BUTCHER" BY GEORGE CONDON IN *CLEVELAND MAGAZINE*, MARCH 1984.

Oil on ragboard

20

ARTIST
Kent H. Barton

DESIGNER
Kent H. Barton

ART DIRECTOR
Kent H. Barton

PUBLICATION
The Miami Herald

PUBLISHER
The Miami Herald Publishing Co. Inc.

ILLUSTRATION FOR ARTICLES ENTITLED "WATT BETRAYED HIS PARTY" BY MORRIS K. UDALL AND "WHY CONSERVATIVES ARE DISENCHANTED" BY RICHARD A. VIGUERIE IN *THE MIAMI HERALD*, OCTOBER 1983.

Scraperboard

21

ARTIST
Bascove

ART DIRECTOR
Bob Ciano

PUBLICATION
Life

PUBLISHER
Time Inc.

ILLUSTRATIONS FOR A SERIES OF COMMENTS ON SOCIAL AND POLITICAL TOPICS ENTITLED "VOICES" IN *LIFE*, DECEMBER 1983

Woodcut with watercolor

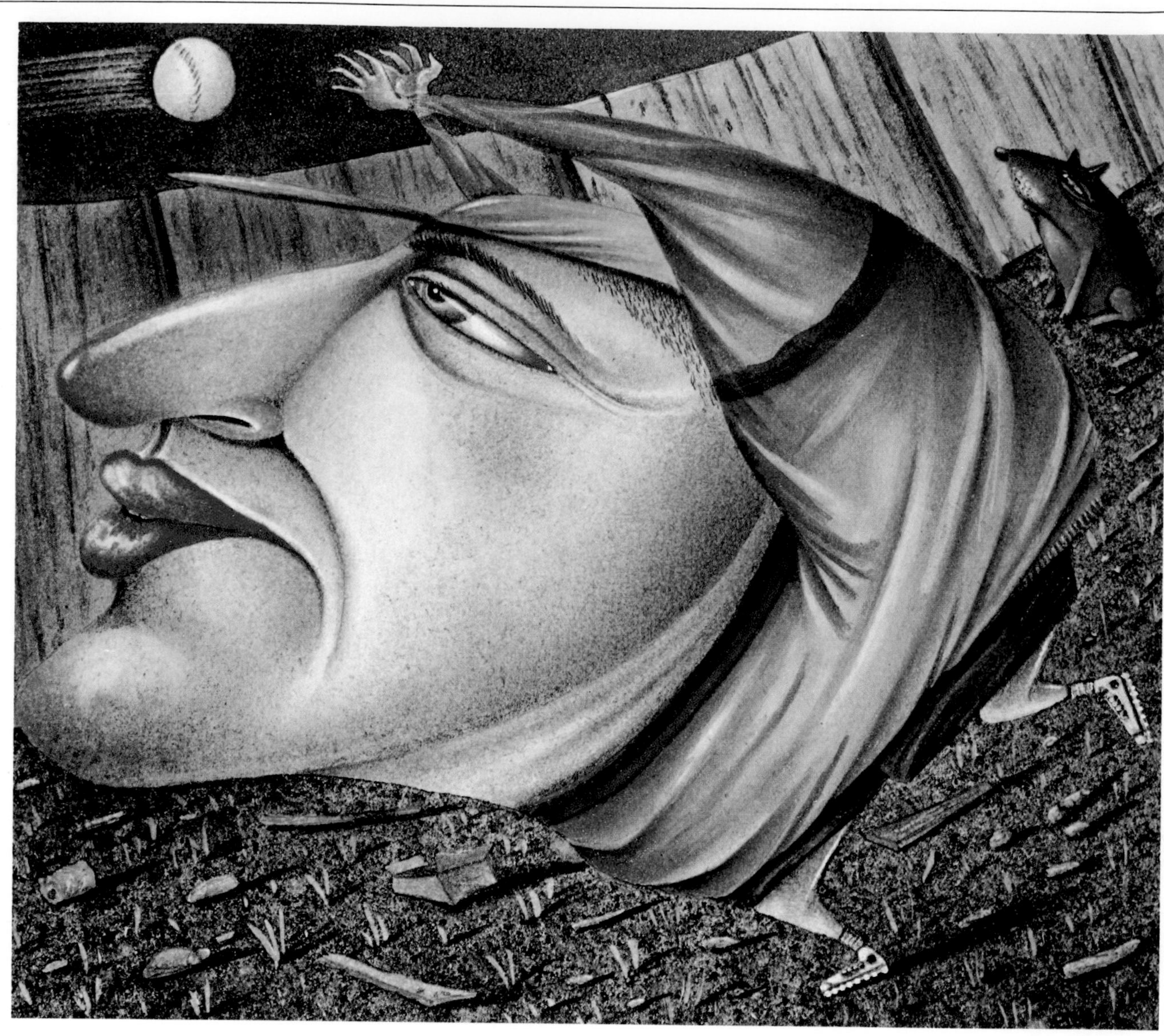

22

ARTIST
Philippe Beha

DESIGNER
Mary Opper

ART DIRECTOR
Arthur Niemi

PUBLICATION
Quest

PUBLISHER
Comac Communications Ltd.

ILLUSTRATION FOR AN ARTICLE ENTITLED "SPORTS: THE GLOVES ARE OFF; BAREHANDED SOFTBALL AND THE SUMMER OF '46" BY HARRY BRUCE IN *QUEST*, MARCH 1983.

Gouache and acrylic

23

ARTIST
Jamie Bennett

DESIGNER
Shari Spier

ART DIRECTOR
Louis Fishauf

PUBLICATION
Executive

PUBLISHER
Airmedia

ILLUSTRATION DEPICTING THE MERCANTILE REVOLUTION ENTITLED "TOWARD THE YEAR 2000" BY ROBERT ARNOLD RUSSEL IN *EXECUTIVE*, JANUARY 1984.

Mixed Media

24

ARTIST
Guy Billout

ART DIRECTOR
Dorothy Wickenden

PUBLICATION
The New Republic Magazine

PUBLISHER
The New Republic Inc.

COVER ILLUSTRATION FOR A STORY ABOUT THE DEATH PENALTY ENTITLED "CONDEMNED TO DEATH" BY DAVID BRUCK IN *THE NEW REPUBLIC MAGAZINE*, DECEMBER 1983.

Watercolor

25

ARTIST
Guy Billout

DESIGNER
Derek W. Ungless

ART DIRECTOR
Derek W. Ungless

PUBLICATION
Rolling Stone

PUBLISHER
Straight Arrow Publishers, Inc.

ILLUSTRATION FOR AN ARTICLE ENTITLED "THE ICE AGE COMETH" BY TIM CAHILL IN *ROLLING STONE*, MAY 1983.

Watercolor

26

ARTIST
Guy Billout

DESIGNERS
Patricia Bradbury/Don Morris

ART DIRECTOR
Robert Best

PUBLICATION
New York Magazine

PUBLISHER
News Group Publications, Inc.

ILLUSTRATION FOR AN ARTICLE ENTITLED "FRIENDSHIP IN THE CITY" BY LINDA WOLFE IN *NEW YORK MAGAZINE*, JULY 1983.

Watercolor

27

ARTIST
Guy Billout

DESIGNER
Judy Garlan

ART DIRECTOR
Judy Garlan

PUBLICATION
The Atlantic Monthly

PUBLISHER
The Atlantic Monthly Co.

SERIES OF FULL-PAGE PAINTINGS BY THE ARTIST APPEARING AS A REGULAR FEATURE IN *THE ATLANTIC MONTHLY.*

Watercolor

28

ARTIST
Patrick Blackwell

DESIGNER
Ronn Campisi

ART DIRECTOR
Ronn Campisi

PUBLICATION
The Boston Globe Magazine

PUBLISHER
Globe Newspaper Co.

"SEASON'S GREETINGS" CHRISTMAS DAY COVER ILLUSTRATION FOR *THE BOSTON GLOBE MAGAZINE*, DECEMBER 1983.

Watercolor

29

ARTIST
Cathie Bleck

ART DIRECTOR
James Noel Smith

PUBLICATION
Westward

PUBLISHER
Dallas Times Herald

ILLUSTRATION FOR AN ARTICLE ABOUT CATS AND CAT LOVERS ENTITLED "LETTING THE CAT OUT OF THE BAG" BY LARRY TRITTEN IN *WESTWARD*, JULY 1983.

Ink and scratchboard

30

ARTIST
Cathie Bleck

DESIGNER
James Noel Smith

ART DIRECTOR
James Noel Smith

PUBLICATION
Dallas Times Herald

PUBLISHER
Dallas Times Herald

ILLUSTRATION FOR A STORY ABOUT RAPE ENTITLED "THE MIND OF THE VICTIM" BY JENNIFER BOETH IN *DALLAS TIMES HERALD,* JUNE 1983.

Scratchboard

31

ARTIST
Braldt Bralds

DESIGNER
Judy Garlan

ART DIRECTOR
Judy Garlan

PUBLICATION
The Atlantic Monthly

PUBLISHER
The Atlantic Monthly Co.

ILLUSTRATION FOR A NON-FICTION PIECE ENTITLED "THE NAKED VULTURE AND THE THINKING APE" BY KENNETH BROWER IN *THE ATLANTIC MONTHLY*, OCTOBER 1983.

Oil

32

ARTIST
Steve Brodner

ART DIRECTOR
Patrick JB Flynn

PUBLICATION
The Progressive

PUBLISHER
The Progressive Inc.

ILLUSTRATION FOR AN ARTICLE ON HUNGER AND POVERTY ENTITLED "BRAZIL! DUNKIN' DONUTS WON'T FEED THE HUNGRY" BY DAMIAN BURNHAM IN *THE PROGRESSIVE*, FEBRUARY 1984.

Pencil, collage, India ink, and oil paint

33

ARTIST
Lou Brooks

DESIGNER
Elizabeth Williams

ART DIRECTOR
Derek W. Ungless

PUBLICATION
Rolling Stone

PUBLISHER
Straight Arrow Publishers, Inc.

ILLUSTRATION FOR AN ARTICLE ENTITLED "STRAY CATS: EIGHTIES CARTOON HEROES" BY PARKE PUTERBAUGH IN *ROLLING STONE*, OCTOBER 1983.

Pen and ink and airbrush

34

ARTIST
Christine Bunn

DESIGNER
B.J. Galbraith

ART DIRECTOR
B.J. Galbraith

PUBLICATION
Radio Guide

PUBLISHER
Saturday Night Publishing Services for the Canadian Broadcasting Corp.

PORTRAITS OF REBECCA WEST AND H.G. WELLS FOR "IN THE HEAT OF THE MORNING" BY MARK CZARNECKI IN *RADIO GUIDE*, SEPTEMBER 1983.

Chalk pastel

35

ARTIST
Christine Bunn

DESIGNER
B.J. Galbraith

ART DIRECTOR
B.J. Galbraith

PUBLICATION
Radio Guide

PUBLISHER
Saturday Night Publishing Services for the Canadian Broadcasting Corp.

PORTRAIT OF DASHIELL HAMMETT FOR AN ARTICLE ENTITLED "DASH OF HAMMETT" BY STEVEN RAUCHMAN IN *RADIO GUIDE*, DECEMBER 1983.

Prismacolor

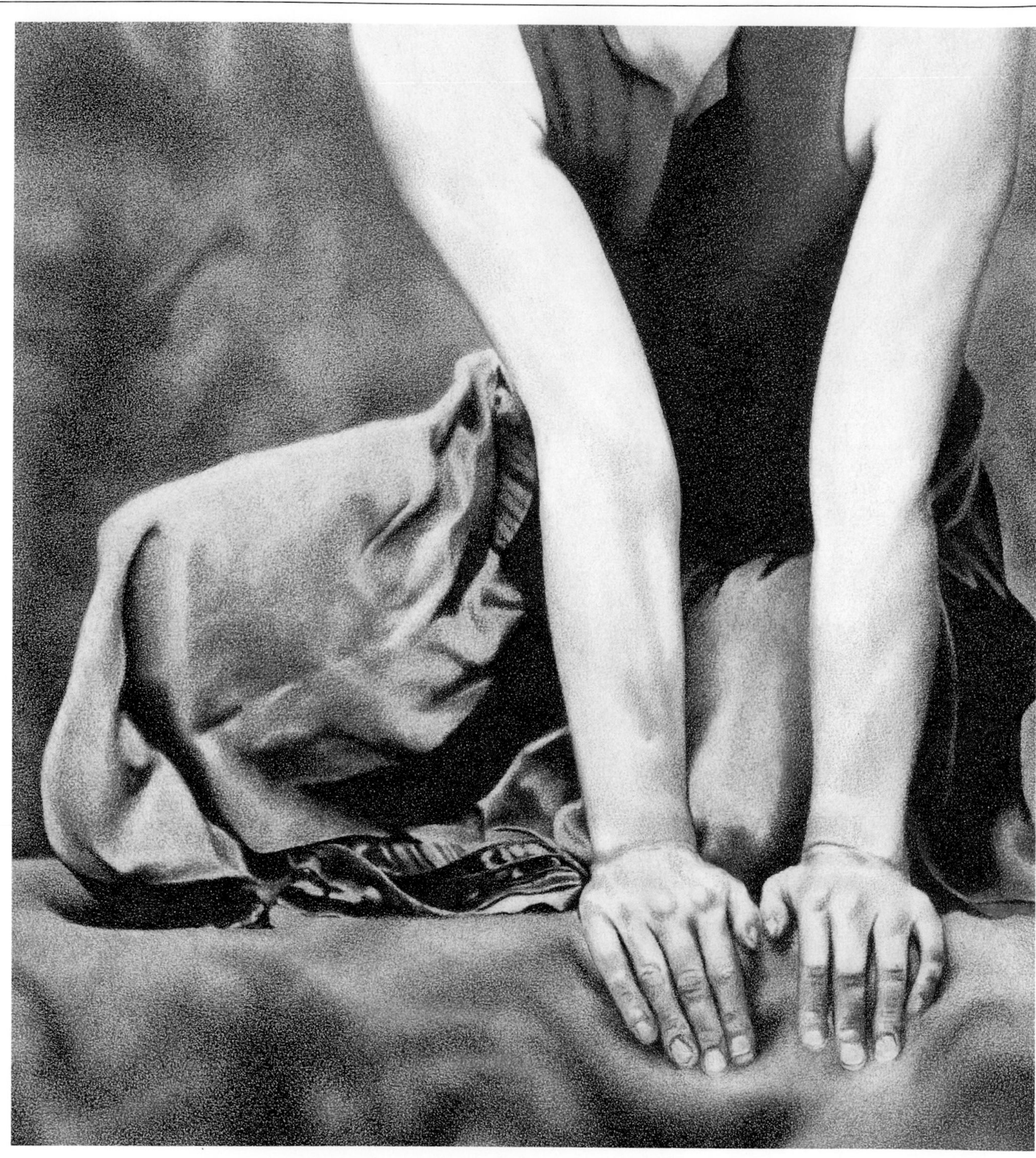

36

ARTIST
Christine Bunn

DESIGNER
Bruce Ramsay

ART DIRECTOR
Louis Fishauf

PUBLICATION
Saturday Night

PUBLISHER
Saturday Night Publishing

ILLUSTRATION FOR A FICTION PIECE ENTITLED "LOULOU" BY MARGARET ATWOOD IN *SATURDAY NIGHT*, JUNE 1983.

Colored pencil

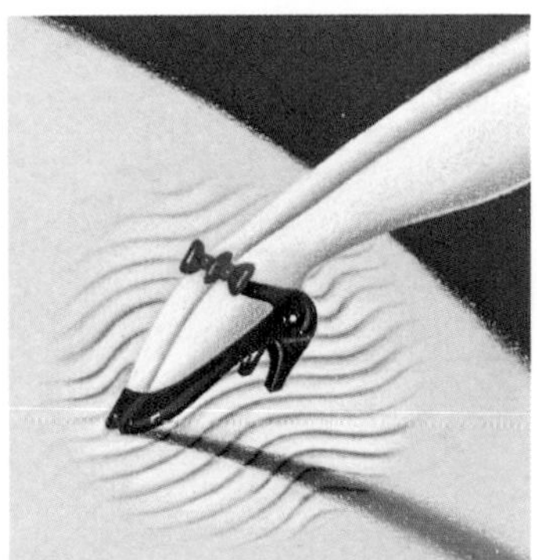

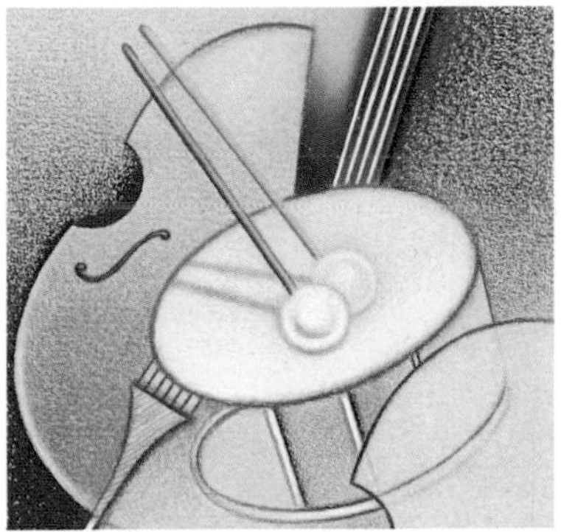

37

ARTIST
Dave Calver

DESIGNERS
Patricia Bradbury/Don Morris

ART DIRECTOR
Robert Best

PUBLICATION
New York Magazine

PUBLISHER
News Group Publications, Inc.

SERIES OF ILLUSTRATIONS FOR "FALL PREVIEW" IN *NEW YORK MAGAZINE*, SEPTEMBER 1983.

Watercolor and pencil

38

ARTIST
Dave Calver

DESIGNERS
David Kampa/Fred Woodward

ART DIRECTOR
Fred Woodward

PUBLICATION
Texas Monthly

PUBLISHER
Texas Monthly, Inc.

ILLUSTRATION FOR AN ARTICLE ENTITLED "PERFECT TEXAS" BY PETER APPLEBOME IN *TEXAS MONTHLY,* MARCH 1984.

Colored pencil

39

ARTIST
Larry W. Carroll

DESIGNER
Larry W. Carroll

ART EDITOR
Paul Serchia

PUBLICATION
News Chronicle

PUBLISHER
John P. Scripps Newspaper

ILLUSTRATION FOR AN ARTICLE ENTITLED "COCAINE: A WORSENING EPIDEMIC SCARS AMERICA" BY MITCHELL S. ROSENTHAL IN *NEWS CHRONICLE*, JANUARY 1984.

Mixed media

40

ARTIST
Steve Carver

ART DIRECTOR
Forbes Linkhorn

PUBLICATION
American Journal of Nursing

PUBLISHER
American Journal of Nursing Co.

ILLUSTRATIONS TO SHOW THE CONTRASTING SYMPTOMS OF ANOREXIA AND BULIMIA FOR AN ARTICLE ENTITLED "AVOIDING THE POWER STRUGGLE" BY ELDINE SANGER AND THERESE CASSINO IN *AMERICAN JOURNAL OF NURSING*, JANUARY 1984.

Acrylic and alkyd

41

ARTIST
Denise Chapman

ART DIRECTOR
Fred Woodward

PUBLICATION
Texas Monthly

PUBLISHER
Texas Monthly, Inc.

ILLUSTRATION FOR A STORY ON HOUSTON'S ALTERNATIVE SPACES AND GALLERIES ENTITLED "PERSONAL SPACE" BY MICHAEL ENNIS IN *TEXAS MONTHLY,* AUGUST 1983.

China marker, colored pencil, and gesso on paper

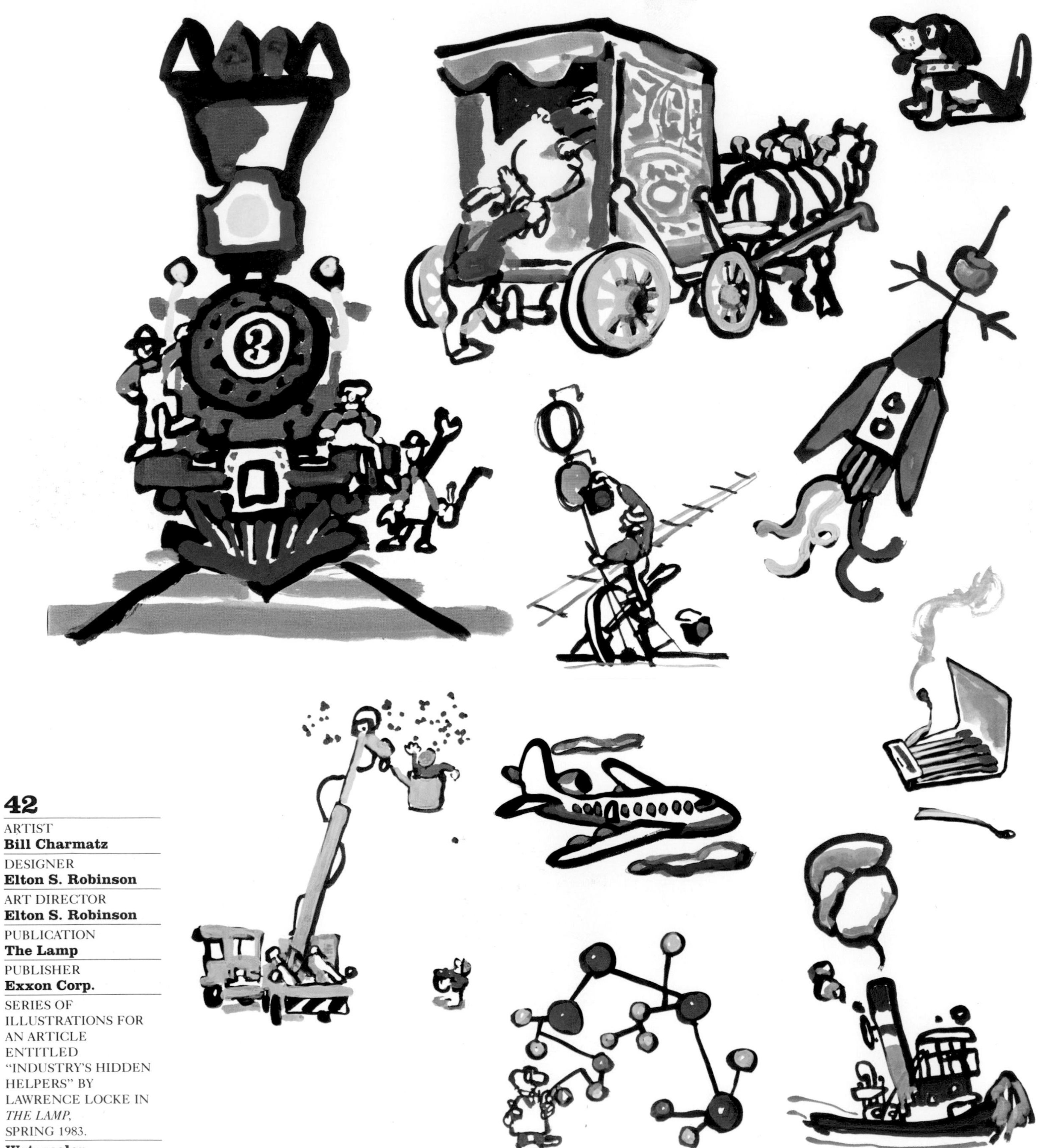

42

ARTIST
Bill Charmatz

DESIGNER
Elton S. Robinson

ART DIRECTOR
Elton S. Robinson

PUBLICATION
The Lamp

PUBLISHER
Exxon Corp.

SERIES OF ILLUSTRATIONS FOR AN ARTICLE ENTITLED "INDUSTRY'S HIDDEN HELPERS" BY LAWRENCE LOCKE IN *THE LAMP*, SPRING 1983.

Watercolor

43

ARTIST
Pete Christman

ART DIRECTOR
Lisa Lytton

PUBLICATION
Artifacts

PUBLISHER
The Savannah College of Art and Design

CENTERFOLD ILLUSTRATION IN *ARTIFACTS*, THE SAVANNAH COLLEGE OF ART AND DESIGN NEWSLETTER, APRIL 1984.

Colored pencil

44

ARTIST
Seymour Chwast

DESIGNER
Judy Garlan

ART DIRECTOR
Judy Garlan

PUBLICATION
The Atlantic Monthly

PUBLISHER
The Atlantic Monthly Co.

COVER ILLUSTRATION FOR AN ARTICLE ENTITLED "LIVING WITH NUCLEAR WEAPONS" BY THE HARVARD NUCLEAR STUDY GROUP IN *THE ATLANTIC MONTHLY,* JUNE 1983.

Cello-tak

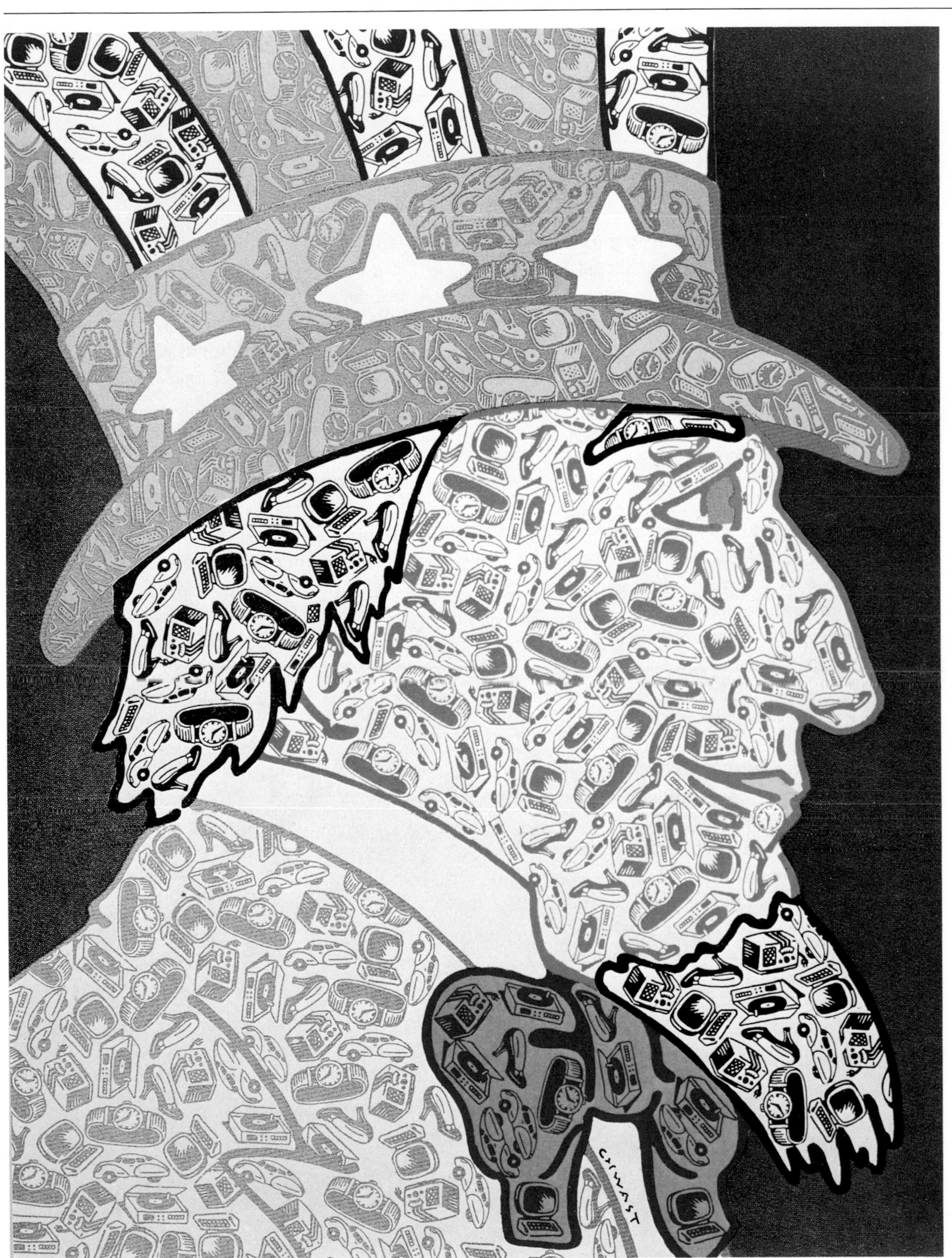

45

ARTIST
Seymour Chwast

DESIGNER
Judy Garlan

ART DIRECTOR
Judy Garlan

PUBLICATION
The Atlantic Monthly

PUBLISHER
The Atlantic Monthly Co.

ILLUSTRATION FOR A NON-FICTION PIECE ENTITLED "THE NEXT AMERICAN FRONTIER" BY ROBERT B. REICH IN *THE ATLANTIC MONTHLY*, APRIL 1983.

Cello-tak

46

ARTIST
Judy Clifford

ART DIRECTOR
Nina Ovryn

PUBLICATION
Review Magazine

PUBLISHER
East West Network Inc.

SERIES OF ILLUSTRATIONS ON FOOD AND FAMOUS BUILDINGS FOR AN ARTICLE ENTITLED "FOOD CITY" BY DONALD DEWEY IN *REVIEW MAGAZINE*, FEBRUARY 1984.

Watercolor

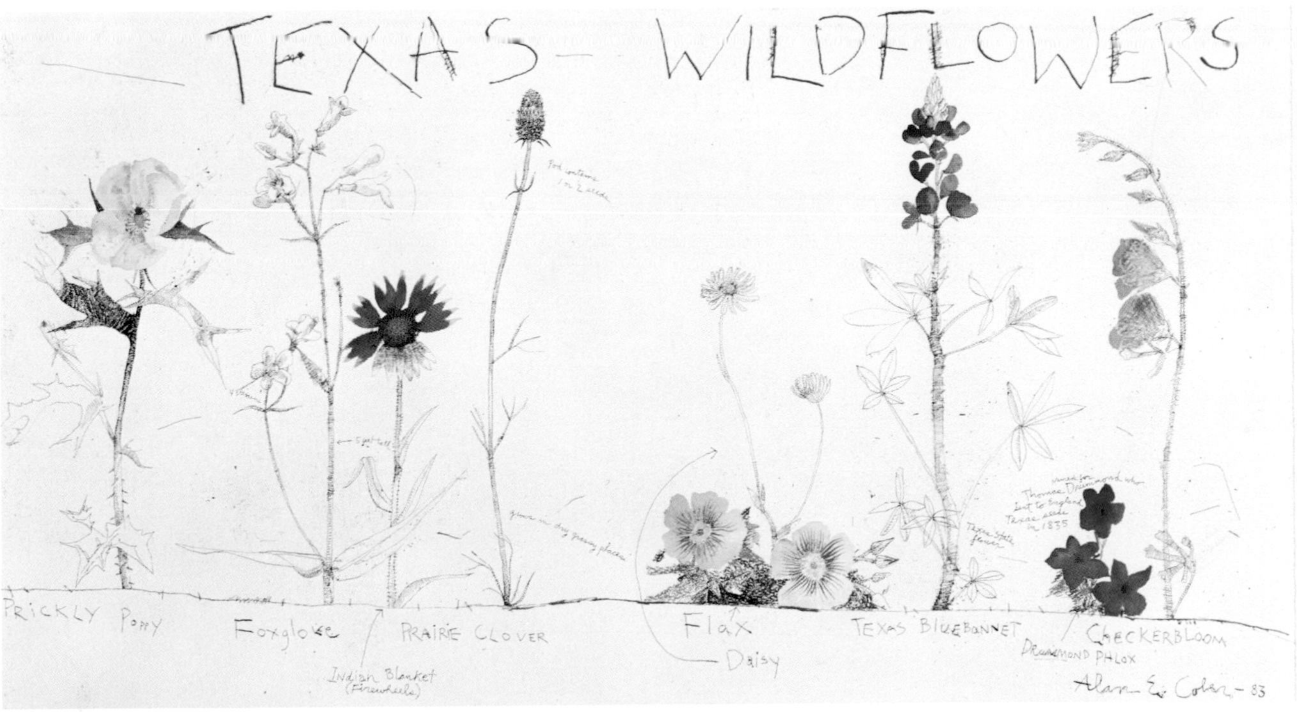

47

ARTIST
Alan E. Cober

ART DIRECTOR
Gary Gretter

PUBLICATION
Sports Afield

PUBLISHER
Hearst Magazines

ILLUSTRATION FOR A STORY ABOUT THE NORTHERN PIKE ENTITLED "ESOX" BY DAVID BOWRING IN *SPORTS AFIELD*, JULY 1983.

Watercolor

ARTIST
Alan E. Cober

ART DIRECTOR
Fred Woodward

PUBLICATION
Westward

PUBLISHER
Dallas Times Herald

ILLUSTRATION FOR AN ARTICLE ENTITLED "TEXAS WILDFLOWERS" IN *WESTWARD*, MARCH 1983.

Ink and watercolor

48

ARTIST
Alan E. Cober

DESIGNER
Howard Kline

ART DIRECTOR
Howard Kline

PUBLICATION
Empire Magazine

PUBLISHER
The Denver Post

ILLUSTRATION FOR AN ARTICLE ON RAPE ENTITLED "THE WORST CRIME" BY VERNA JONES IN *EMPIRE MAGAZINE*, JANUARY 1983.

Ink, pencil, and watercolor

49

ARTIST
Alan E. Cober

DESIGNER
Fred Woodward

ART DIRECTOR
Fred Woodward

PUBLICATION
Texas Monthly

PUBLISHER
Texas Monthly, Inc.

ILLUSTRATION FOR AN ARTICLE ENTITLED "HI, I'M JIMMYY DEAN, AND I'D LIKE YOU TO TRY MY PURE PORK SAUSAGE" BY FRYAR CALHOUN IN *TEXAS MONTHLY,* AUGUST 1983.

Watercolor, ink, and pencil

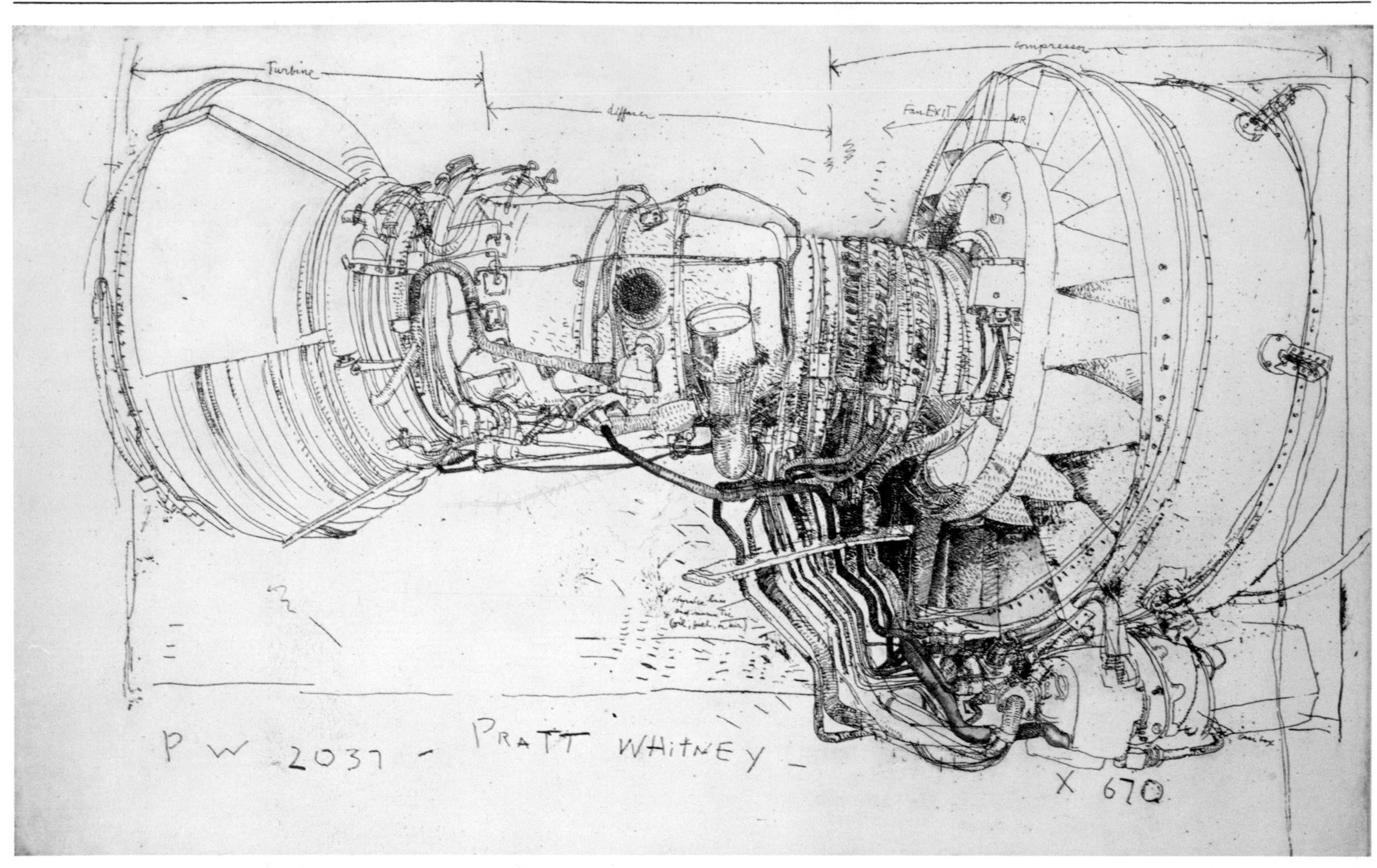

50

ARTIST
Alan E. Cober

DESIGNER
Elton S. Robinson

ART DIRECTOR
Elton S. Robinson

PUBLICATION
The Lamp

PUBLISHER
Exxon Corp.

ILLUSTRATION FOR AN ARTICLE ENTITLED "ENGINE-UITY" BY JULIET McGHIE IN *THE LAMP*, WINTER 1983.

Pen, ink, and watercolor

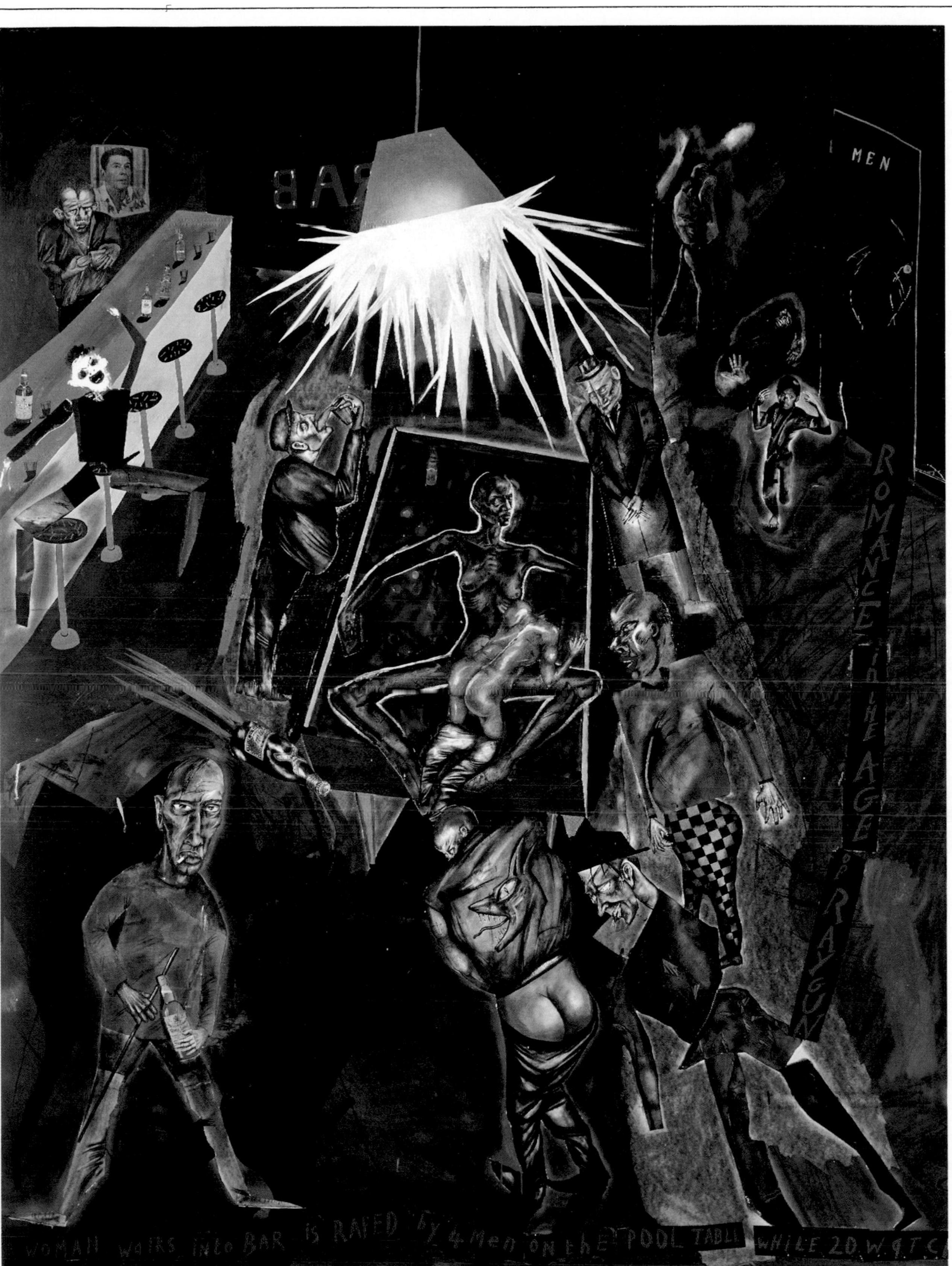

51

ARTIST
Sue Coe

DESIGNER
Martha Geering

ART DIRECTOR
Louise Kollenbaum

PUBLICATION
Mother Jones

PUBLISHER
Foundation for National Progress

ONE OF A SERIES OF ILLUSTRATIONS FOR AN ARTICLE ENTITLED "MOODS FOR MODERNS" IN *MOTHER JONES*, JULY 1983.

Graphite

52

ARTIST
Sue Coe

DESIGNER
Dian-Aziza Ooka

ART DIRECTOR
Louise Kollenbaum

PUBLICATION
Mother Jones

PUBLISHER
Foundation for National Progress

ILLUSTRATION FOR AN ARTICLE ENTITLED "DARK VISIONS—THE ART OF SUE COE" BY LOUISE KOLLENBAUM IN *MOTHER JONES*, AUGUST 1983.

Graphite

53

ARTIST
John Collier

ART DIRECTOR
James Noel Smith

PUBLICATION
Westward

PUBLISHER
Dallas Times Herald

COVER ILLUSTRATION FOR A FEATURE ENTITLED "TO FIND A MOCKINGBIRD: THE SEARCH FOR HARPER LEE" BY DREW JUBERA IN *WESTWARD*, DECEMBER 1983.

Pastel

54

ARTIST
Ray-Mel Cornelius

ART DIRECTOR
James Noel Smith

PUBLICATION
Westward

PUBLISHER
Dallas Times Herald

COVER ILLUSTRATION FOR AN ARTICLE ENTITLED "GIMME CAPS" BY THOM MARSHALL IN *WESTWARD*, OCTOBER, 1983.

Acrylic

55

ARTIST
Jerome Couelle

DESIGNER
Jolene Cuyler

ART DIRECTOR
Louis Fishauf

PUBLICATION
Saturday Night

PUBLISHER
Saturday Night Publishing

ILLUSTRATION FOR A POEM ENTITLED "THE HEMINGWAY HOUSE IN HAVANA" BY JOYCE NELSON IN *SATURDAY NIGHT*, APRIL 1984

Acrylic

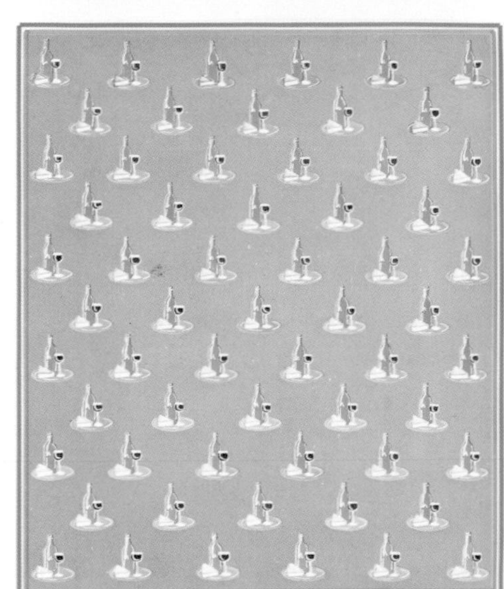
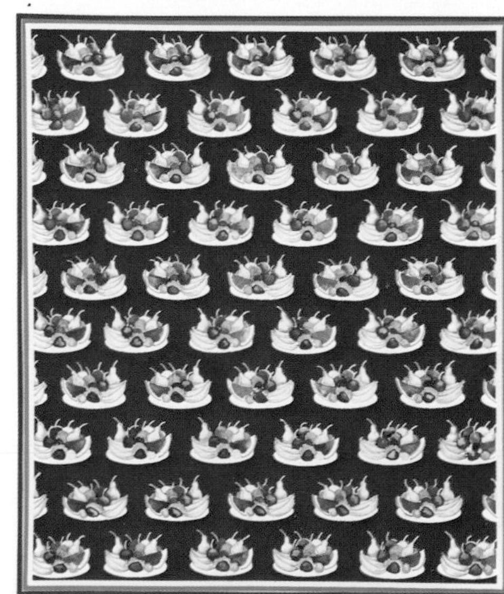
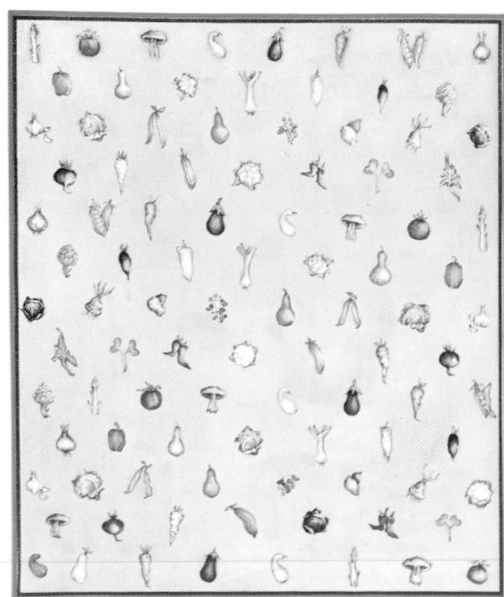
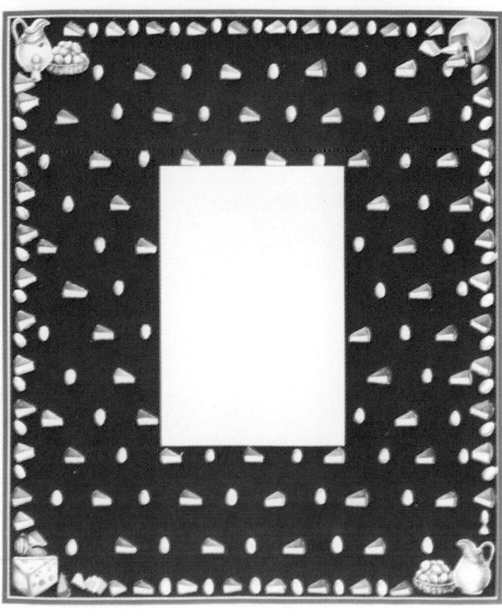

56

ARTIST
Neverne K. Covington

DESIGNER
Neverne K. Covington

ART DIRECTORS
Aralyn Adare/Peggy Stark

PUBLICATION
Floridian Magazine

PUBLISHER
St. Petersburg Times Publishing Co.

SERIES OF BORDER THEME ILLUSTRATIONS FOR A WEEKLY FEATURE ENTITLED "CUISINE, CUISINE" IN *FLORIDIAN MAGAZINE*, JANUARY AND FEBRUARY 1983.

Gouache and watercolor

57

ARTIST
Kinuko Y. Craft

ART DIRECTOR
Rudolph Hoglund

PUBLICATION
Time

PUBLISHER
Time Inc.

COVER ILLUSTRATION FOR AN ARTICLE ENTITLED "HOMECOMING, THE RETURN OF THE POLISH POPE" IN *TIME*, JUNE 1983.

Egg tempera on gold leaf panel

58

ARTIST
John Craig

DESIGNER
Bett McLean

ART DIRECTOR
Andrew Epstein

PUBLICATION
Veterinary Practice Management

PUBLISHER
13-30 Corp.

ILLUSTRATION FOR AN ARTICLE ON TIME MANAGEMENT ENTITLED "STAYING IN HIGH GEAR WITHOUT BURNING OUT" BY JOANNE KELLEHER IN *VETERINARY PRACTICE MANAGEMENT,* WINTER 1983/84.

Collage

59

ARTIST
Robert Crawford

DESIGNER
Kerig Pope

ART DIRECTOR
Tom Staebler

PUBLICATION
Playboy

PUBLISHER
Playboy Enterprises

ILLUSTRATION FOR AN ARTICLE ABOUT SO-CALLED FRIENDS WHO EAGERLY BED ESTRANGED SPOUSES ENTITLED "WHAT ARE FRIENDS FOR?" BY ART BUCHWALD IN *PLAYBOY,* JANUARY 1984.

Acrylic

60

ARTIST
José Cruz

ART DIRECTOR
Greg Paul

PUBLICATION
The Plain Dealer Magazine

PUBLISHER
The Plain Dealer Publications Co.

COVER ILLUSTRATION FOR AN ARTICLE ENTITLED "CLEVELAND JAZZ BLOWS HOT AND COOL" IN *THE PLAIN DEALER MAGAZINE*, JANUARY 1983.

Acrylic and glitter

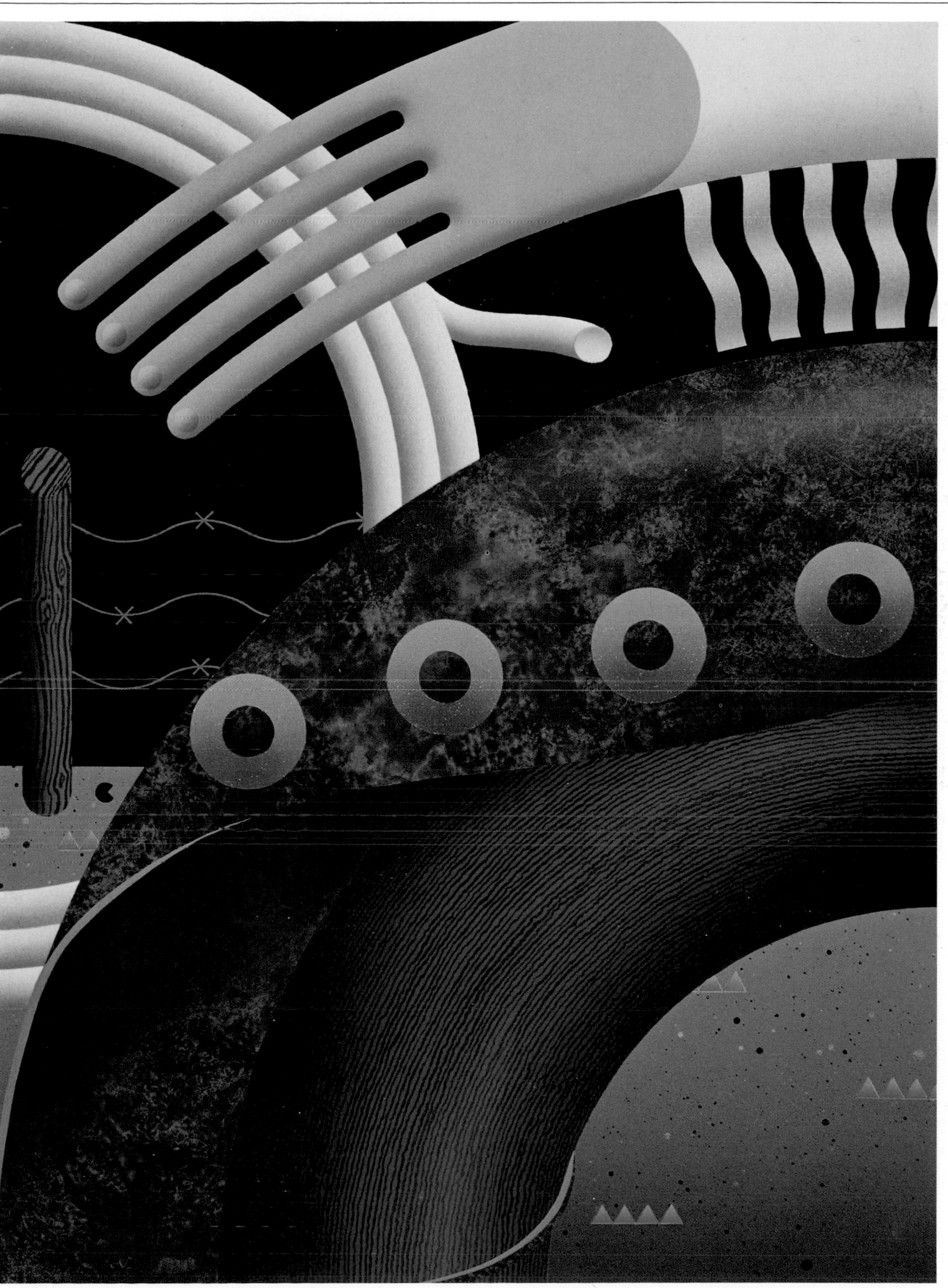

61

ARTIST
José Cruz

ART DIRECTOR
Fred Woodward

PUBLICATION
Texas Monthly

PUBLISHER
Texas Monthly, Inc.

ILLUSTRATION SHOWING THE ARTIST'S INTERPRETATION OF THE TERM "WESTERN ART" IN *TEXAS MONTHLY*, NOVEMBER 1983.

Acrylic

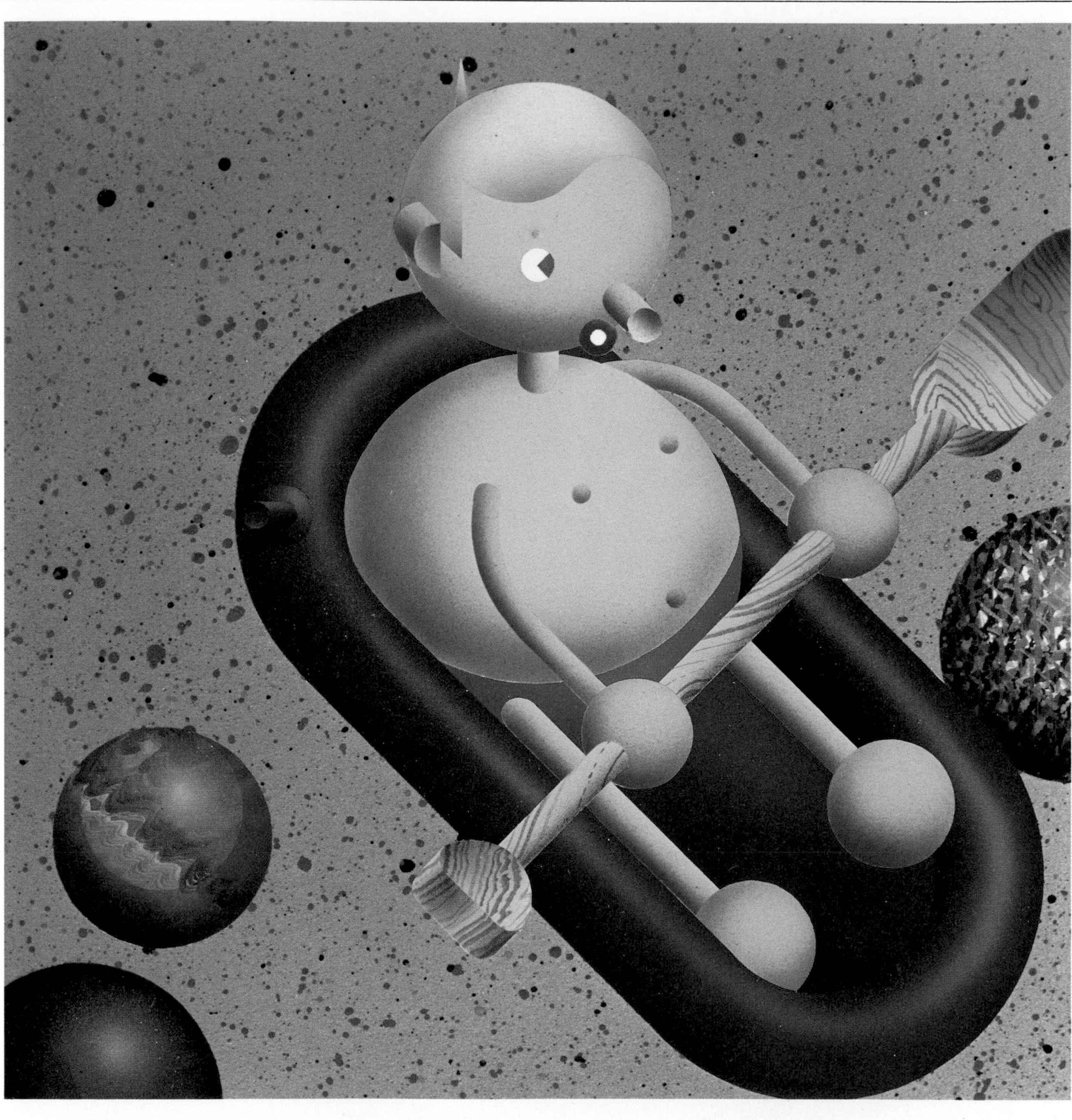

62

ARTIST
José Cruz

DESIGNER
José Cruz

ART DIRECTOR
Ginny Pitrie

PUBLICATION
Dallas Life

PUBLISHER
Dallas Morning News

ILLUSTRATION DEPICTING SUMMER FUN FOR "THE DISCOVER PAGE" IN *DALLAS LIFE*, JUNE 1983.

Acrylic

63

ARTIST
Tom Curry

DESIGNER
Fred Woodward

ART DIRECTOR
Tom Curry

PUBLICATION
Texas Monthly

PUBLISHER
Texas Monthly, Inc.

ILLUSTRATION SHOWING THE ARTIST'S INTERPRETATION OF THE TERM "WESTERN ART" IN *TEXAS MONTHLY*, DECEMBER 1983.

Acrylic

64

ARTIST
Tom Curry

DESIGNER
Tom Curry

ART DIRECTOR
Greg Paul

PUBLICATION
The Plain Dealer Magazine

PUBLISHER
The Plain Dealer Publications Co.

ILLUSTRATION FOR AN ARTICLE ON DOUBLETALK IN BROADCASTING ENTITLED "NOW, TO REPEAT THAT REITERATION AGAIN" BY JIM WILKERSON IN *THE PLAIN DEALER MAGAZINE*, JULY 1983.

Acrylic

65

ARTIST
Peter de Sève

ART DIRECTOR
Patricia Bradbury

PUBLICATION
New York

PUBLISHER
News Group Publications Inc.

ILLUSTRATION FOR AN ARTICLE ENTITLED "SOUR GRAPES" BY ALEXIS BESPALOFF IN *NEW YORK*, NOVEMBER 1983.

Watercolor and ink

66

ARTIST
Blair Drawson

DESIGNER
Robert Priest

ART DIRECTOR
Robert Priest

PUBLICATION
Esquire

PUBLISHER
Esquire Associates

ILLUSTRATION FOR AN ARTICLE ENTITLED "THE BIRTH OF BEBOP" BY RALPH ELLISON IN *ESQUIRE*, JUNE 1983.

Watercolor

67

ARTIST
Blair Drawson

DESIGNER
Shari Spier

ART DIRECTOR
Louis Fishauf

PUBLICATION
Commentator

PUBLISHER
Saturday Night Contract Publishing

ILLUSTRATIONS FOR AN ARTICLE ON RELATIONS BETWEEN GOVERNMENT, BUSINESS, AND LABOR ENTITLED "ONE VOICE AMONG THREE SOLITUDES" IN *COMMENTATOR*, SPRING 1983.

Watercolor

68

ARTIST
Blair Drawson

DESIGNER
Shari Spier

ART DIRECTOR
Louis Fishauf

PUBLICATION
Executive

PUBLISHER
Airmedia

COVER AND INSIDE ILLUSTRATION FOR AN ARTICLE ENTITLED "RULING THE HOME ROOST" BY WILLIAM HOZY IN *EXECUTIVE*, MAY 1983.

Watercolor and ink

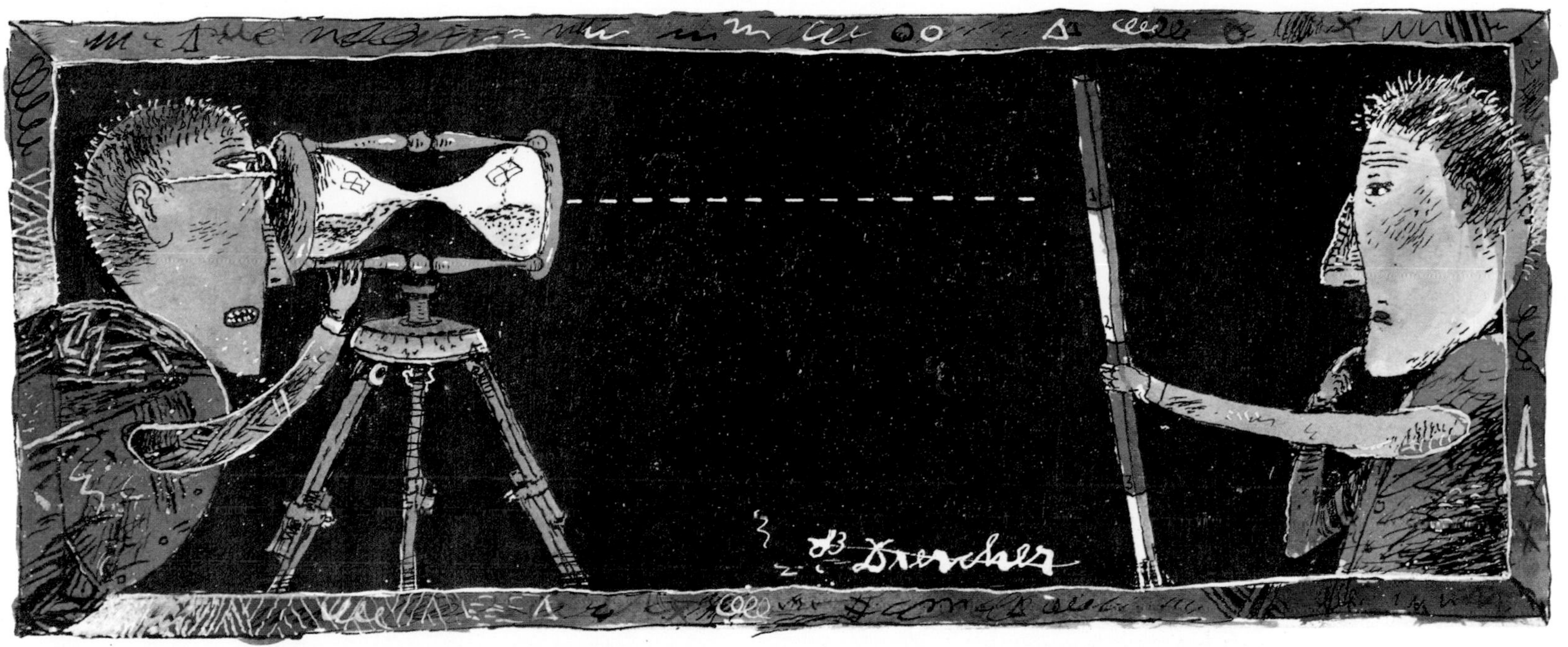

69

ARTIST
Henrik Drescher

DESIGNER
John Cohoe

ART DIRECTOR
John Cohoe

PUBLICATION
GEO

PUBLISHER
Knapp Communications Corp.

ILLUSTRATION FOR A SCIENTIFIC STORY ENTITLED "THE METER IS REDEFINED IN TERMS OF TIME" BY JOHN BERENDT IN Geo, JANUARY 1984.

Pen and ink and watercolor

ARTIST
Henrik Drescher

ART DIRECTOR
Elizabeth Vanitalie

PUBLICATION
The Movies

ILLUSTRATION FOR AN ARTICLE ENTITLED "NEVER CRY AUTHOR" BY MARK JACOBSON IN *THE MOVIES*, NOVEMBER 1983.

Ink and watercolor

70

ARTIST
Henrik Drescher

DESIGNER
Patrick JB Flynn

ART DIRECTOR
Patrick JB Flynn

PUBLICATION
The Progressive

PUBLISHER
The Progressive, Inc.

ILLUSTRATION FOR AN ARTICLE ENTITLED "THE GREENS: A NEW KIND OF POLITICS TAKES ROOT IN GERMAN SOIL" BY WILLIAM SWEET IN *THE PROGRESSIVE*, MAY 1983.

Brush, pen and ink

71

ARTIST
Henrik Drescher

DESIGNER
Dian-Aziza Ooka

ART DIRECTOR
Louise Kollenbaum

PUBLICATION
Mother Jones

PUBLISHER
Foundation for National Progress

ILLUSTRATION FOR "THE SMILE WARS" BY ARLIE HOCHSCHILD IN *MOTHER JONES*, DECEMBER 1983.

Watercolor and ink

72

ARTIST
Henrik Drescher

ART DIRECTOR
Steven Heller

PUBLICATION
The New York Times Book Review

PUBLISHER
The New York Times Co.

ILLUSTRATION FOR AN ARTICLE ENTITLED "WASHINGTON AND THE POOR" BY HAROLD L. WILENSKY IN *THE NEW YORK TIMES BOOK REVIEW,* JULY 1983.

Ink

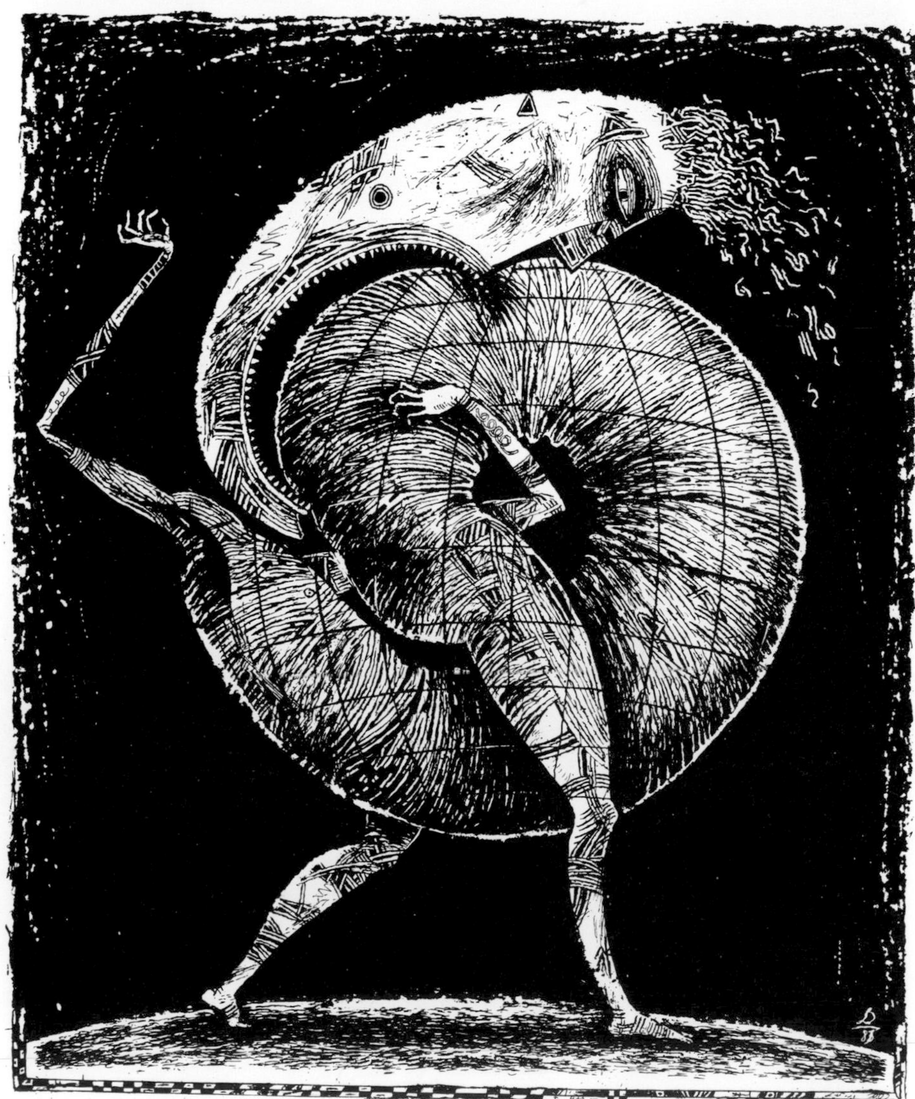

ARTIST
Henrik Drescher

DESIGNER
Alice Cook

ART DIRECTOR
Alice Cook

PUBLICATION
Intervention

COVER ILLUSTRATION ON THE THEME OF INTERVENTION IN CENTRAL AMERICA FOR *INTERVENTION,* 1984.

Ink

73

ARTIST
Andrzej Dudzinski

DESIGNER
Ronn Campisi

ART DIRECTOR
Ronn Campisi

PUBLICATION
The Boston Globe Magazine

PUBLISHER
Globe Newspaper Co.

ILLUSTRATION FOR AN ARTICLE ENTITLED "AMERICA'S PROFILE" BY CHARLES KENNEY IN *THE BOSTON GLOBE MAGAZINE*, MARCH 1984.

Oil crayon

74

ARTIST
Andrzej Dudzinski

ART DIRECTOR
Barbara Lish

PUBLICATION
Avenue Magazine

PUBLISHER
Avenue Magazine, Inc.

ILLUSTRATION FOR AN ARTICLE ENTITLED "SANTA'S CHILDREN" BY ITALO CALVINO IN *AVENUE MAGAZINE*, DECEMBER/JANUARY 1984.

Charcoal and pastel

75

ARTIST
Nina Duran

DESIGNER
Marcia Wright

ART DIRECTOR
Marcia Wright

PUBLICATION
TWA Ambassador

PUBLISHER
Trans World Airlines

ILLUSTRATION FOR A STORY ON DESSERT WINES ENTITLED "JUST DESSERTS" BY CHARLES LOCKWOOD IN *TWA AMBASSADOR*, FEBRUARY 1983.

Oil

76

ARTIST
Sean Earley

DESIGNER
Fred Woodward

ART DIRECTOR
Fred Woodward

PUBLICATION
Texas Monthly

PUBLISHER
Texas Monthly, Inc.

ILLUSTRATION DEPICTING A TEXAS CON MAN WHO FOOLED EVERYONE FROM STATE LEGISLATORS TO THE PENTAGON FOR AN ARTICLE ENTITLED "THE BIG CON" BY BYRON HARRIS IN *TEXAS MONTHLY*, SEPTEMBER 1983.

Acrylic

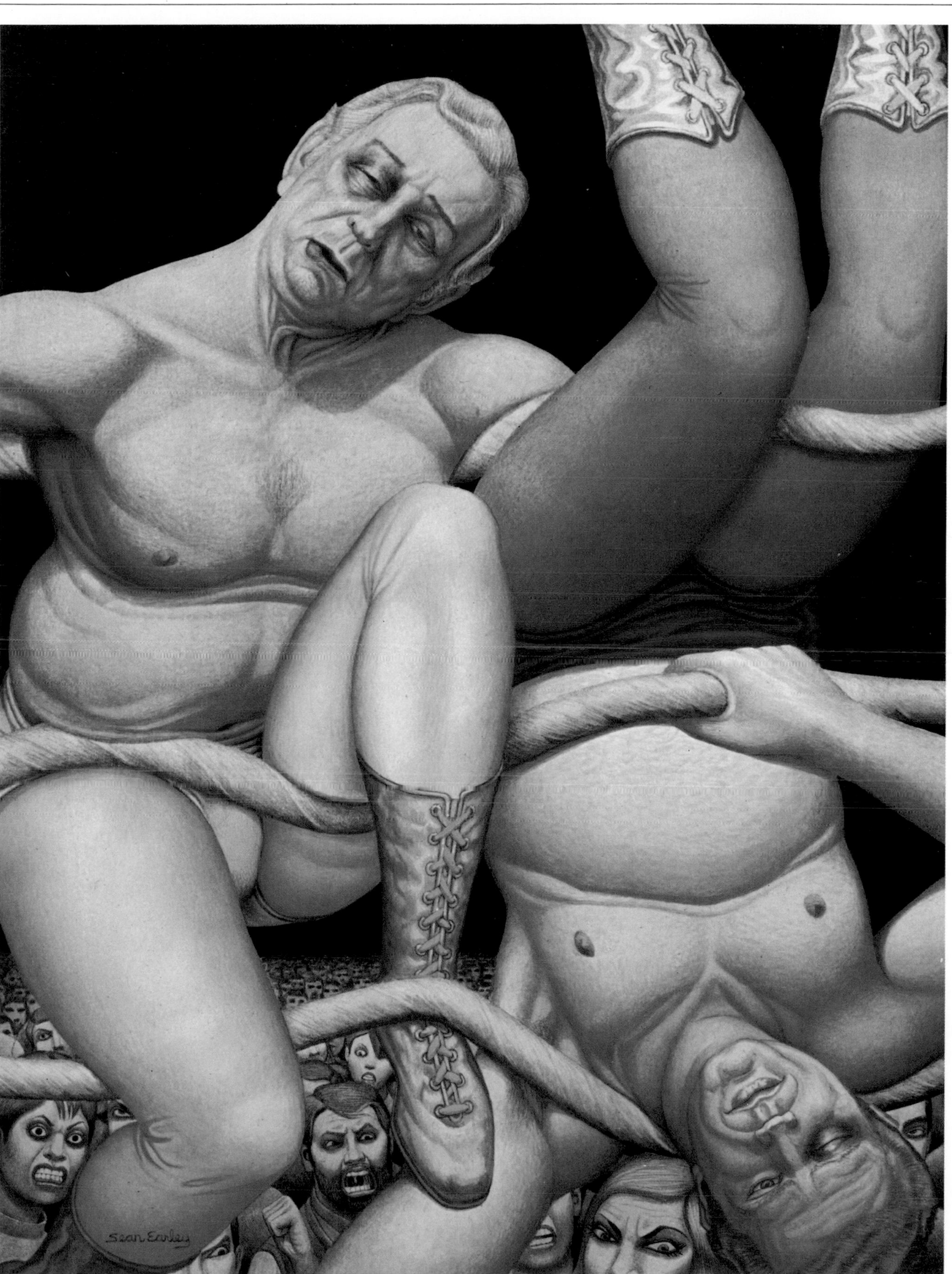

77

ARTIST
Sean Earley

DESIGNERS
David Kampa/Fred Woodward

ART DIRECTOR
Fred Woodward

PUBLICATION
Texas Monthly

PUBLISHER
Texas Monthly, Inc.

ILLUSTRATION FOR AN ARTICLE ABOUT DEVELOPERS VS. A SMALL NEIGHBORHOOD GROUP ENTITLED "I BEAT BEN BARNES AND JOHN CONNALLY IN A FAIR FIGHT" BY KAYE NORTHCOTT IN *TEXAS MONTHLY*, MARCH 1984.

Acrylic

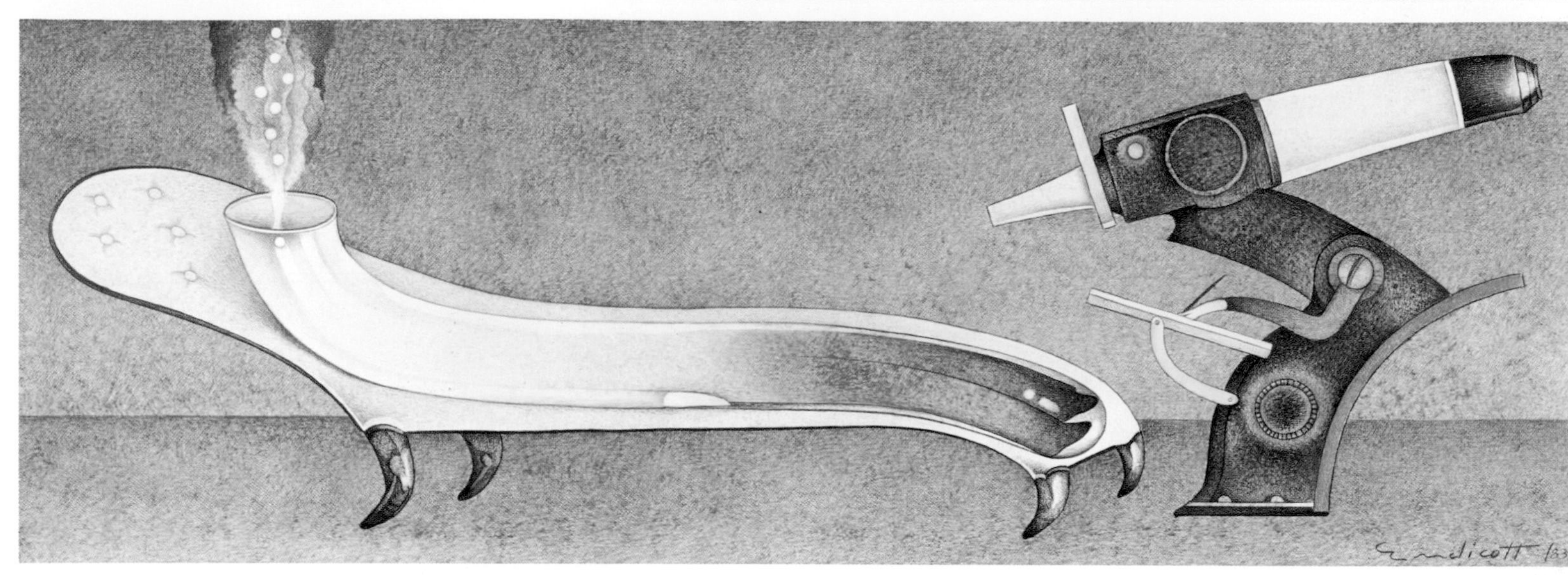

78

ARTIST
James Endicott

DESIGNER
Judy Garlan

ART DIRECTOR
Judy Garlan

PUBLICATION
The Atlantic Monthly

PUBLISHER
The Atlantic Monthly Co.

ILLUSTRATION FOR A NON-FICTION PIECE ENTITLED "BIOLOGY AND MENTAL ILLNESS" BY JOSEPH ALPER IN *THE ATLANTIC MONTHLY,* DECEMBER 1983.

Watercolor

79

ARTIST
Randall Enos

DESIGNER
Ronn Campisi

ART DIRECTOR
Ronn Campisi

PUBLICATION
The Boston Globe Magazine

PUBLISHER
Globe Newspaper Co.

COVER ILLUSTRATION FOR A FEATURE ENTITLED "GLOBE PHOTO CONTEST WINNERS" IN *THE BOSTON GLOBE MAGAZINE*, OCTOBER 1983.

Linocut and collage

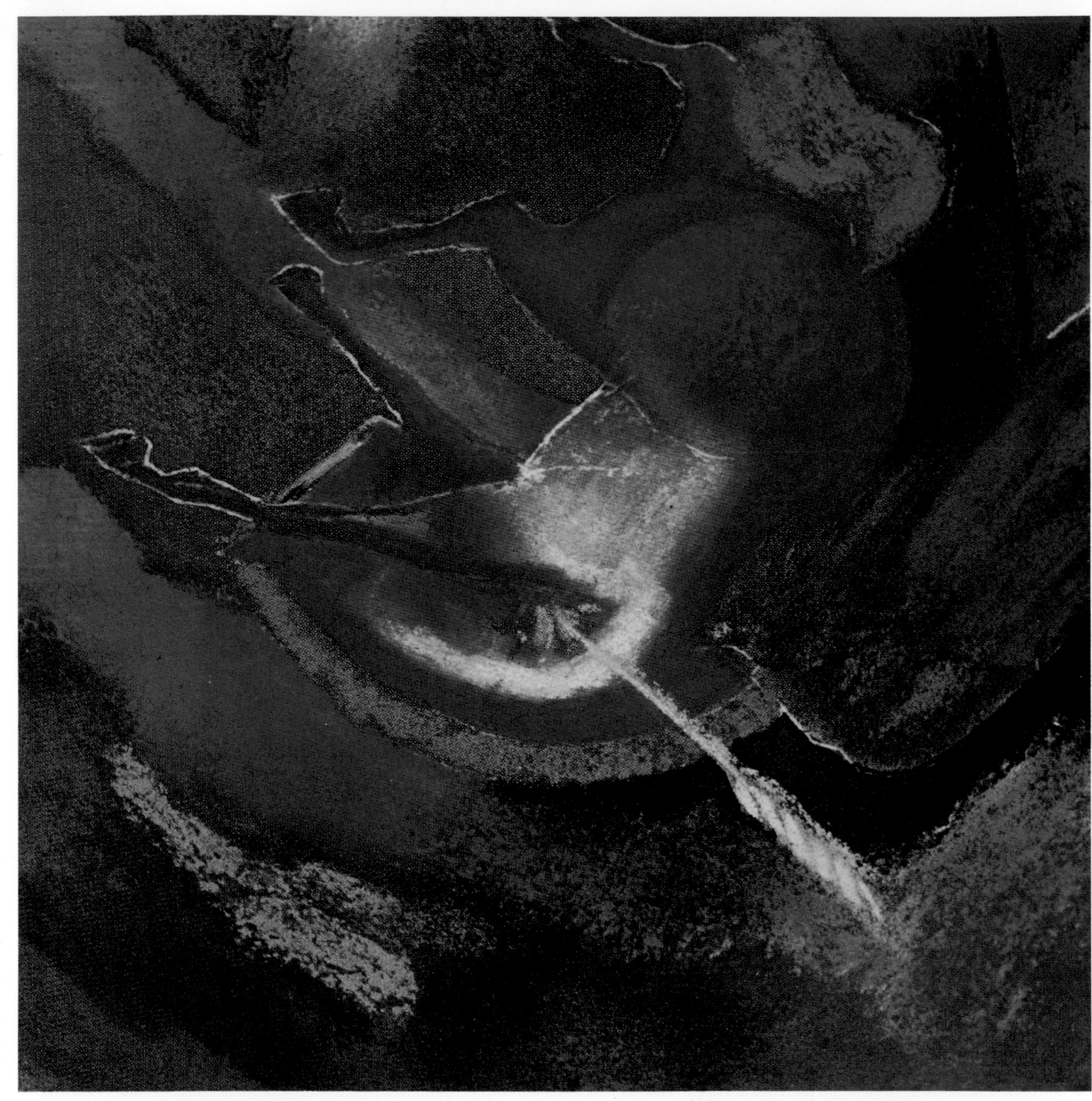

80

ARTIST
Vivienne Flesher

DESIGNER
David Kampa

ART DIRECTOR
Fred Woodward

PUBLICATION
Texas Monthly

PUBLISHER
Texas Monthly, Inc.

ILLUSTRATION FOR AN ARTICLE ABOUT DALLAS AFTER THE ASSASSINATION OF JOHN F. KENNEDY ENTITLED "WHY DO THEY HATE US SO MUCH?" BY LAWRENCE WRIGHT IN *TEXAS MONTHLY*, NOVEMBER 1983.

Pastel and watercolor

81

ARTIST
Vivienne Flesher

DESIGNER
Robert Best

ART DIRECTORS
Patricia Bradbury/Don Morris

PUBLICATION
New York Magazine

PUBLISHER
News Group Publications Inc.

ILLUSTRATION FOR AN ARTICLE ENTITLED "BREAST FEEDING" BY JANE WHOLEY IN *NEW YORK MAGAZINE*, OCTOBER 1983.

Pastel

82

ARTIST
Dagmar Frinta

DESIGNER
Marcia Wright

ART DIRECTOR
Marcia Wright

PUBLICATION
TWA Ambassador

PUBLISHER
Trans World Airlines

ILLUSTRATION FOR AN ESSAY ENTITLED "STORIES OF CHRISTMAS PAST: CHRISTMAS IN MAINE" BY ROBERT P. TRISTRAM COFFIN IN *TWA AMBASSADOR*, DECEMBER 1983.

Mixed media

83

ARTIST
Dagmar Frinta

DESIGNER
Ronn Campisi

ART DIRECTOR
Ronn Campisi

PUBLICATION
The Boston Globe Magazine

PUBLISHER
Globe Newspaper Co.

COVER ILLUSTRATION FOR A FEATURE ENTITLED "STRUGGLE & CELEBRATION: FOUR STORIES OF FATHERING" BY DAVID MEHEGAN IN *THE BOSTON GLOBE MAGAZINE*, JUNE 1983.

Paper collage, pen and ink, and watercolor

84

ARTIST
Dagmar Frinta

DESIGNER
Mary Challinor

ART DIRECTOR
Rodney Williams

PUBLICATION
Science 83

PUBLISHER
American Association for the Advancement of Science

ILLUSTRATION FOR AN ARTICLE ENTITLED "SUICIDE SIGNALS" BY MAYA PINES IN *SCIENCE 83*, OCTOBER 1983.

Mixed media

85

ARTIST
Dagmar Frinta

DESIGNER
Wayne Fitzpatrick

ART DIRECTOR
Wayne Fitzpatrick

PUBLICATION
Science 84

PUBLISHER
American Association for the Advancement of Science

ILLUSTRATION FOR AN ARTICLE ENTITLED "DR. COLEY'S TOXINS" BY JUNE GOODFIELD IN *SCIENCE 84*, APRIL 1984.

Mixed media

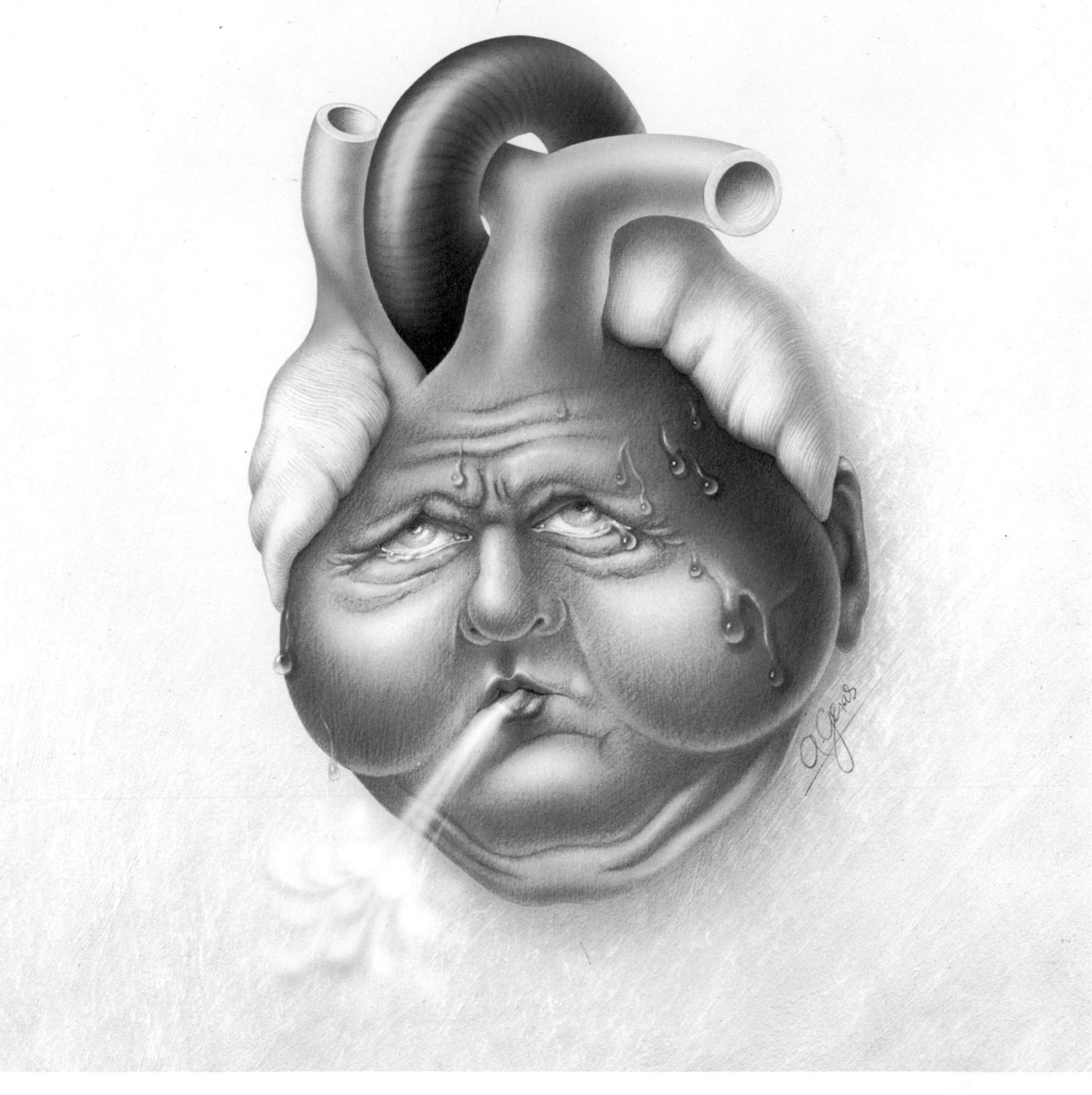

86

ARTIST
Audra Geras

ART DIRECTOR
Audra Geras

PUBLICATION
Illustrated Medicine

PUBLISHER
Wynwood Publishing Inc.

COVER ILLUSTRATION FOR AN ARTICLE ENTITLED "CHRONIC HEART FAILURE: ADVANCES IN CLINICAL MANAGEMENT" BY WILSON S. COLUCCI, M.D. IN *ILLUSTRATED MEDICINE*, JUNE 1983.

Mixed media

87

ARTIST
Robert Giusti

DESIGNER
Janice Fudyma

DESIGN GROUP
Bernhardt Fudyma Design Group

PUBLICATION
Grace Digest

PUBLISHER
W.R. Grace & Co.

ILLUSTRATION FOR AN ARTICLE ENTITLED "SUPERBULL—ABS DELIVERS THE MALE" BY JOYCE COLE IN *GRACE DIGEST*, SPRING/SUMMER 1983.

Acrylic on canvas

88

ARTIST
Bob Goldstrom

DESIGNER
James T. Walsh

ART DIRECTOR
James T. Walsh

PUBLICATION
Emergency Medicine

PUBLISHER
Fischer Medical Publications

ILLUSTRATION FOR AN ARTICLE ON ELECTRICAL INJURIES ENTITLED "OF VOLTS & BOLTS" BY MARY ANN COOPER, M.D. IN *EMERGENCY MEDICINE*, APRIL 1983.

Oil

89

ARTIST
Scott Gordley

DESIGNER
Miriam Smith

ART DIRECTOR
Miriam Smith

PUBLICATION
The Newsday Magazine

PUBLISHER
Newsday Inc.

ILLUSTRATION FOR A STORY ABOUT A MENTALLY RETARDED WOMAN ENTITLED "MILLIE'S VISIT HOME" BY MILLICENT PINDEK AND JAMIE PASTOR BOLNICK IN *THE NEWSDAY MAGAZINE*, NOVEMBER 1983.

Pastel

90

ARTIST
Dale Gottlieb

ART DIRECTOR
Tina Adamek

PUBLICATION
Postgraduate Medicine

PUBLISHER
McGraw Hill Publishing Co.

ILLUSTRATION FOR AN ARTICLE ENTITLED "MAMMALIAN BITES" BY JAMES HAWKINS, PAUL M. PARIS, AND R.D. STEWART IN *POSTGRADUATE MEDICINE*, JUNE 1983.

Watercolor

91

ARTIST
Alexa Grace

DESIGNER
Charles Churchward

ART DIRECTORS
Yolanda Como/Charles Churchward/Shirley Lee

PUBLICATION
Vanity Fair

PUBLISHER
Condé-Nast Publications Inc.

ILLUSTRATION FOR AN ARTICLE ENTITLED "GHOST HUNTING" BY ANN ARENSBERG IN *VANITY FAIR*, DECEMBER 1983.

Porcelain, paint, and pastel

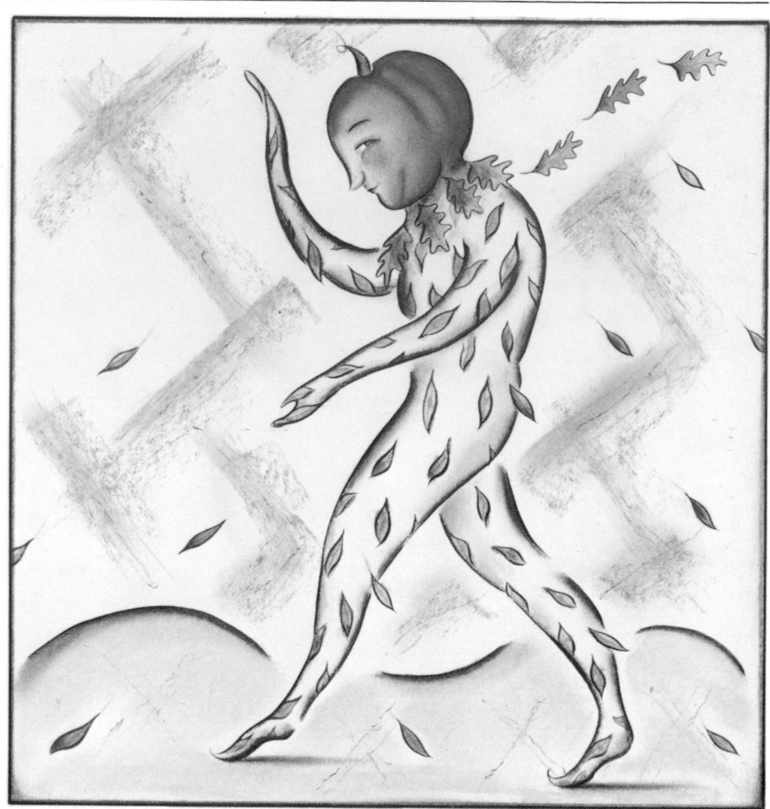

92

ARTIST
Alexa Grace
DESIGNER
Ronn Campisi
ART DIRECTOR
Ronn Campisi
PUBLICATION
The Boston Globe Magazine
PUBLISHER
Globe Newspaper Co.
ILLUSTRATION FOR AN ARTICLE ENTITLED "AUTUMN, REFLECTIONS ON THE CHANGING SEASON" BY GAIL CALDWELL IN *THE BOSTON GLOBE MAGAZINE*, OCTOBER 1983
Pastel and watercolor

ARTIST
Alexa Grace
DESIGNER
Fred Woodward
ART DIRECTOR
Fred Woodward
PUBLICATION
Dallas Times Herald
PUBLISHER
Dallas Times Herald
ILLUSTRATION FOR AN ARTICLE ENTITLED "PIZZA WITH EVERYTHING" BY JOE RHODES IN *DALLAS TIMES HERALD*, MARCH 1983.
Pastel, watercolor, and colored pencil

93

ARTIST
Alexa Grace

ART DIRECTOR
Riki Allred

PUBLICATION
Northeast

PUBLISHER
The Hartford Courant

COVER ILLUSTRATION FOR AN ARTICLE ENTITLED "LIFE OF A FREELANCE WRITER" BY LINDA CASE IN *NORTHEAST*, MARCH 1984.

Porcelain, paint, pastel, and paper

94

ARTIST
Melissa Grimes

DESIGNER
Nancy McMillen

ART DIRECTOR
Nancy McMillen

PUBLICATION
Texas Monthly

PUBLISHER
Texas Monthly, Inc.

ILLUSTRATION FOR A STORY ABOUT THREE BLACK REVOLUTIONARIES OF THE 60'S ENTITLED "THE BAD BROTHER" BY GARY CARTWRIGHT IN *TEXAS MONTHLY,* MAY 1983.

Photocollage, colored paper, and gouache

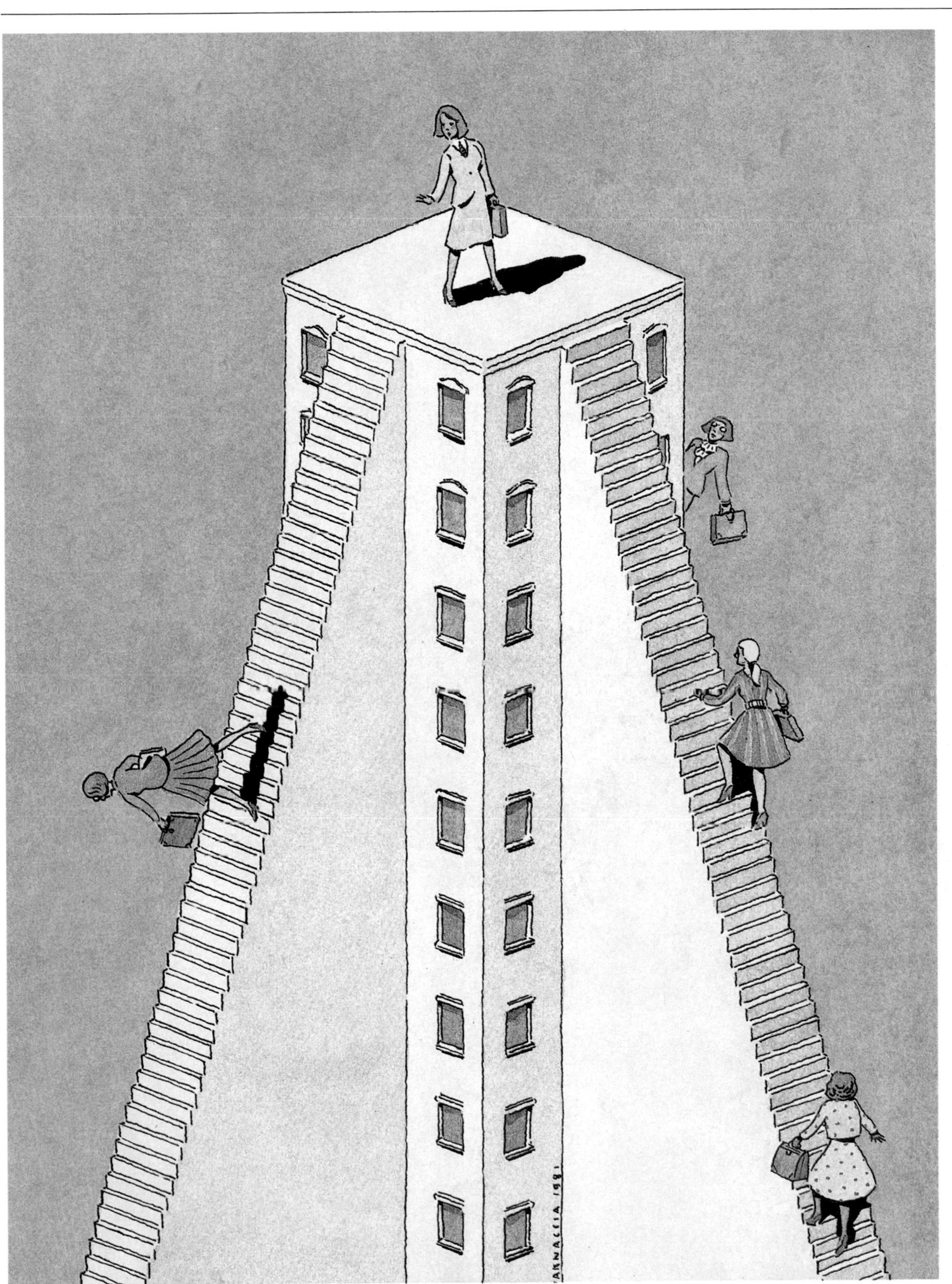

95

ARTIST
Steven Guarnaccia

ART DIRECTOR
Sue H. Llewellyn

PUBLICATION
Business World Women

PUBLISHER
Ziff Davis Publishing

ILLUSTRATION DEPICTING WOMEN IN PROFESSIONAL POSITIONS FOR "UPWARD BOUND" BY ROSABETH MOSS KANTER, PhD IN *BUSINESS WORLD WOMEN*, DECEMBER 1983.

Watercolor

96

ARTIST
Michael Hampshire

ART DIRECTOR
J. Robert Teringo

PUBLICATION
National Geographic Magazine

PUBLISHER
National Geographic Society

ILLUSTRATION DEPICTING THE CUSTOM OF SELLING INDULGENCES FOR AN ARTICLE ABOUT MARTIN LUTHER, ENTITLED "THE WORLD OF LUTHER" BY MERLE SEVERY IN *NATIONAL GEOGRAPHIC MAGAZINE*, OCTOBER 1983.

Acrylic

97

ARTIST
Greg Harlin

DESIGNER
Valerie Greenhouse

ART DIRECTOR
Valerie Greenhouse

PUBLICATION
Mortgage Banking

PUBLISHER
Harrison Communications

ILLUSTRATION FOR AN ARTICLE ENTITLED "NEW ROUTES FOR TITLE INSURERS" BY JOHN GOODE AND RUSSELL W. JORDAN, III IN *MORTGAGE BANKING*, MARCH 1984.

Watercolor

98

ARTIST
Ron Hauge

DESIGNER
Timothy McCarthy

ART DIRECTOR
Michael Grossman

PUBLICATION
National Lampoon

PUBLISHER
The National Lampoon Inc.

SERIES OF ILLUSTRATIONS ENTITLED "RON HAUGE'S YEAR OF REJECTED NEW YORKER COVERS" IN *NATIONAL LAMPOON*, DECEMBER 1983.

Mixed media

99

ARTIST
Philip Hays

DESIGNER
Nancy Butkus

ART DIRECTOR
Nancy Butkus

PUBLICATION
California Magazine

PUBLISHER
New West Communications Corp.

COVER ILLUSTRATION FOR A STORY ON A FEMINIST LEADER SERVING TIME IN PRISON ENTITLED "NO REGRETS" BY KATE COLEMAN IN *CALIFORNIA MAGAZINE*, MAY 1983.

Watercolor

100

ARTIST
Sandra Hendler

DESIGNER
Sandra Hendler

ART DIRECTOR
Bill Marr

PUBLICATION
Philadelphia Inquirer Magazine

PUBLISHER
Philadelphia Inquirer

ILLUSTRATION FOR AN ARTICLE ENTITLED "UGLY IS MORE THAN SKIN DEEP" BY WILLIAM ECEBARGER IN *PHILADELPHIA INQUIRER MAGAZINE*, NOVEMBER 1983.

Colored pencil

101

ARTIST
John Hersey

ART DIRECTOR
Mick Wiggins

PUBLICATION
PC World

PUBLISHER
CW Communications, Inc.

ILLUSTRATION DEPICTING A TOUR THROUGH TELECOMMUNICATION SYSTEMS FOR AN ARTICLE ENTITLED "COMMUNICATIONS CONCEPTS" BY W. DAVID SCHWADER IN *PC WORLD*, APRIL 1984.

Gouache

102

ARTIST
Brad Holland

ART DIRECTORS
Barbara Solowan/Bernadette Gillen

PUBLICATION
City Woman

PUBLISHER
Comac Communications Ltd.

ILLUSTRATION FOR AN ARTICLE ENTITLED "PREGNANT THOUGHTS" BY JOANNE KATES IN *CITY WOMAN*, SPRING 1984.

Acrylic

103

ARTIST
Brad Holland

DESIGNER
Dian-Aziza Ooka

ART DIRECTOR
Louise Kollenbaum

PUBLICATION
Mother Jones

PUBLISHER
Foundation for National Progress

ILLUSTRATION FOR AN ARTICLE ENTITLED "THE WILD BIRDS" BY WENDELL BERRY IN *MOTHER JONES*, APRIL 1984.

Acrylic

104

ARTIST
Brad Holland

DESIGNER
Bruce Hansen

ART DIRECTOR
Tom Staebler

PUBLICATION
Playboy

PUBLISHER
Playboy Enterprises, Inc.

ILLUSTRATION FOR A STORY ON MUHAMMAD ALI ENTITLED "SHADOWBOXER" BY MARK KRAM IN *PLAYBOY*, JANUARY 1984.

Acrylic

ARTIST
Brad Holland

DESIGNER
Skip Williamson

ART DIRECTOR
Tom Staebler

PUBLICATION
Playboy

PUBLISHER
Playboy Enterprises, Inc.

ILLUSTRATION FOR AN ARTICLE ENTITLED "EYE TO EYE WITH MR. T." BY D. KEITH MANO IN *PLAYBOY*, SEPTEMBER 1983.

Acrylic

105

ARTIST
Brad Holland

DESIGNER
Bett McLean

ART DIRECTOR
Andrew Epstein

PUBLICATION
The Best of Business

PUBLISHER
13-30 Corp.

ILLUSTRATION FOR AN ARTICLE ENTITLED "CORPORATE STRESS AND THE BLACK EXECUTIVE" BY BEBE MOORE CAMPBELL IN *THE BEST OF BUSINESS*, SPRING 1983.

Acrylic

106

ARTIST
Brad Holland

DESIGNER
Ken Kendrick

ART DIRECTORS
Roger Black/Ken Kendrick

PUBLICATION
The New York Times Magazine

PUBLISHER
The New York Times Co.

ILLUSTRATION FOR AN ARTICLE ENTITLED "THE RUSH TO DEREGULATE" BY MARTIN AND SUSAN J. TOLCHIN IN *THE NEW YORK TIMES MAGAZINE*, AUGUST 1983.

Acrylic

107

ARTIST
Brad Holland

DESIGNER
Mary Challinor

ART DIRECTOR
Mary Challinor

PUBLICATION
Science 84

PUBLISHER
American Association for the Advancement of Science

ILLUSTRATION FOR AN ARTICLE ENTITLED "INFANTICIDE" BY BARBARA BURKE IN *SCIENCE 84*, MAY 1984.

Acrylic

108

ARTIST
Brad Holland

ART DIRECTOR
Tom Lunde

PUBLICATION
Newsweek

PUBLISHER
Washington Post Co.

ILLUSTRATION FOR AN ARTICLE ENTITLED "DIVORCE AMERICAN STYLE" BY ARIC PRESS IN *NEWSWEEK*, JANUARY 1983.

Acrylic

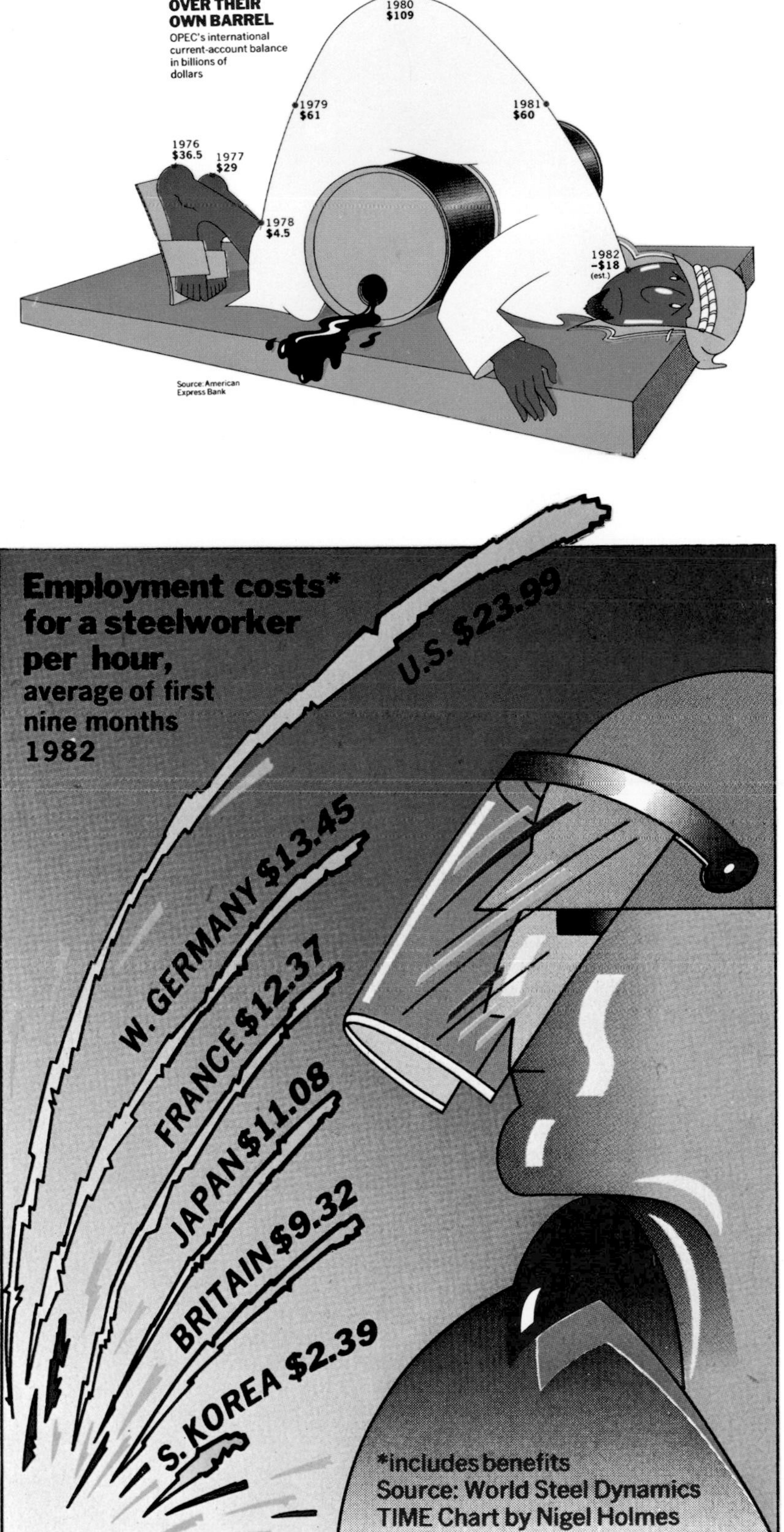

109

ARTIST
Nigel Holmes

DESIGNER
Nigel Holmes

ART DIRECTOR
Nigel Holmes

PUBLICATION
Time

PUBLISHER
Time Inc.

ILLUSTRATION FOR AN ARTICLE ENTITLED "THE HUMBLING OF OPEC" BY CHARLES ALEXANDER IN *TIME*, FEBRUARY 1983.

Black line and computer coloring and airbrush

ARTIST
Nigel Holmes

DESIGNER
Nigel Holmes

ART DIRECTOR
Nigel Holmes

PUBLICATION
Time

PUBLISHER
Time Inc.

ILLUSTRATION FOR AN ARTICLE ENTITLED "BIG STEEL'S WINTER OF WOES" BY CHRISTOPHER BYRON IN *TIME*, JANUARY 1983.

Black line and computer coloring and airbrush

110

ARTIST
Thomas Hunt

DESIGNER
Louis Fishauf

ART DIRECTOR
Louis Fishauf

PUBLICATION
Saturday Night

PUBLISHER
Saturday Night Publishing

ILLUSTRATION FOR AN ARTICLE ENTITLED "DEADLY WEAPON" BY CARSTEN STROUD IN *SATURDAY NIGHT*, OCTOBER 1983.

Pencil

111

ARTIST
Jeff Jackson

DESIGNER
Mary Opper

ART DIRECTOR
Arthur Niemi

PUBLICATION
Quest

PUBLISHER
Comac Communications Ltd.

ILLUSTRATION FOR A STORY ON THE CANADIAN FASHION INDUSTRY ENTITLED "CLOTHES ENCOUNTERS" BY MATTHEW HART IN *QUEST*, DECEMBER 1983.

Colored paper

112

ARTIST
Jeff Jackson

DESIGNER
Barbara Solowan

ART DIRECTOR
Barbara Solowan

PUBLICATION
City Woman

PUBLISHER
Comac Communications Ltd.

ILLUSTRATION FOR AN ARTICLE ENTITLED "MANAGING MEN—NINE TO FIVE AND AFTER" BY SHEILA KIERAN IN *CITY WOMAN*, SPRING 1983.

Pastel

113

ARTIST
Frances Jetter

DESIGNER
Ronn Campisi

ART DIRECTOR
Ronn Campisi

PUBLICATION
The Boston Globe Magazine

PUBLISHER
Globe Newspaper Co.

ILLUSTRATION FOR AN ARTICLE ENTITLED "AMERICA'S PROFILE" BY CHARLES KENNEY IN *THE BOSTON GLOBE MAGAZINE*, MARCH 1984.

Linocut and collage

114

ARTIST
Frances Jetter

DESIGNER
Susan Reinhardt

ART DIRECTOR
Susan Reinhardt

PUBLICATION
The Dial

PUBLISHER
Public Broadcasting Communications, Inc.

ILLUSTRATION ABOUT A WOMAN'S IDENTIFICATION WITH MEDEA'S VENGEANCE FOR AN ARTICLE ENTITLED "WOMEN'S ANGER" BY LISA SCHWARTZBAUM IN *THE DIAL*, APRIL 1983.

Linocut and collage

115

ARTIST
David A. Johnson

DESIGNER
Ken Kendrick

ART DIRECTOR
Ken Kendrick

PUBLICATION
The New York Times Magazine

PUBLISHER
The New York Times Co.

ILLUSTRATION FOR AN ARTICLE ENTITLED "EGYPT'S ANGRY ISLAMIC MILITANTS" BY SANA HASAN IN *THE NEW YORK TIMES MAGAZINE*, NOVEMBER 1983.

Ink

116

ARTIST
David A. Johnson

ART DIRECTOR
Steven Heller

PUBLICATION
The New York Times Book Review

PUBLISHER
The New York Times Co.

ILLUSTRATION FOR A BOOK REVIEW ENTITLED "PROUST BEFORE HE BUILT HIS MONUMENT" BY JOHN WEIGHTMANN IN *THE NEW YORK TIMES BOOK REVIEW,* MAY, 1983.

Black ink

ARTIST
David A. Johnson

DESIGNER
Steven Heller

ART DIRECTOR
Steven Heller

PUBLICATION
The New York Times Book Review

PUBLISHER
The New York Times Co.

ILLUSTRATION FOR A REVIEW OF A THOMAS MANN BOOK ENTITLED "THE ARTIST IN POLITICS" BY WALTER LAQUEUR IN *THE NEW YORK TIMES BOOK REVIEW,* 1983.

Black ink

117

ARTIST
Gary Kelley

DESIGNER
Gary Bernloehr

ART DIRECTOR
Gary Bernloehr

PUBLICATION
Florida Trend Magazine

PUBLISHER
Florida Trend Inc.

ILLUSTRATION FOR AN ARTICLE ENTITLED "HOW SMALL BANKS PLAN TO AVOID GETTING TRAMPLED" BY JOHN CRADDOCK IN *FLORIDA TREND MAGAZINE*, OCTOBER 1983.

Pastel

118

ARTIST
Gary Kelley

DESIGNERS
Fred Woodward/David Kampa

ART DIRECTOR
Fred Woodward

PUBLICATION
Texas Monthly

PUBLISHER
Texas Monthly, Inc.

ILLUSTRATION FOR AN ARTICLE ENTITLED "THE TEXAS FOOD MANIFESTO" BY ALISON COOK IN *TEXAS MONTHLY*, DECEMBER 1983.

Pastel

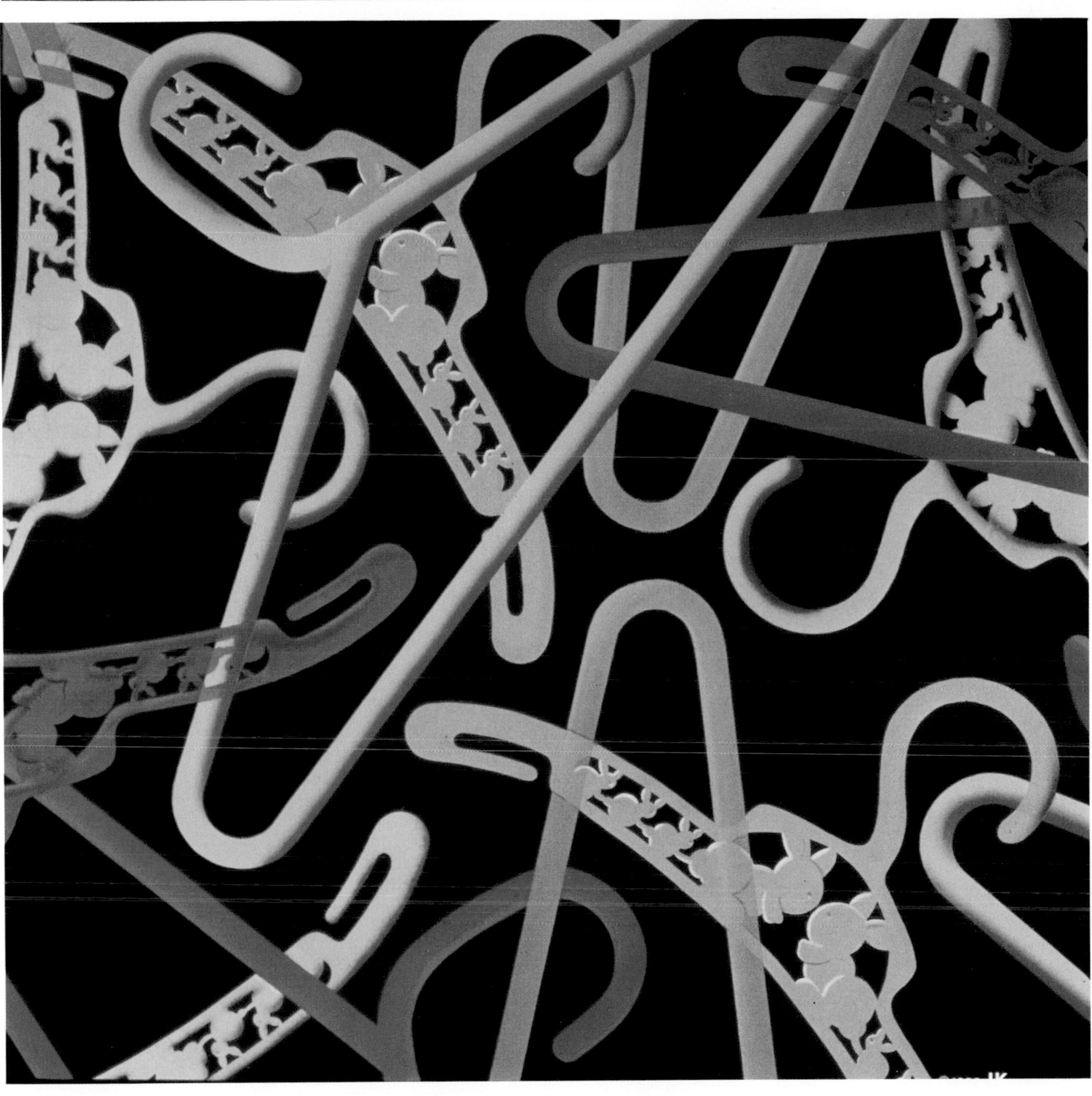

119

ARTIST
Julia King

DESIGNER
Julia King

ART DIRECTOR
Ginny Pitre

PUBLICATION
Dallas Life

PUBLISHER
Dallas Morning News

ILLUSTRATION FOR A SHORT STORY ENTITLED "WARDROBE PLANNING" IN *DALLAS LIFE MAGAZINE*, FEBRUARY 1983.

Acrylic

120

ARTIST
Renee Klein

DESIGNER
Stephen Doyle

ART DIRECTOR
Derek W. Ungless

PUBLICATION
Rolling Stone

PUBLISHER
Straight Arrow Publishers, Inc.

ILLUSTRATION FOR A RECORD REVIEW ENTITLED "FUNKY REGGAE: NEW MUSIC FROM THE ISLANDS" BY DEBBY MILLER IN *ROLLING STONE*, MAY 1983.

Linoleum block print

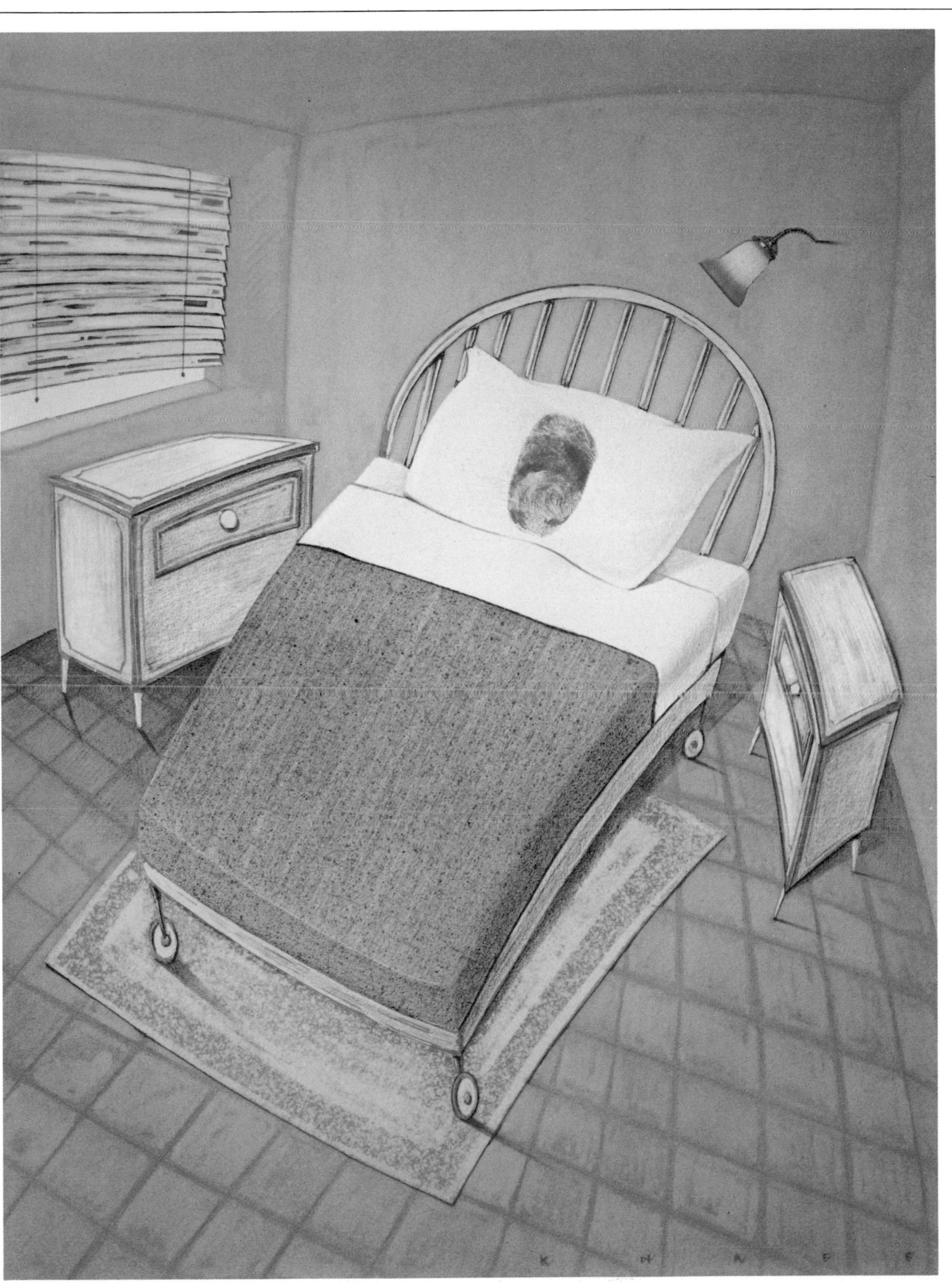

121

ARTIST
Jean-Christian Knaff

DESIGNER
Jean-Christian Knaff

ART DIRECTOR
Daniele Lebel

PUBLICATION
L'Actualité

PUBLISHER
McClean Hunter

ILLUSTRATION FOR AN ARTICLE ENTITLED "L'HOTEL DIEU DES TORTURES" (HOSPITAL FOR POLITICALLY TORTURED PEOPLE) BY SYLVIE HALPERN IN *L'ACTUALITÉ*, JANUARY 1984.

Watercolor and mixed media

122

ARTIST
Jean-Christian Knaff

ART DIRECTOR
Jocelyne Fournel

PUBLICATION
Montreal Ce Mois-Ci

PUBLISHER
MCM Publishing Co.

COVER ILLUSTRATION FOR *MONTREAL CE MOIS-CI* (THIS MONTH IN MONTREAL), 1983.

Watercolor and mixed media

123

ARTIST
George F. Kocar

DESIGNER
Sam Capuano

ART DIRECTOR
Greg Paul

PUBLICATION
The Plain Dealer Magazine

PUBLISHER
The Plain Dealer Publications Co.

ILLUSTRATION FOR AN ARTICLE ENTITLED "ROCKY IN RIGHT" BY JAY KEGLEY IN *THE PLAIN DEALER MAGAZINE*, JUNE 1983.

Acrylic

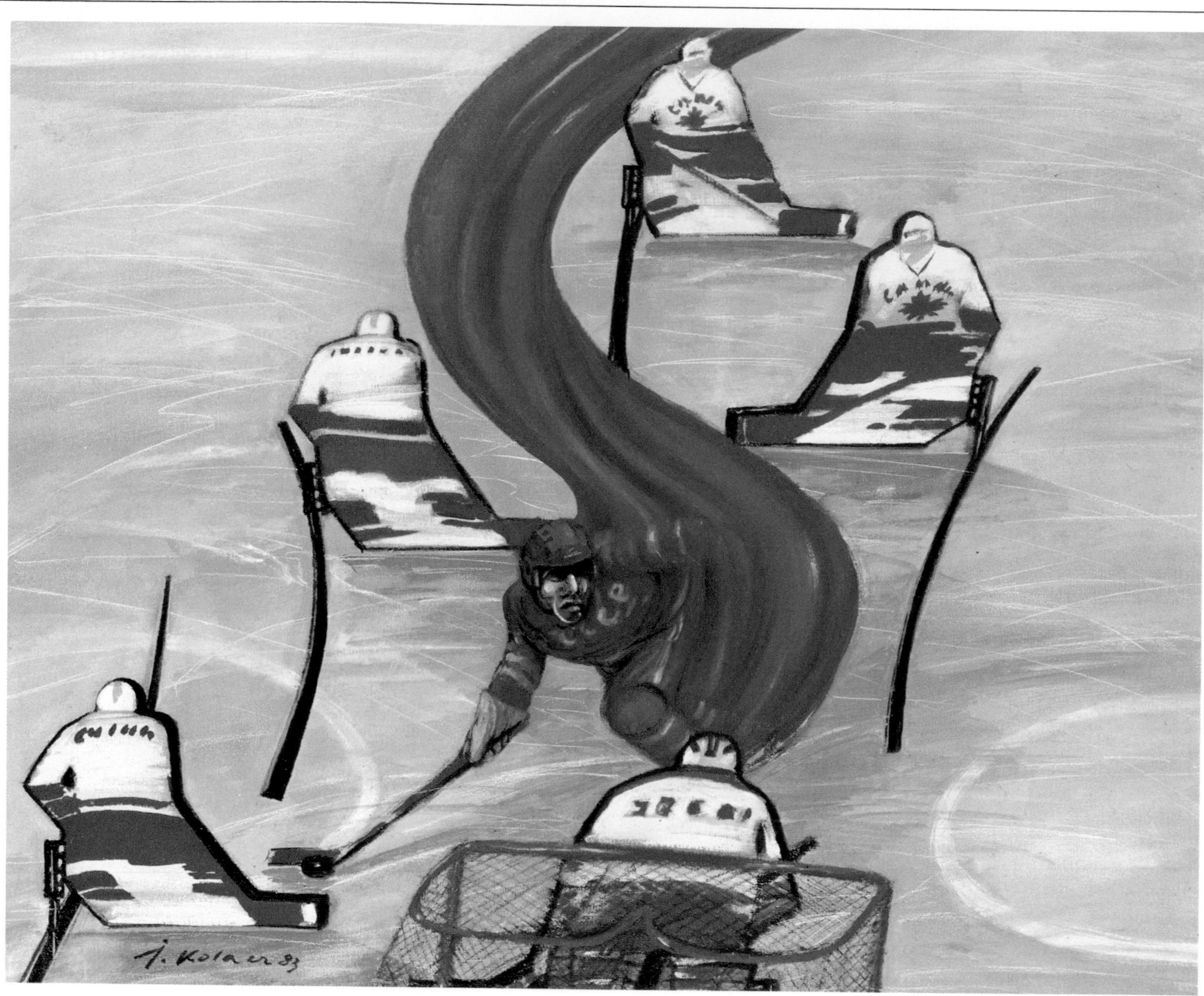

124

ARTIST
Jerzy Kolacz

DESIGNER
Jolene Cuyler

ART DIRECTOR
Louis Fishauf

PUBLICATION
Saturday Night

PUBLISHER
Saturday Night Publishing

ILLUSTRATION FOR AN ARTICLE ENTITLED "BREAKING AWAY" BY KEN DRYDEN IN *SATURDAY NIGHT*, OCTOBER 1983.

Acrylic

125

ARTIST
Edward Koren

DESIGNER
Nancy Duckworth

ART DIRECTOR
Nancy Butkus

PUBLICATION
California Magazine

PUBLISHER
New West Communications Corp.

ILLUSTRATION FOR AN ARTICLE ENTITLED "ANIMAL HOSPITAL" BY DELIA EPHRON IN *CALIFORNIA MAGAZINE*, MAY 1983.

Pen and ink

126

ARTIST
Stephen Kroninger

DESIGNERS
Marianne Gaffney/Michael Grossman

ART DIRECTOR
Michael Grossman

PUBLICATION
National Lampoon

PUBLISHER
The National Lampoon Inc.

ILLUSTRATION FOR AN ARTICLE ENTITLED "EVERY BOY'S GUIDE TO HIS OWN RAT PACK" BY MIMI POND IN *NATIONAL LAMPOON*, MARCH 1984.

Collage

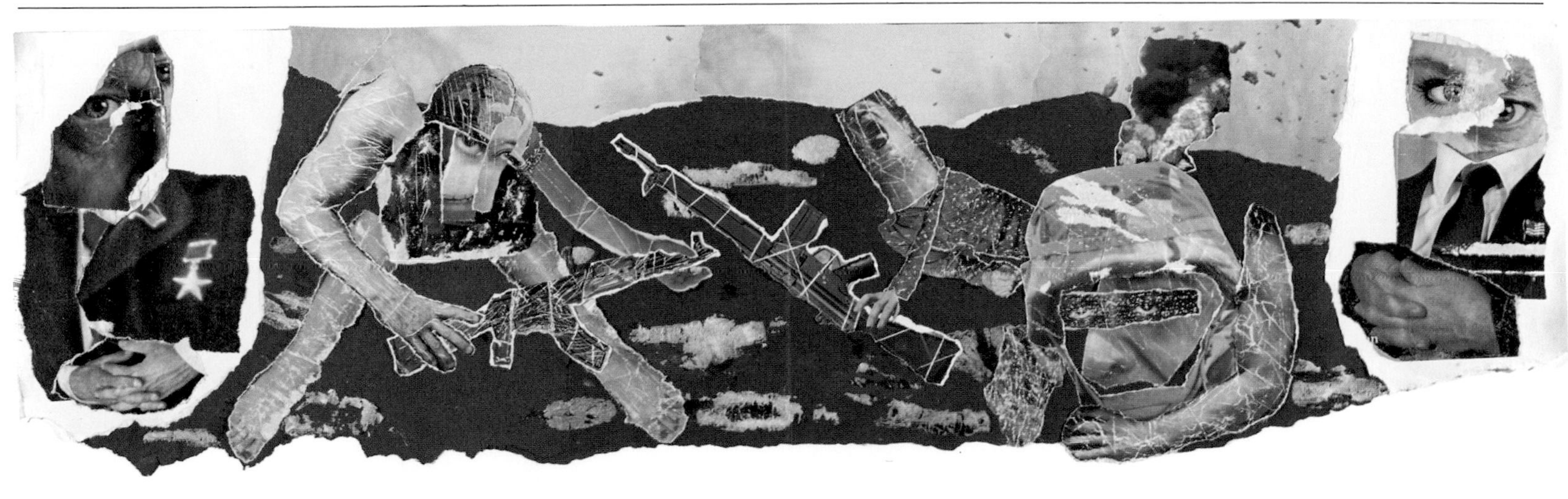

127

ARTIST
Stephen Kroninger

DESIGNER
Patrick JB Flynn

ART DIRECTOR
Patrick JB Flynn

PUBLICATION
The Progressive

PUBLISHER
The Progressive, Inc.

ILLUSTRATION DEPICTING THE IDEA OF CONVENTIONAL NUCLEAR WEAPONRY FOR AN ARTICLE ENTITLED "LEAPING THE FIREBREAK" BY MICHAEL KLARE IN *THE PROGRESSIVE*, SEPTEMBER 1983.

Photo-collage

128

ARTIST
Mark Kseniak

DESIGNER
Marcia Wright

ART DIRECTOR
Barbara Koster

PUBLICATION
TWA Ambassador

PUBLISHER
Webb Company

ILLUSTRATION FOR AN ARTICLE ENTITLED "B-SCHOOL BLUES" BY CLAUDIA H. DEUTSCH IN *TWA AMBASSADOR*, DECEMBER 1983.

Pen and ink and Cello-tak

129

ARTIST
Kuniyasu

DESIGNER
Elizabeth Williams

ART DIRECTOR
Derek W. Ungless

PUBLICATION
Rolling Stone

PUBLISHER
Straight Arrow Publishers, Inc.

ILLUSTRATION FOR AN ARTICLE ENTITLED "EURYTHMICS AND THE LANGUAGE OF LOVE" BY CHRISTOPHER CONNELLY IN *ROLLING STONE*, FEBRUARY 1984.

Pastel

130

ARTIST
Anita Kunz

DESIGNER
Louis Fishauf

ART DIRECTOR
Louis Fishauf

PUBLICATION
Saturday Night

PUBLISHER
Saturday Night Publishing

ILLUSTRATION FOR AN ARTICLE ENTITLED "AGENT OF THE HOLOCAUST" BY SOL LITMAN IN *SATURDAY NIGHT*, JULY 1983.

Gouache and watercolor

131

ARTIST
Anita Kunz

DESIGNER
B.J. Galbraith

ART DIRECTOR
B.J. Galbraith

PUBLICATION
Radio Guide

PUBLISHER
Saturday Night Publishing Services for the Canadian Broadcasting Corp.

COVER ILLUSTRATION FOR A FEATURE ENTITLED "MUSIC TO LISTEN FOR" BY KENNETH WINTERS IN *RADIO GUIDE*, JULY 1983.

Watercolor and gouache

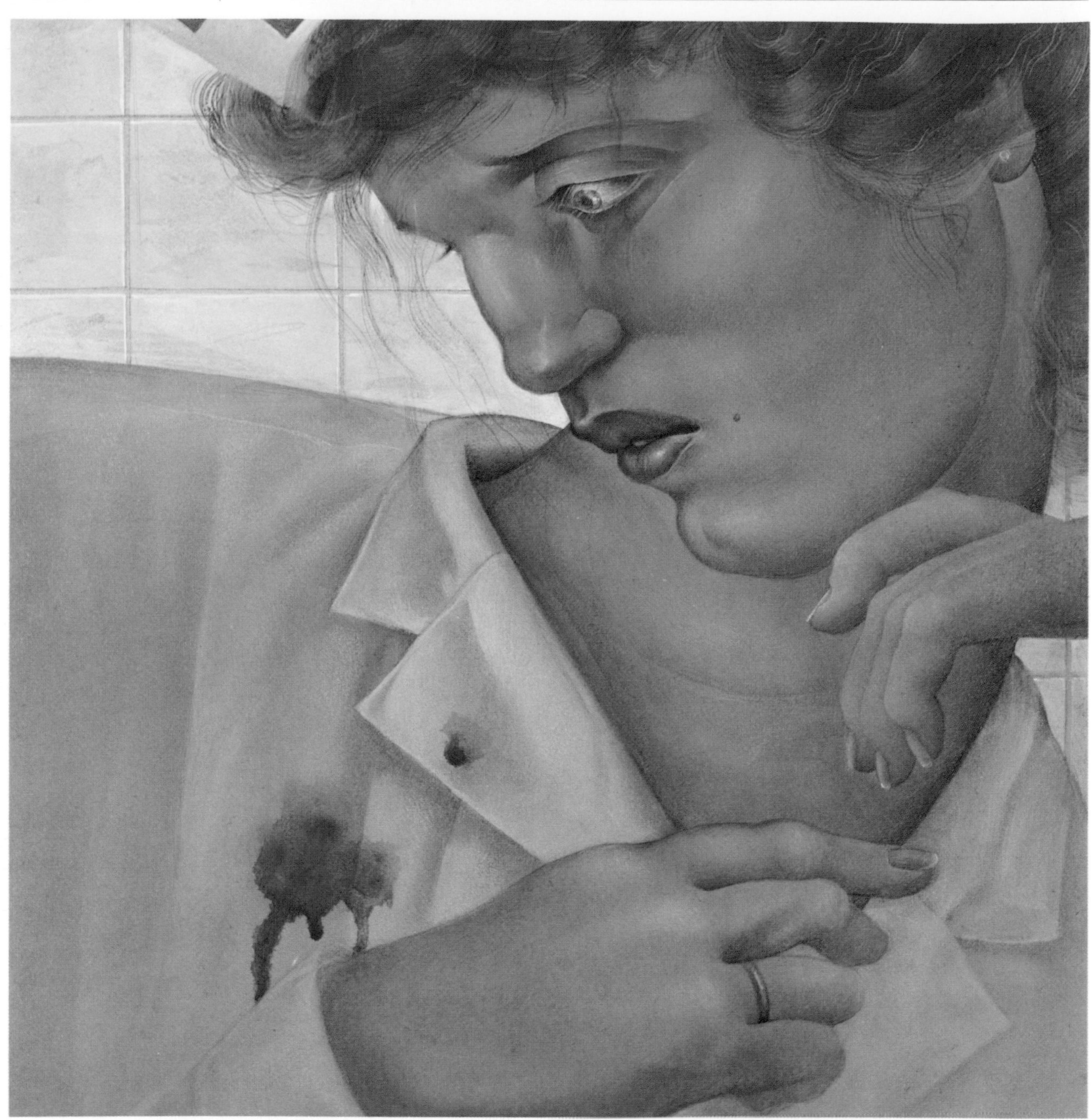

132

ARTIST
Anita Kunz

DESIGNER
Arthur Niemi

ART DIRECTOR
Arthur Niemi

PUBLICATION
Quest

PUBLISHER
Comac Communications Ltd.

ILLUSTRATION DEPICTING THE HORRORS OF NURSING ENTITLED "SILENT NIGHTINGALES" BY CARSTEN STROUD IN *QUEST*, MARCH 1983.

Watercolor and gouache

133

ARTIST
Anita Kunz

ART DIRECTOR
Fred Woodward

PUBLICATION
Westward

PUBLISHER
Dallas Times Herald

ILLUSTRATION FOR A PROFILE ON RAY CHARLES ENTITLED "LET THE GOOD TIMES ROLL" BY PETER GURALNICK IN *WESTWARD*, MAY 1983.

Watercolor and gouache

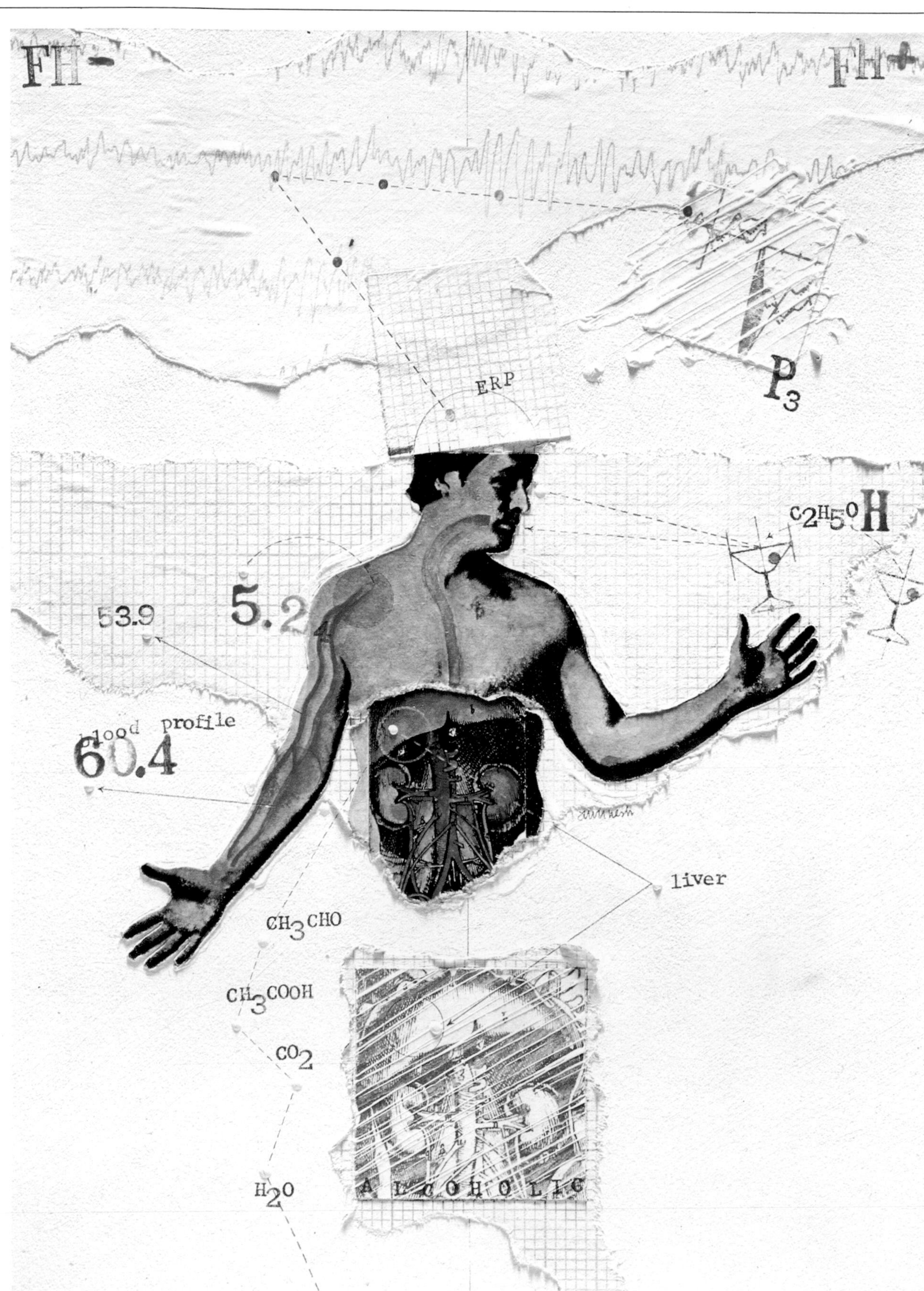

134

ARTIST
David Lesh

DESIGNER
Rodney Williams

ART DIRECTOR
Rodney Williams

PUBLICATION
Science 83

PUBLISHER
American Association for the Advancement of Science

ILLUSTRATION FOR AN ARTICLE ENTITLED "TELLTALE METABOLISM OF ALCOHOLICS" BY MICHAEL WATTERLOND IN *SCIENCE 83*, JUNE 1983.

Mixed media

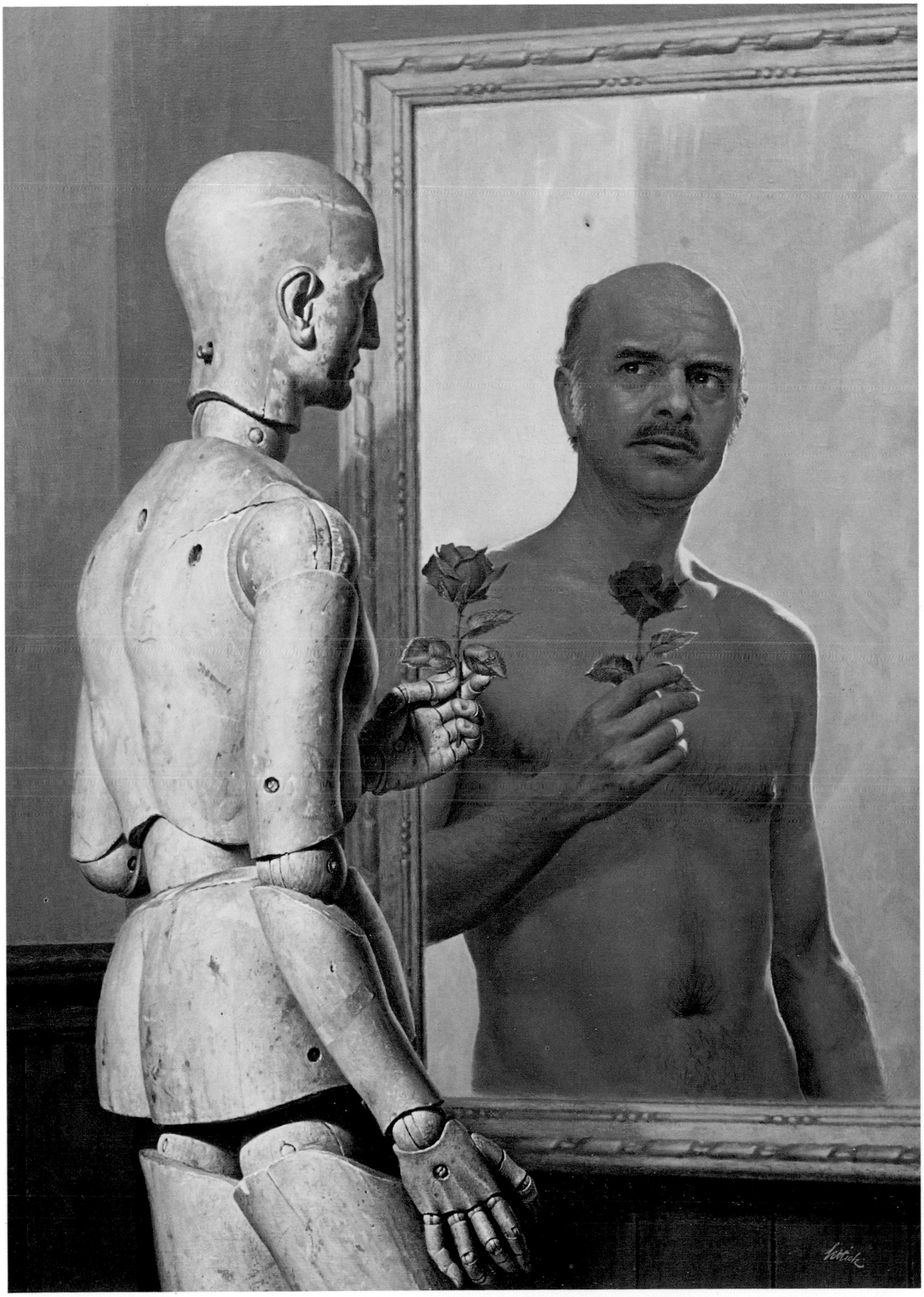

135

ARTIST
Birney Lettick

ART DIRECTOR
Elizabeth Woodson

PUBLICATION
Omni

PUBLISHER
Omni Publications International Ltd.

ILLUSTRATION FOR AN ARTICLE ENTITLED "MORNING CHILD" BY GARDNER DOZOIS IN *OMNI*, JANUARY 1984.

Oil

136

ARTIST
David Levine

DESIGNER
Lloyd Ziff

ART DIRECTOR
Lloyd Ziff

PUBLICATION
Vanity Fair

PUBLISHER
Condé-Nast Publications Inc.

PORTRAIT OF GLEN GOULD FOR AN ARTICLE ENTITLED "THE MUSIC ITSELF" BY EDWARD W. SAID IN *VANITY FAIR*, MAY 1983.

Pen and ink

137

ARTIST
Ron Lightburn

ART DIRECTOR
Peter Manning

PUBLICATION
Western Living Magazine

PUBLISHER
Comac Communications Ltd.

ILLUSTRATION FOR A RESTAURANT REVIEW COLUMN ENTITLED "CAKES AND ALE" BY JURGEN GOTHE IN *WESTERN LIVING MAGAZINE*, JULY 1983.

Colored pencil

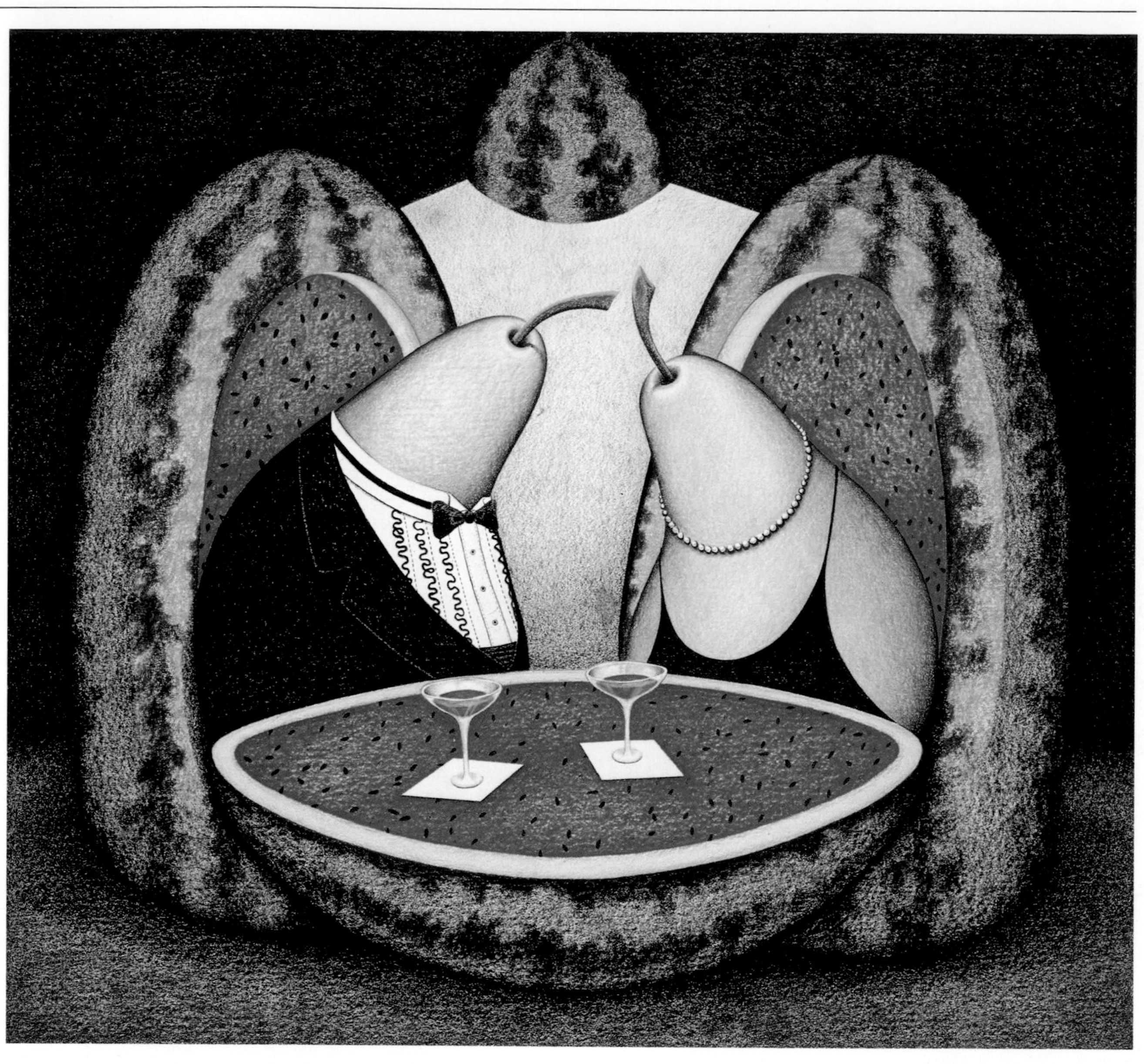

138

ARTIST
John C. Long

DESIGNER
John C. Long

ART EDITOR
Michael J. Ban

PUBLICATION
Michigan Magazine

PUBLISHER
Detroit News

ILLUSTRATION FOR A HUMOROUS ARTICLE FOR NEW YEAR'S EVE DAY ENTITLED "ROMANTIC PAIR" IN *MICHIGAN MAGAZINE*, JANUARY 1984.

Colored pencil

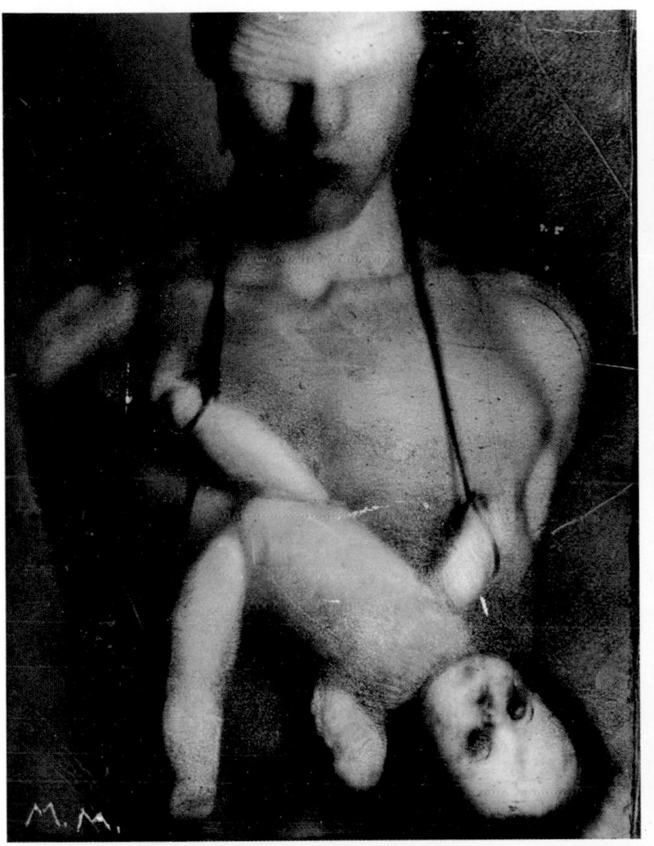

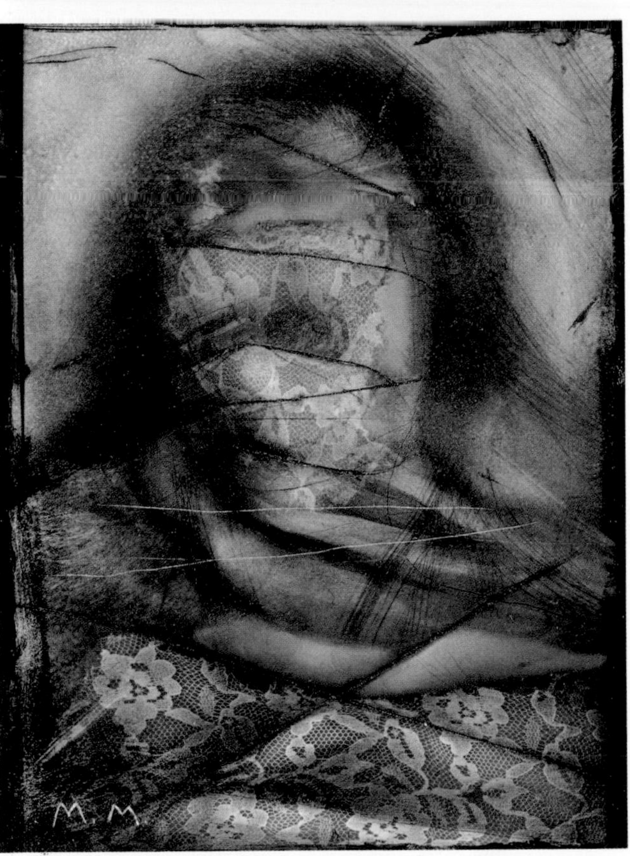

139

ARTIST
Matt Mahurin

DESIGNER
Irene Ramp

ART DIRECTOR
Rudy Hoglund

PUBLICATION
Time

PUBLISHER
Time Inc.

SERIES OF ILLUSTRATIONS FOR AN ARTICLE ENTITLED "PRIVATE VIOLENCE" BY KURT ANDERSEN IN *TIME*, SEPTEMBER 1983.

Oil on photographs

140

ARTIST
Matt Mahurin

ART DIRECTOR
Theo Kouvatos

PUBLICATION
Playboy

PUBLISHER
Playboy Enterprises, Inc.

PORTRAIT FOR AN ARTICLE ENTITLED "INTERVIEW WITH WILLIAM HURT" BY E. JEAN CARROL IN *PLAYBOY*, FEBRUARY 1984.

Oil

141

ARTIST
Matt Mahurin

ART DIRECTOR
Riki Allred

PUBLICATION
Northeast

PUBLISHER
The Hartford Courant

ILLUSTRATION FOR AN ARTICLE ENTITLED "THE CAT LADY" BY MARY ELIZABETH MINEGAR IN *NORTHEAST*, DECEMBER 1983.

Oil

142

ARTIST
Matt Mahurin

DESIGNER
Derek W. Ungless

ART DIRECTOR
Derek W. Ungless

PUBLICATION
Rolling Stone

PUBLISHER
Straight Arrow Publishers, Inc.

ILLUSTRATION FOR AN ARTICLE ENTITLED "BUDDY HOLLY: NO STRINGS ATTACHED" BY KURT LODER IN *ROLLING STONE*, MARCH 1983.

Oil

143

ARTIST
Matt Mahurin

DESIGNER
Elizabeth Williams

ART DIRECTOR
Derek W. Ungless

PUBLICATION
Rolling Stone

PUBLISHER
Straight Arrow Publishers, Inc.

ILLUSTRATION FOR AN ARTICLE ENTITLED "THE YEAR IN MUSIC" BY DAVID ROSENTHAL IN *ROLLING STONE*, DECEMBER 1983-JANUARY 1984.

Oil

144

ARTIST
Mark Marek

ART DIRECTOR
Michael Grossman

PUBLICATION
National Lampoon

PUBLISHER
The National Lampoon Inc.

"THE ADVENTURES OF HERCULES AMONGST THE NORTH AMERICANS," A COMIC STRIP IN *NATIONAL LAMPOON*, FEBRUARY 1984.

Pen and ink and pantone paper

145

ARTIST
Mark Marek

DESIGNER
Elizabeth Williams

ART DIRECTOR
Derek W. Ungless

PUBLICATION
Rolling Stone

PUBLISHER
Straight Arrow Publishers, Inc.

ILLUSTRATION FOR AN ARTICLE ENTITLED "GEORGE CLINTON AND COMPANY RECAPTURE THE DANCE-FLOOR CROWN" BY DEBBY MILLER IN *ROLLING STONE*, MARCH 1984.

Ink and pantone

146

ARTIST
Mark Marek

DESIGNER
Elizabeth Williams

ART DIRECTOR
Derek W. Ungless

PUBLICATION
Rolling Stone

PUBLISHER
Straight Arrow Publishers, Inc.

COVER ILLUSTRATION FOR A SUPPLEMENT ENTITLED "COLLEGE PAPERS" BY CAROLYN WHITE IN *ROLLING STONE*, MARCH 1984.

Amberlith and mechanical tints

147

ARTIST
Mark Marek

DESIGNER
Mark Marek

ART DIRECTOR
Manhattan Design

PUBLICATION
Christmas Rapping Paper

PUBLISHER
Manhattan Design

ILLUSTRATION FOR AN ARTICLE ENTITLED "THE SAVAGE CHEF" BY PETER GORMAN IN THE COOKING SECTION OF *CHRISTMAS RAPPING PAPER*, JANUARY 1983.

Ink and pantone

148

ARTIST
Mark Marek

DESIGNER
Elizabeth Williams

ART DIRECTOR
Derek W. Ungless

PUBLICATION
Rolling Stone

PUBLISHER
Straight Arrow Publishers, Inc.

ILLUSTRATION FOR AN ARTICLE ENTITLED "TERMINAL EDUCATION" BY PHIL BERTONI IN *ROLLING STONE*, MARCH 1984.

Ink and pantone

149

ARTIST
Eugene Mihaesco

ART DIRECTOR
Tina Adamek

PUBLICATION
Postgraduate Medicine

PUBLISHER
McGraw Hill Publishing Co.

ILLUSTRATION FOR AN ARTICLE ENTITLED "MILD HYPERTENSION" BY EDWARD D. FREIS, M.D. IN *POSTGRADUATE MEDICINE*, JANUARY 1983.

Pastel

150

ARTIST
Eugene Mihaesco

DESIGNER
Tom Bentkowski

ART DIRECTOR
Rudy Hoglund

PUBLICATION
Time

PUBLISHER
Time Inc.

SERIES OF ILLUSTRATIONS FOR AN ARTICLE ABOUT THE TURNING POINTS IN GEORGE ORWELL'S LIFE ENTITLED "THAT YEAR IS ALMOST HERE" BY PAUL GRAY IN *TIME*, NOVEMBER 1983.

Pen and ink

151

ARTIST
Eugene Mihaesco

DESIGNER
Irene Ramp

ART DIRECTOR
Rudy Hoglund

PUBLICATION
Time

PUBLISHER
Time Inc.

ILLUSTRATION FOR AN ARTICLE ENTITLED "STRESS: CAN WE COPE?" BY CLAUDIA WALLIS IN *TIME*. JUNE 1983.

Pencil and watercolor

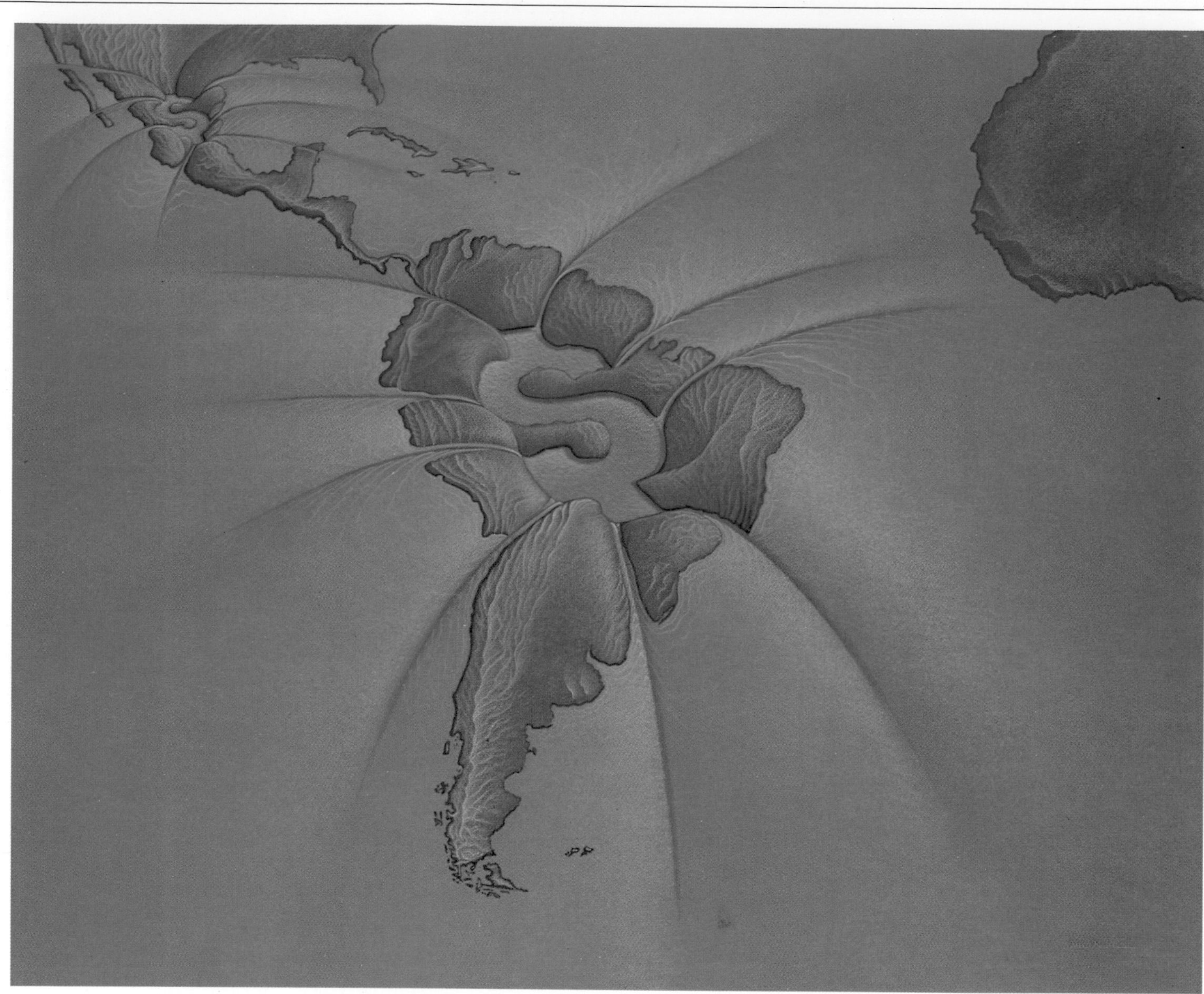

152

ARTIST
David Montiel

ART DIRECTOR
Bett McLean

PUBLICATION
Best of Business

PUBLISHER
13-30 Corp.

ILLUSTRATION FOR AN ARTICLE ENTITLED "LATIN AMERICAN DEBT" IN *BEST OF BUSINESS*, JUNE 1983.

Acrylic

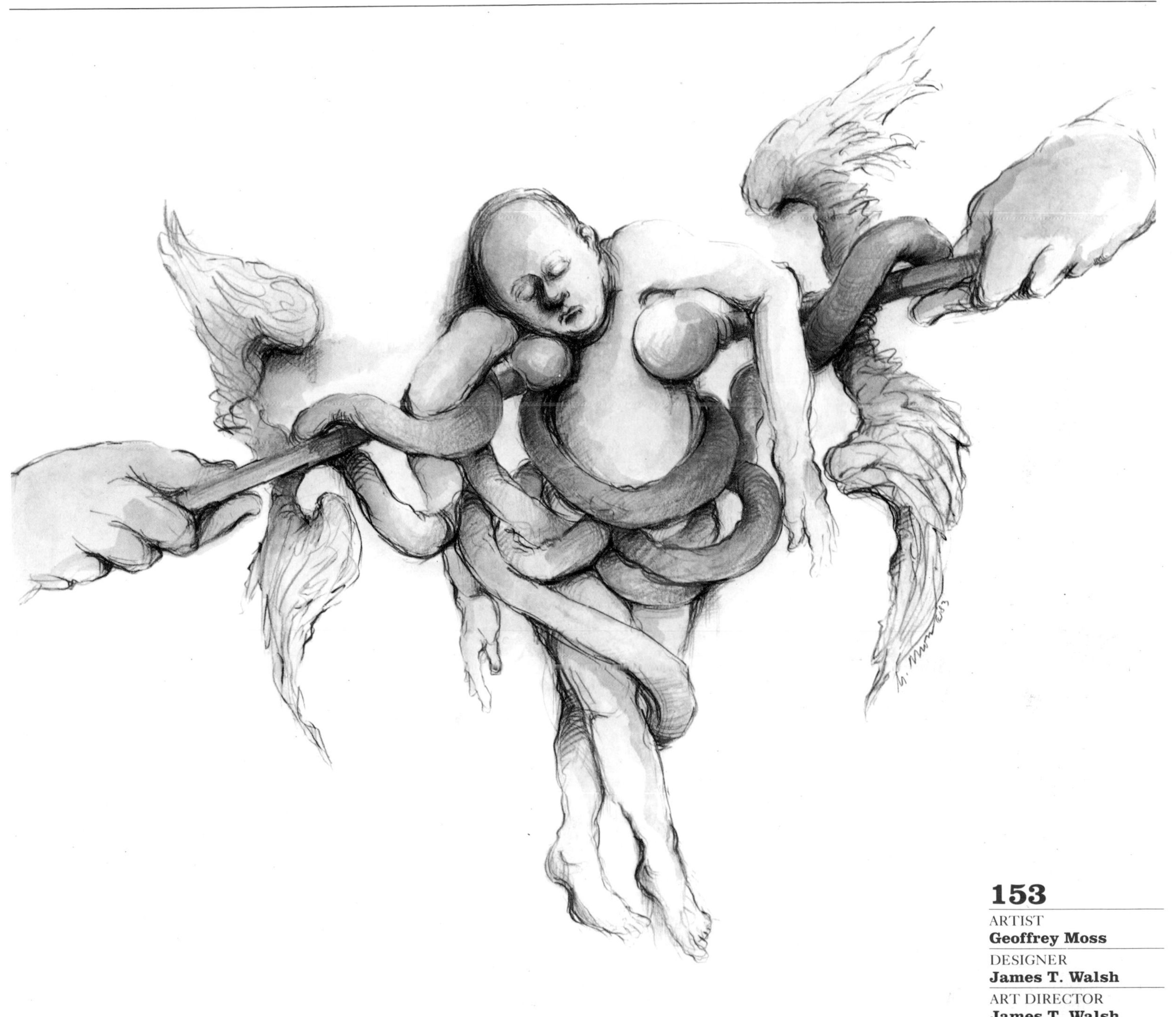

153

ARTIST
Geoffrey Moss

DESIGNER
James T. Walsh

ART DIRECTOR
James T. Walsh

PUBLICATION
Emergency Medicine

PUBLISHER
Fischer Medical Publications

ILLUSTRATION FOR AN ARTICLE ENTITLED "TRAUMA CONTROVERSIES: SHOCK" BY JOHN HEINEGG IN *EMERGENCY MEDICINE*, MARCH 1983.

Watercolor

154

ARTIST
San Murata

DESIGNER
San Murata

ART DIRECTOR
Jonathan Rogers

PUBLICATION
Avenue Magazine

PUBLISHER
Bloor Publishing

COVER ILLUSTRATION FOR *AVENUE MAGAZINE*, MARCH 1984.

Gouache

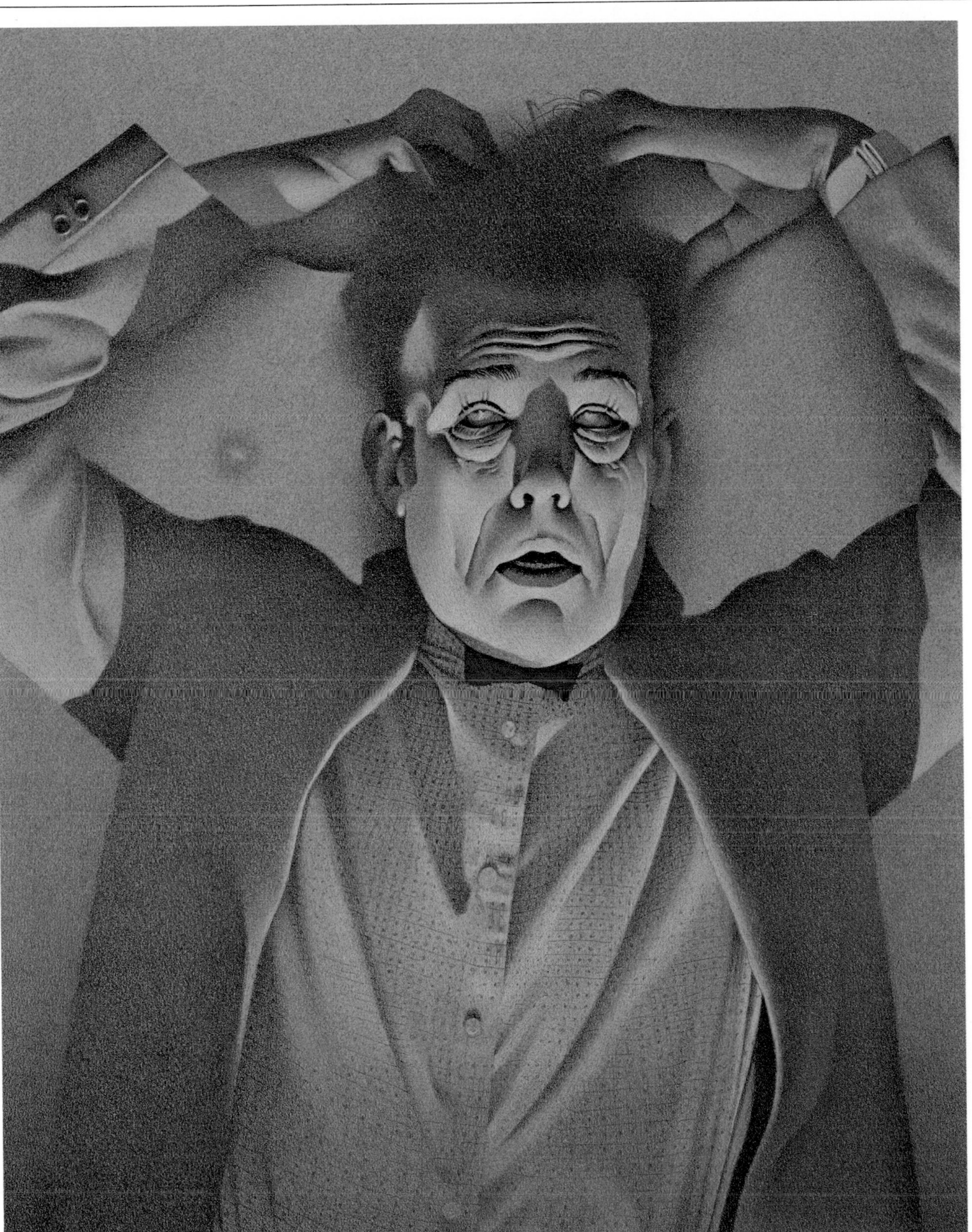

155

ARTIST
Bill Nelson

DESIGNER
Bill Nelson

ART DIRECTOR
Bill Nelson

PUBLICATION
Throttle Magazine

PUBLISHER
Throttle Inc.

COVER ILLUSTRATION FOR *THROTTLE MAGAZINE*, DECEMBER 1983.

Colored pencil on charcoal paper

156

ARTIST
Barbara Nessim

DESIGNER
Wynn Dan

ART DIRECTOR
Paula Greif

PUBLICATION
Mademoiselle

PUBLISHER
Condé-Nast Publications Inc.

ILLUSTRATION SHOWING REFLEXOLOGY SPOTS FOR AN ARTICLE ENTITLED "THE SOUL OF YOUR FOOT" IN *MADEMOISELLE*, MARCH 1984.

Watercolor, pen and ink, and gouache

157

ARTIST
Mel Odom

DESIGNER
Kerig Pope

ART DIRECTOR
Tom Staebler

PUBLICATION
Playboy

PUBLISHER
Playboy Enterprises, Inc.

ILLUSTRATION FOR A STORY ENTITLED "THE TRAIL OF YOUR BLOOD ON THE SNOW" BY GABRIEL GARCIA MARQUEZ IN *PLAYBOY,* JANUARY 1984.

Colored pencil

158

ARTIST
Robert Andrew Parker

DESIGNER
Barbara Koster

ART DIRECTOR
Barbara Koster

PUBLICATION
TWA Ambassador

PUBLISHER
Trans World Airlines

ILLUSTRATION FOR AN ARTICLE ENTITLED "THE RETURN TO ELEGANT HOTEL DINING: LA RECOLTÉ" BY CHARLES LOCKWOOD IN *TWA AMBASSADOR*, AUGUST 1983.

Etching

159

ARTIST
Judy Pedersen

ART DIRECTOR
Barbara Lish

PUBLICATION
Avenue Magazine

PUBLISHER
Avenue Magazine, Inc.

ILLUSTRATION FOR A STORY ENTITLED "THE LOST SUITOR" BY JOYCE CAROL OATES IN *AVENUE MAGAZINE*, FEBRUARY 1984.

Pastel

160

ARTIST
Judy Pedersen

DESIGNER
Fred Woodward

ART DIRECTOR
Fred Woodward

PUBLICATION
Westward

PUBLISHER
Dallas Times Herald

ILLUSTRATION FOR AN ARTICLE ENTITLED "MY MOTHER" BY NORMA BRADLEY ALLEN IN *WESTWARD*, MAY 1983.

Pastel

161

ARTIST
Mark Penberthy

DESIGNER
Mark Penberthy

ART DIRECTOR
Derek W. Ungless

PUBLICATION
Rolling Stone

PUBLISHER
Straight Arrow Publishers Inc.

ILLUSTRATION FOR A REVIEW ENTITLED "RECORDS: LIONEL RICHIE'S LATIN HUSTLE" BY DON SHEWEY IN *ROLLING STONE* FOR THE ALBUM "CAN'T SLOW DOWN," JANUARY 1983.

Acrylic

162

ARTIST
Mark Penberthy

DESIGNER
Mark Penberthy

ART DIRECTOR
Ralph Stello

PUBLICATION
U.S. Pharmacist

PUBLISHER
Jobson Publishing

COVER ILLUSTRATION FOR A FEATURE ENTITLED "REYE'S SYNDROME" BY RALF G. RAHWAN, PhD IN *U.S. PHARMACIST*, DECEMBER 1983.

Acrylic

163

ARTIST
Paola Piglia

DESIGNER
Gary Mele

ART DIRECTOR
Kati Korpijaakko

PUBLICATION
Ms

PUBLISHER
Ms Foundation for Education and Communication, Inc.

ILLUSTRATION FOR AN ARTICLE ENTITLED "BASTARD CHILD" BY PAULA K. GOVER-LEFFINGWELL IN *MS*, OCTOBER 1983.

Watercolor and gouache

164

ARTIST
Glenn Priestley

DESIGNER
Jolene Cuyler

ART DIRECTOR
Louis Fishauf

PUBLICATION
Saturday Night

PUBLISHER
Saturday Night Publishing

ILLUSTRATION FOR THE POEM "RYE & PICKEREL" BY ERIN MOURÉ IN *SATURDAY NIGHT*, FEBRUARY 1984.

Oil

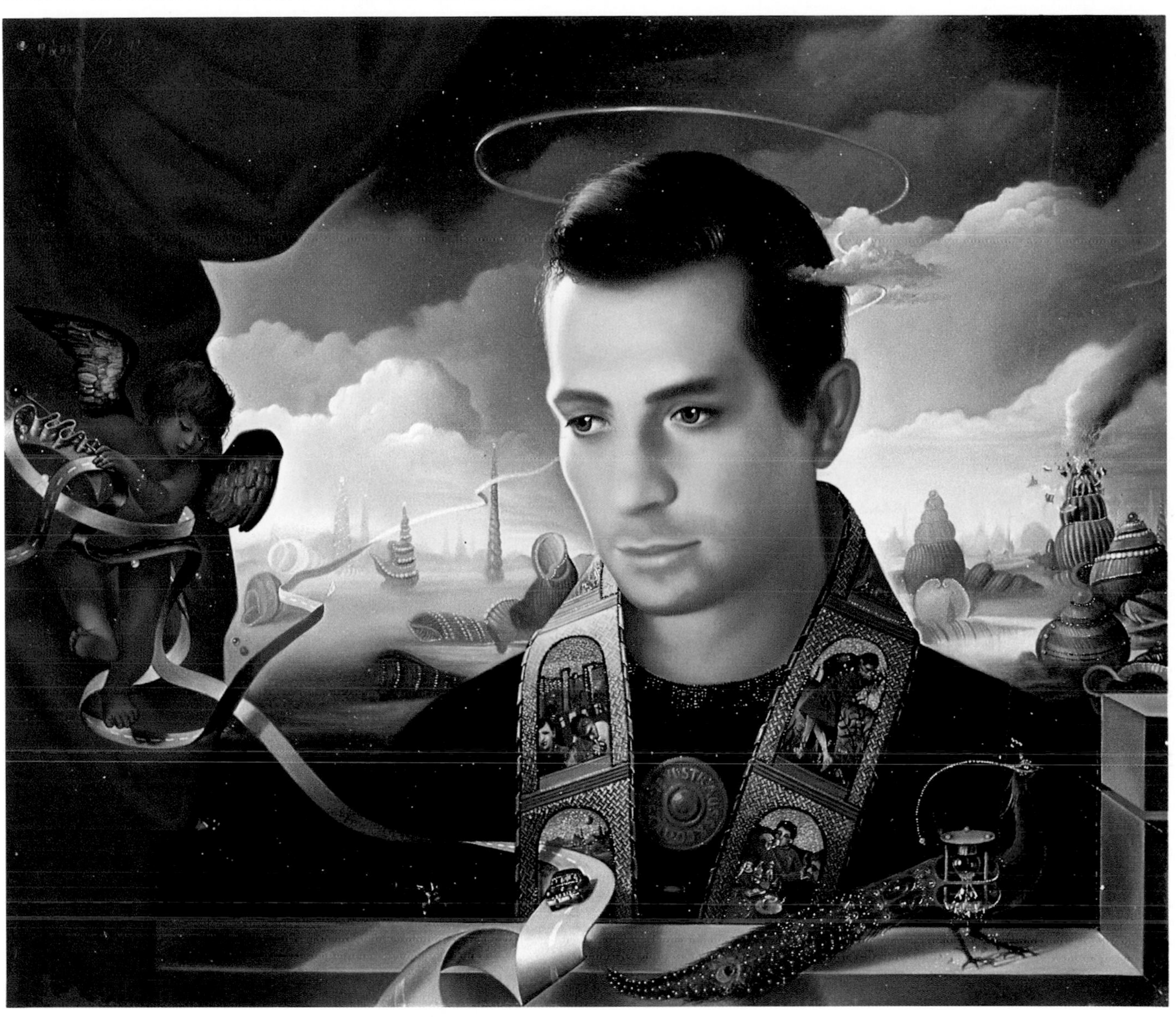

165

ARTIST
Rallé

DESIGNER
John Miller

ART DIRECTOR
April Silver

PUBLICATION
Esquire

PUBLISHER
Esquire Associates

ILLUSTRATION FOR AN ARTICLE ENTITLED "IS THERE ANY END TO KEROUAC HIGHWAY?" BY KEN KESEY IN *ESQUIRE*, DECEMBER 1983.

Oil

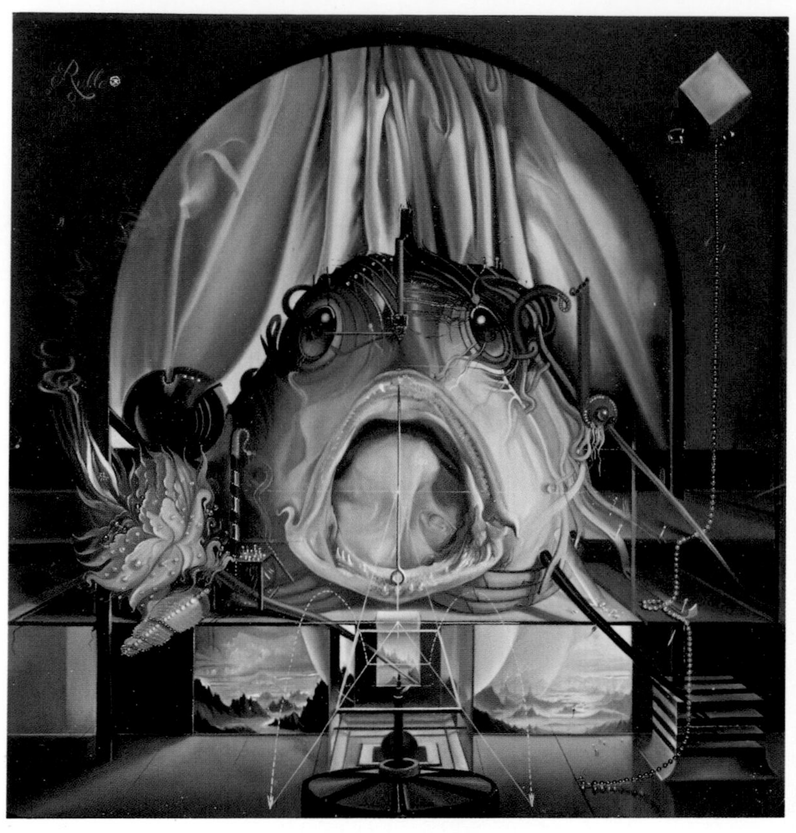

166

ARTIST
Rallé

ART DIRECTOR
Elizabeth Woodson

PUBLICATION
Omni

PUBLISHER
Omni Publications International, Ltd.

ILLUSTRATIONS FOR AN ARTICLE ENTITLED "OMINOUS ICONS" BY KATHLEEN DILETTANTE IN *OMNI*, SEPTEMBER 1983.

Oil

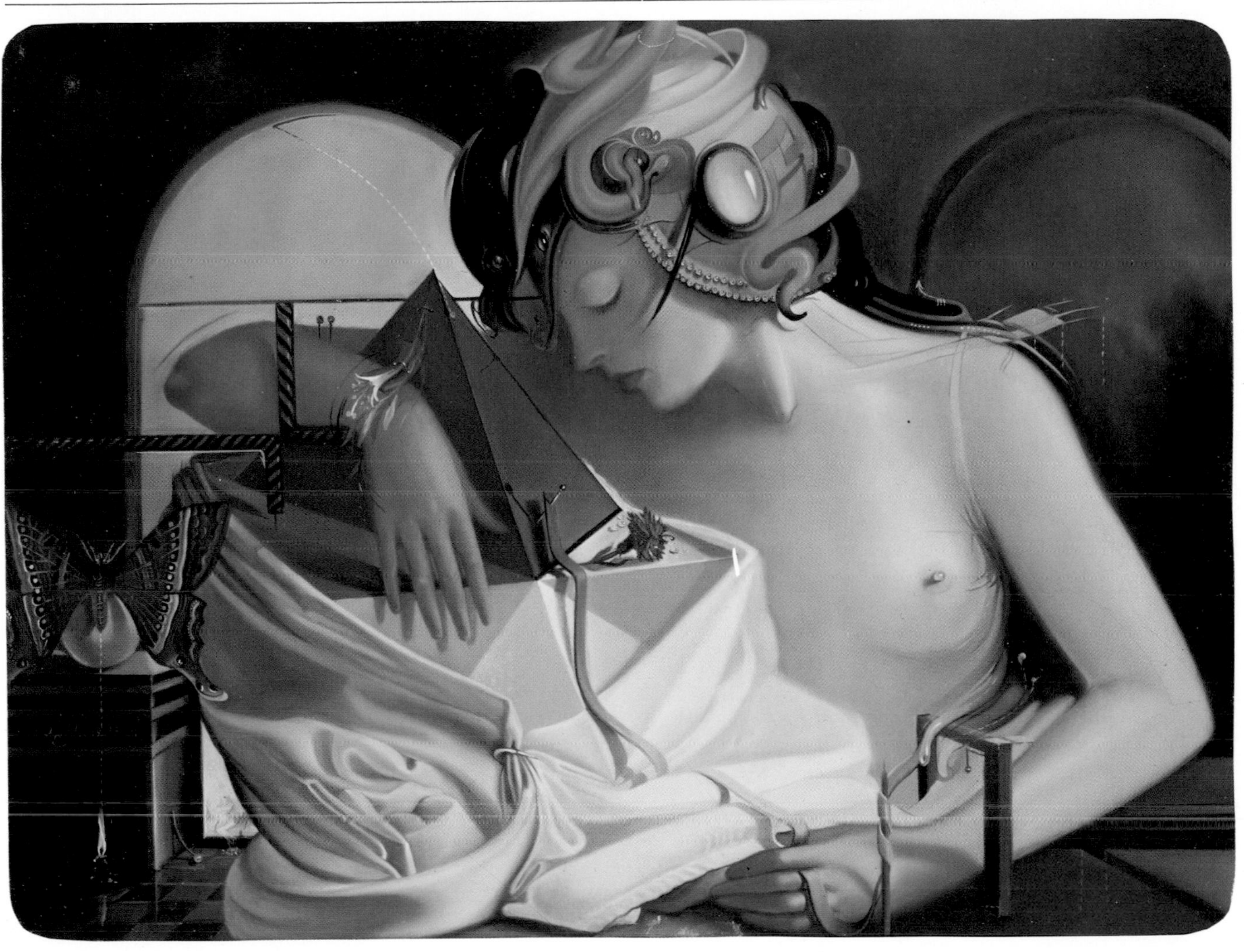

167

ARTIST
Rallé

ART DIRECTOR
Elizabeth Woodson

PUBLICATION
Omni

PUBLISHER
Omni Publications International Ltd.

ILLUSTRATION FOR AN ARTICLE ENTITLED "OMINOUS ICONS" BY KATHLEEN DILETTANTE IN *OMNI*, SEPTEMBER 1983.

Oil

168

ARTIST
Scott Reynolds

DESIGNER
Riki Allred

ART DIRECTOR
Riki Allred

PUBLICATION
Northeast

PUBLISHER
The Hartford Courant

ILLUSTRATION FOR AN ARTICLE ENTITLED "SUNDAY IN THE PARK" BY BEL KAUFMAN IN *NORTHEAST*, OCTOBER 1983.

Oil paint and pastel

169

ARTIST
Richard Schlecht

ART DIRECTOR
Jan Adkins

PUBLICATION
National Geographic Magazine

PUBLISHER
National Geographic Society

ILLUSTRATION FOR AN ARTICLE ENTITLED "HAMILTON AND SCOURGE: GHOST SHIPS OF THE WAR OF 1812" BY DANIEL A. NELSON IN *NATIONAL GEOGRAPHIC MAGAZINE*, MARCH 1983.

Watercolor

170

ARTIST
Collette Slade

DESIGNER
Dugald Stermer

ART DIRECTORS
Dugald Stermer/Barbara Cady

PUBLICATION
Gifts &

PUBLISHER
Teleflora Publishing Inc.

ILLUSTRATION FOR A STORY ABOUT A LEGENDARY RETAILER ENTITLED "THE DOGE OF THE DEARLY PRICED ITEM" BY BARBARA CADY IN *GIFTS &*, MAY 1983.

Oil

171

ARTIST
Douglas Smith

DESIGNER
Elizabeth Williams

ART DIRECTOR
Derek W. Ungless

PUBLICATION
Rolling Stone

PUBLISHER
Straight Arrow Publishers Inc.

ILLUSTRATION FOR A REVIEW ENTITLED "GUITARS RULE IN THIS BIG COUNTRY" BY KURT LODER IN *ROLLING STONE*, SEPTEMBER 1983.

Scratchboard

172

ARTIST
Douglas Smith

DESIGNER
Ronn Campisi

ART DIRECTOR
Ronn Campisi

PUBLICATION
The Boston Globe Magazine

PUBLISHER
Globe Newspaper Co.

ILLUSTRATION OF A RIGHT WHALE FOR AN ARTICLE ENTITLED "ON THE RIGHT TRACK" BY SUSAN ORLEAN IN *THE BOSTON GLOBE MAGAZINE*, NOVEMBER 1983.

Scratchboard

173

ARTIST
Elwood H. Smith

ART DIRECTOR
John Twohey

PUBLICATION
Chicago Tribune Magazine

PUBLISHER
Chicago Tribune Co.

COVER ILLUSTRATION FOR A FEATURE CALLED "HOT DIGGETY DOGS!" BY RICH BOWEN AND DICK FAY IN *CHICAGO TRIBUNE MAGAZINE*, JUNE 1983.

Watercolor and ink

174

ARTIST
Elwood H. Smith

ART DIRECTOR
James Noel Smith

PUBLICATION
Westward

PUBLISHER
Dallas Times Herald

COVER ILLUSTRATION FOR COLLEGE ISSUE OF *WESTWARD*, SEPTEMBER 1983.

Pen and ink and watercolor

175

ARTIST
Elwood H. Smith

DESIGNER
Louis Fishauf

ART DIRECTOR
Louis Fishauf

PUBLICATION
Saturday Night

PUBLISHER
Saturday Night Publishing

COVER ILLUSTRATION FOR AN ARTICLE ENTITLED "IS GOVERNMENT SPENDING OUT OF CONTROL?" BY GEORGE GALT IN *SATURDAY NIGHT*, FEBRUARY 1983.

Watercolor

176

ARTIST
Jeff Smith

DESIGNER
Fred Woodward

ART DIRECTOR
Fred Woodward

PUBLICATION
Texas Monthly

PUBLISHER
Texas Monthly, Inc.

SERIES OF ILLUSTRATIONS FOR AN ARTICLE ABOUT A BRUTAL MURDER ENTITLED "LOVE AND DEATH IN SILICON PRAIRIE" BY JOHN BLOOM AND JIM ATKINSON IN *TEXAS MONTHLY*, JANUARY AND FEBRUARY 1984.

Watercolor

177

ARTIST
Lane Smith

DESIGNER
Mike Keegan

ART DIRECTOR
Massiss Araradian

PUBLICATION
California Living Magazine

PUBLISHER
L.A. Herald Examiner

ILLUSTRATION FOR A HUMOROUS STORY ABOUT A JEWISH SPRUCE CHRISTMAS TREE ENTITLED "THE GREATEST JOB IN THE WORLD" BY DONALD CARROLL IN *CALIFORNIA LIVING MAGAZINE*, DECEMBER 1983.

Alkyd

178

ARTIST
Edward Sorel

DESIGNER
Judy Garlan

ART DIRECTOR
Judy Garlan

PUBLICATION
The Atlantic Monthly

PUBLISHER
The Atlantic Monthly Co.

ILLUSTRATIONS FOR A SERIES ENTITLED "FIRST ENCOUNTERS" BY NANCY CALDWELL SOREL IN *THE ATLANTIC MONTHLY*, 1983 AND 1984.

Mixed media

179

ARTIST
Greg Spalenka

DESIGNER
Rosemarie Sohmer

ART DIRECTOR
Derek W. Ungless

PUBLICATION
Rolling Stone

PUBLISHER
Straight Arrow Publishers Inc.

ILLUSTRATION FOR AN ARTICLE ENTITLED "ELVIS COSTELLO: TOO MUCH YAKETY-YAK" BY CHRISTOPHER CONNELLY IN *ROLLING STONE*, SEPTEMBER 1983.

Oil

180

ARTIST
Greg Spalenka

DESIGNER
Greg Paul

ART DIRECTOR
Greg Paul

PUBLICATION
The Plain Dealer Magazine

PUBLISHER
The Plain Dealer Publications Co.

ILLUSTRATION FOR A STORY ENTITLED "MAN TO MAN, FATHER TO SON" BY BILL SAMMON IN *THE PLAIN DEALER MAGAZINE*, JUNE 1983.

Oil and acrylic

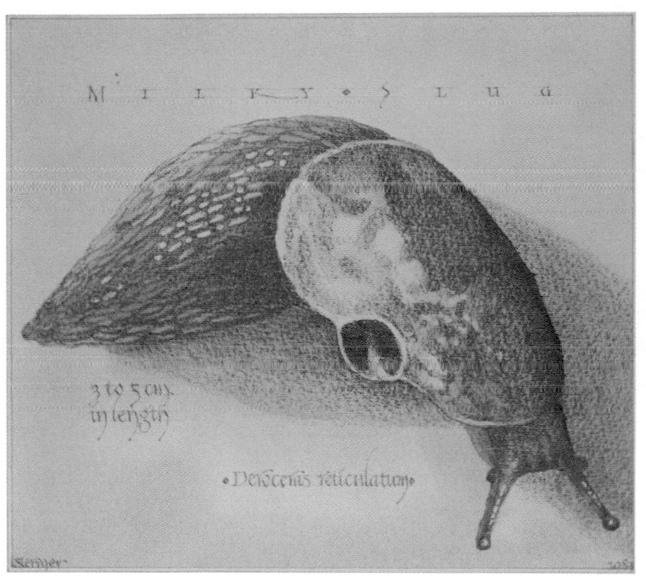

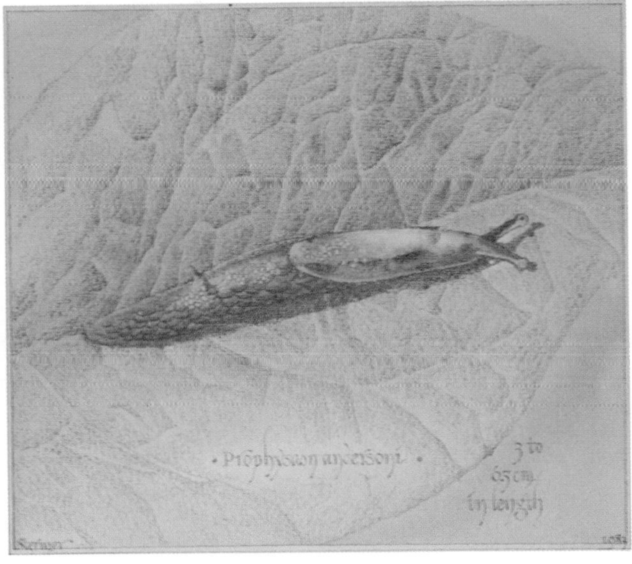

181

ARTIST
Dugald Stermer

DESIGNER
Dugald Stermer

ART DIRECTOR
Robyn Ricks

PUBLICATION
Pacific Northwest

PUBLISHER
Pacific Search

ILLUSTRATIONS DEPICTING VARIOUS SPECIES OF SLUG FOR "THE LIVES OF A SLUG" BY RICK GAUGER IN *PACIFIC NORTHWEST*, MAY 1983.

Pencil and watercolor

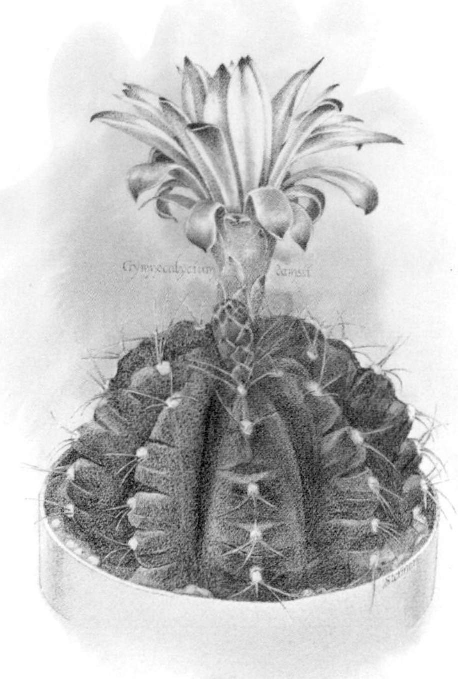

182

ARTIST
Dugald Stermer

DESIGNER
Dugald Stermer

ART DIRECTORS
Dugald Stermer/Barbara Cady

PUBLICATION
Flowers &

PUBLISHER
Teleflora/Flowers &

ILLUSTRATIONS FOR MONTHLY ARTICLES BY THE ARTIST ENTITLED "CACTI/A SERIES OF PORTRAITS" IN *FLOWERS &*, 1983.

Pencil and watercolor

183

ARTIST
Dugald Stermer

DESIGNER
Douglas May

ART DIRECTOR
Douglas May

PUBLICATION
Cuisine Magazine

PUBLISHER
CBS Publications

ILLUSTRATION FOR AN ARTICLE ENTITLED "PEPPER: THE SPICE OF LIFE" BY LESLIE LAND IN *CUISINE MAGAZINE*, MARCH 1984.

Watercolor and colored pencil

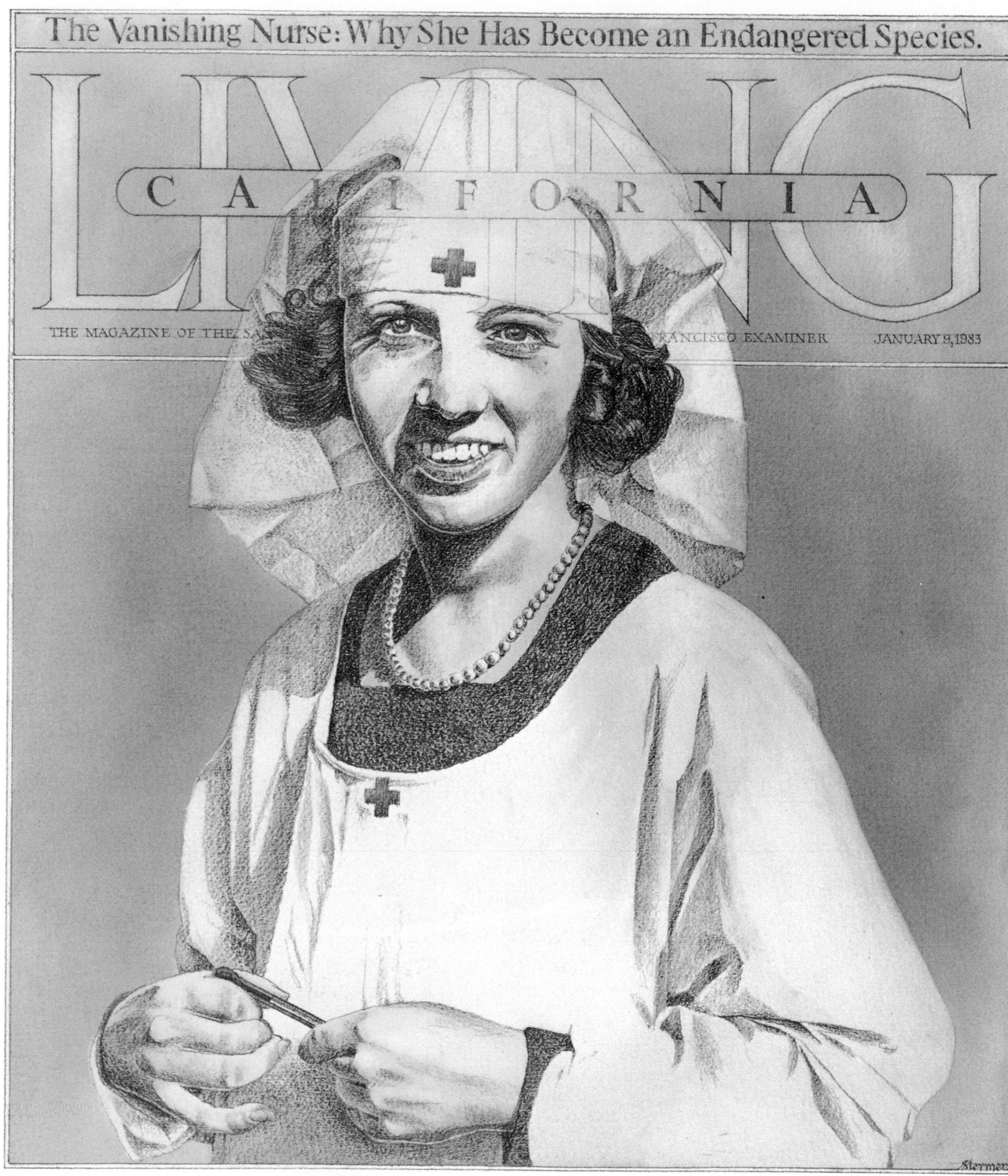
The Vanishing Nurse: Why She Has Become an Endangered Species.
LIVING
CALIFORNIA
THE MAGAZINE OF THE SA
RANCISCO EXAMINER
JANUARY 9, 1983

184

ARTIST
Dugald Stermer

DESIGNER
Dugald Stermer

ART DIRECTORS
Dugald Stermer/Bill Prochnow

PUBLICATION
California Living Magazine

PUBLISHER
San Francisco Examiner

COVER ILLUSTRATION FOR A FEATURE ENTITLED "THE VANISHING NURSE" IN *CALIFORNIA LIVING MAGAZINE*, JANUARY 1983.

Pencil and watercolor

185

ARTIST
Randy Stevens

DESIGNER
Lloyd Ziff

ART DIRECTOR
Lloyd Ziff

PUBLICATION
Vanity Fair

PUBLISHER
Condé-Nast Publications Inc.

ILLUSTRATION FOR AN ARTICLE ENTITLED "THE PROMISCUOUS SELF" BY WALKER PERCY IN *VANITY FAIR*, MAY 1983.

Pastel, pencil, and sparkles

186

ARTIST
Barron Storey

ART DIRECTOR
Jan Adkins

PUBLICATION
National Geographic Magazine

PUBLISHER
National Geographic Society

ILLUSTRATION FOR AN ARTICLE ENTITLED "NATURE'S DWINDLING TREASURES: RAIN FORESTS" BY PETER T. WHITE IN *NATIONAL GEOGRAPHIC MAGAZINE*, JANUARY 1983

Oil

187

ARTIST
Mark Strathy

DESIGNER
Derek W. Ungless

ART DIRECTOR
Derek W. Ungless

PUBLICATION
Rolling Stone

PUBLISHER
Straight Arrow Publishers, Inc.

ILLUSTRATION FOR AN ARTICLE ENTITLED "FALLING IN LOVE AGAIN: THE RICHARD AND LINDA THOMPSON STORY" BY KURT LODER IN *ROLLING STONE*, MARCH 1984

Oil

THE HEADSTAND

a short Novella

WITH PICTURES

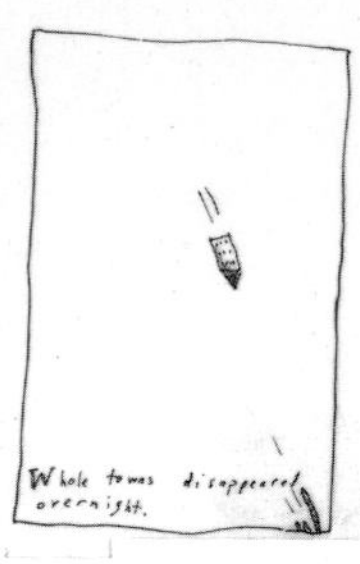

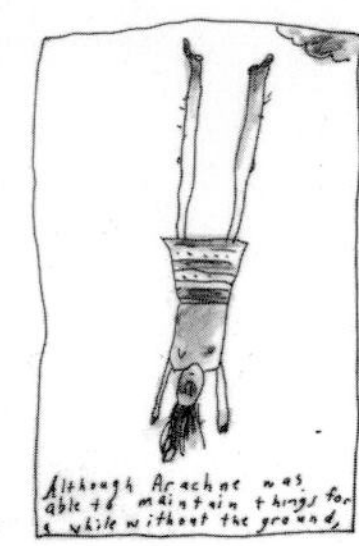

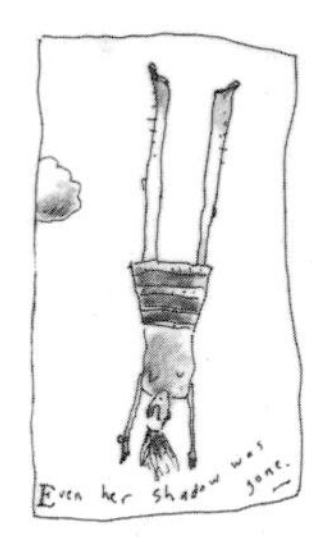

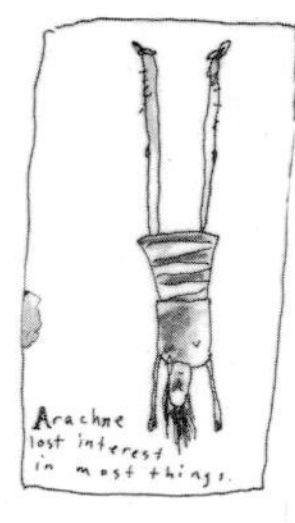

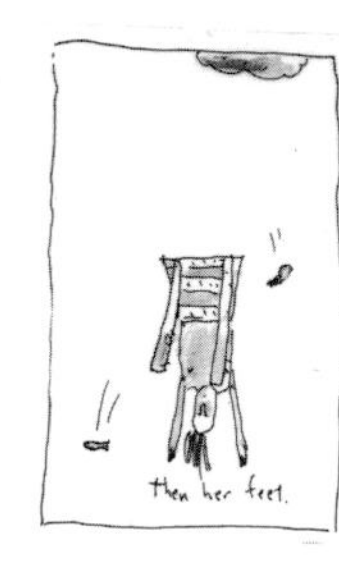

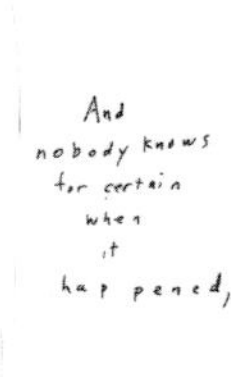

188

ARTIST
Bonnie Timmons

ART DIRECTOR
Howard Kline

PUBLICATION
Empire Magazine

PUBLISHER
The Denver Post

ILLUSTRATION FOR A SHORT STORY BY THE ARTIST ENTITLED "THE HEADSTAND" IN *EMPIRE MAGAZINE*, JANUARY 1983.

Ink and pencil

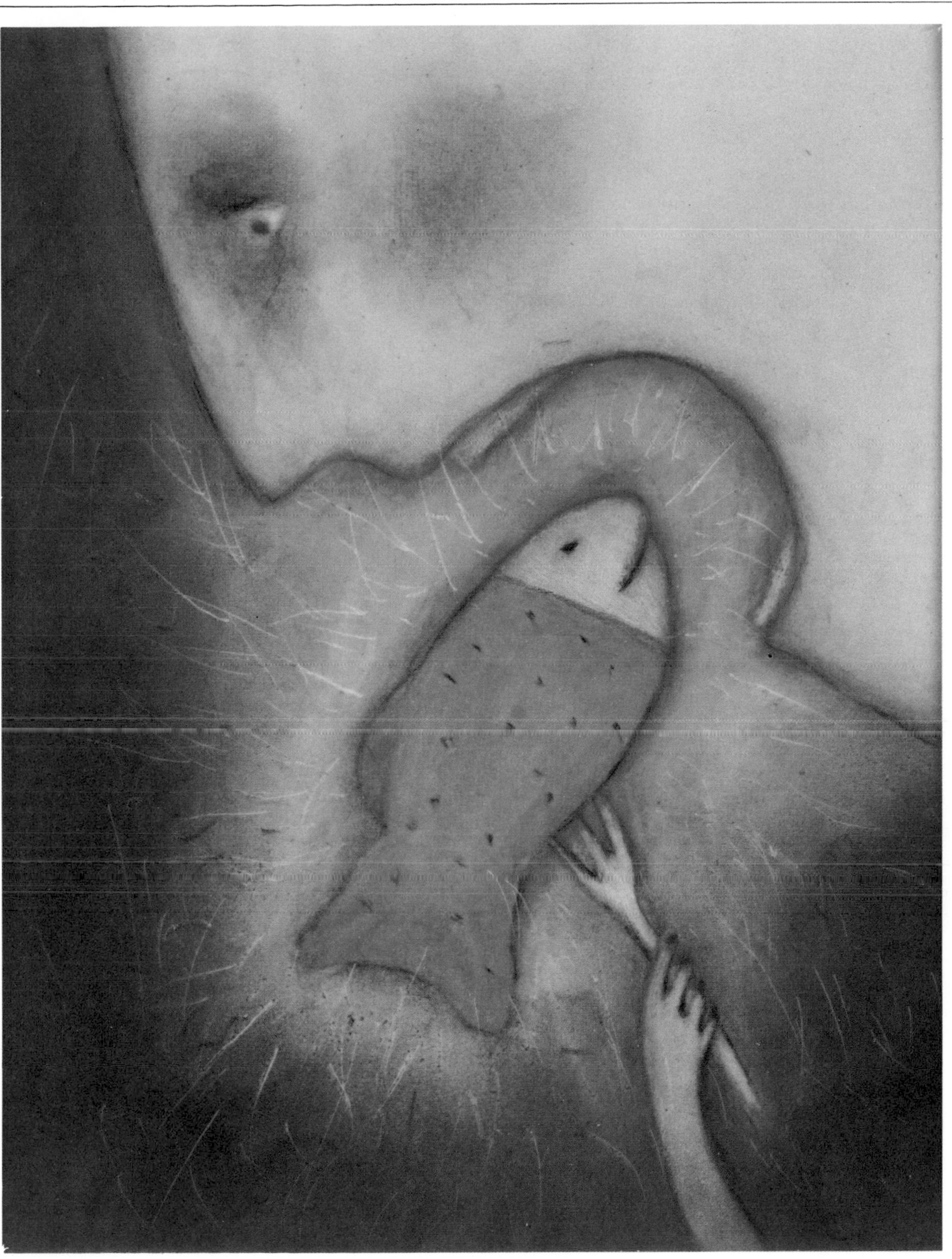

189

ARTIST
Bonnie Timmons

DESIGNERS
Tim Gabor/Kandy Littrell

ART DIRECTOR
Hans Teensma

PUBLICATION
New England Monthly

PUBLISHER
New England Monthly, Inc.

ILLUSTRATION FOR AN ARTICLE ON PRESERVING FOOD BY RADIATION ENTITLED "URPING IN PROVIDENCE" IN *NEW ENGLAND MONTHLY*, APRIL 1984.

Watercolor

190

ARTIST
James Tughan

DESIGNER
Barbara Solowan

ART DIRECTOR
Barbara Solowan

PUBLICATION
City Woman

PUBLISHER
Commac Communications Ltd.

ILLUSTRATION FOR AN ARTICLE ENTITLED "FOLLOW THE LEADER" BY WENDY DENNIS IN *CITY WOMAN*, SUMMER 1983.

Chalk pastel

191

ARTIST
James Tughan

DESIGNER
James Tughan

ART DIRECTOR
Gillian Tsintziras

PUBLICATION
The Goodlife Magazine

PUBLISHER
Selective Media Ventures

ILLUSTRATION FOR AN ARTICLE ENTITLED "THE FRESH DELICIOUS DAZZLE OF A DINNER FROM GREECE" BY ANNE LINDSAY IN *THE GOODLIFE MAGAZINE*, SUMMER 1983.

Chalk pastel

192

ARTIST
James Tughan

DESIGNER
James Tughan

ART DIRECTOR
Gillian Tsintziras

PUBLICATION
The Goodlife Magazine

PUBLISHER
Selective Media Ventures

ILLUSTRATION FOR AN ARTICLE ENTITLED "BEAUTIFUL DOWNTOWN BUFFALO" BY DICK BROWN IN *THE GOODLIFE MAGAZINE*, FEBRUARY 1984.

Colored pencil

193

ARTIST
Paul D. Turnbaugh

DESIGNER
Jill Novak

ART DIRECTOR
Greg Clark

PUBLICATION
Christian Living

PUBLISHER
David C. Cook Publishing

COVER ILLUSTRATION SHOWING HOW FAR WE'VE COME SINCE PASCAL'S TIME FOR AN ARTICLE ENTITLED "CALCULATIONS OF A COMPUTER INVENTOR" BY STEPHEN BOARD IN *CHRISTIAN LIVING*, MARCH 1984.

Airbrush

194

ARTIST
Jean Tuttle

DESIGNER
Marcia Wright

ART DIRECTOR
Marcia Wright

PUBLICATION
TWA Ambassador

PUBLISHER
Trans World Airlines

ILLUSTRATION TO ACCOMPANY AN ALLEGORY ON COMPUTERS ENTITLED "ARTIFICIAL INTELLIGENCE: THE CASE AGAINST THE THINKING MACHINE" BY PAUL FROILAND IN *TWA AMBASSADOR*, FEBRUARY 1983.

Scratchboard

195

ARTIST
Jean Tuttle

DESIGNER
Bruce Ramsay

ART DIRECTOR
Louis Fishauf

PUBLICATION
Saturday Night

PUBLISHER
Saturday Night Publishing

ILLUSTRATION FOR A POEM ENTITLED "THE WEDDING OF TWO MUSICIANS" BY DAVID MacFARLANE IN *SATURDAY NIGHT*, SEPTEMBER 1983.

Mechanical color

196

ARTIST
Andy Warhol

DESIGNER
Kerig Pope

ART DIRECTOR
Tom Staebler

PUBLICATION
Playboy

PUBLISHER
Playboy Enterprises Inc.

ILLUSTRATION FOR A MEMOIR ENTITLED "REMEMBERING TENNESSEE" BY TRUMAN CAPOTE IN *PLAYBOY*, JANUARY 1984.

Serigraph

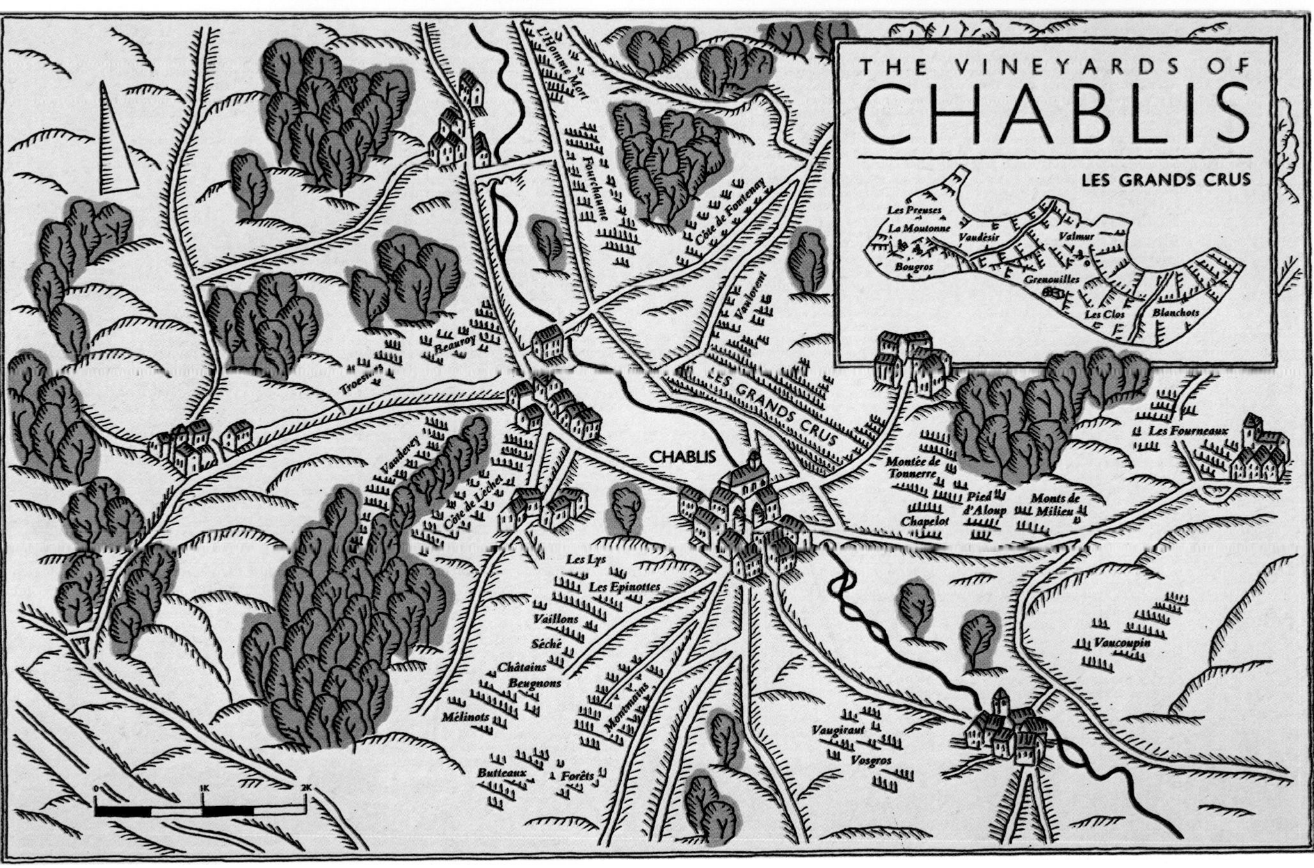

197

ARTIST
Philippe Weisbecker
DESIGNER
Wendy Palitz
ART DIRECTOR
Wendy Palitz
PUBLICATION
Savvy Magazine
PUBLISHER
Savvy Co.
ILLUSTRATION FOR A FEATURE ENTITLED "TO B-SCHOOL OR NOT TO B-SCHOOL?" BY ELAINE F. WEISS IN *SAVVY MAGAZINE*, DECEMBER 1983.
Pen with overlays

ARTIST
Philippe Weisbecker
DESIGNER
Douglas May
ART DIRECTOR
Douglas May
PUBLICATION
Cuisine Magazine
PUBLISHER
CBS Publications
ILLUSTRATION SHOWING THE LOCATIONS OF LOCAL VINEYARDS FOR AN ARTICLE ENTITLED "A CHABLIS PRIMER" BY HUGH JOHNSON IN *CUISINE MAGAZINE*, APRIL 1984.
Pen and ink with painted overlays

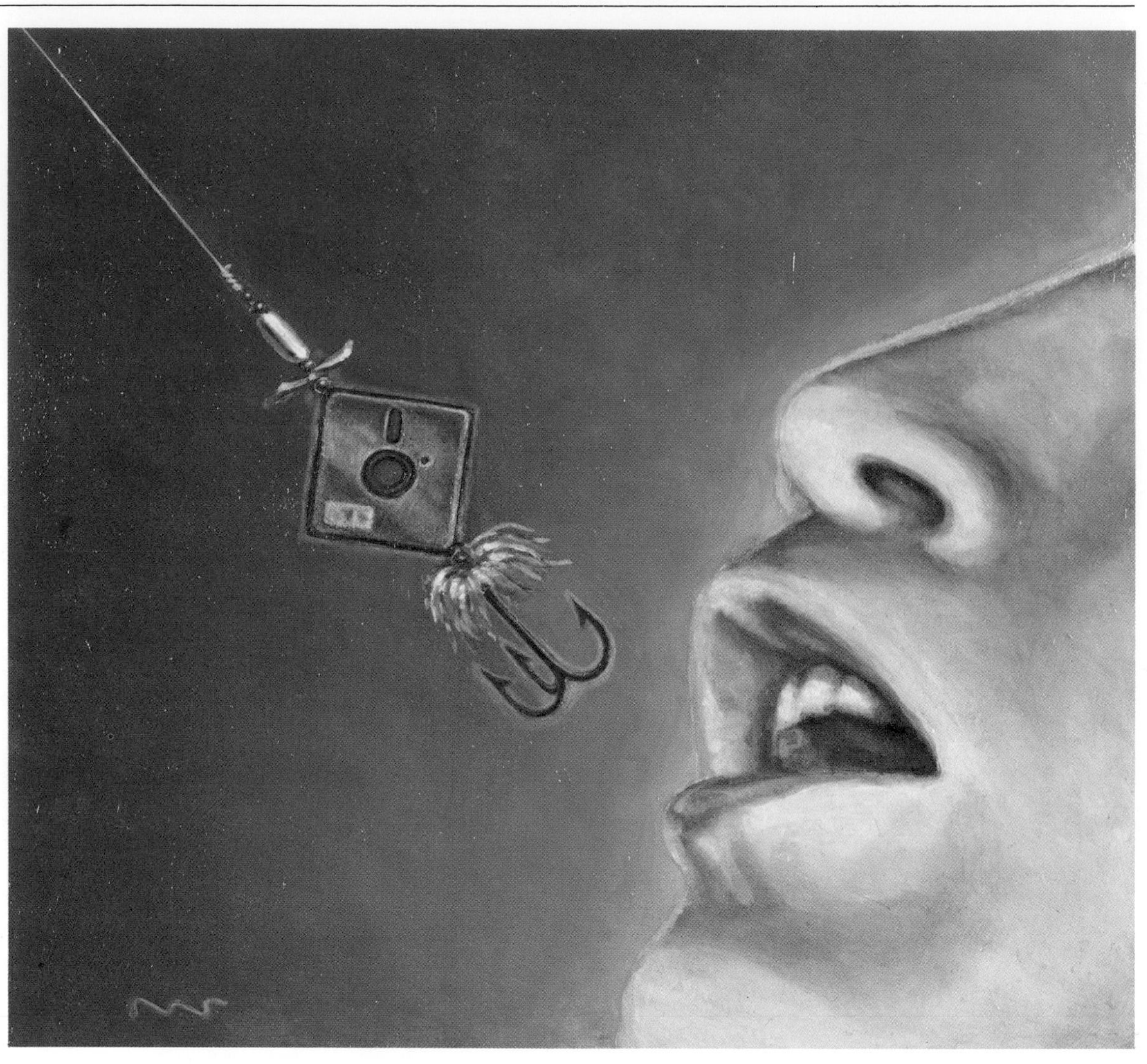

198

ARTIST
Mick Wiggins

ART DIRECTOR
Mick Wiggins

PUBLICATION
PC World

PUBLISHER
CW Communications, Inc.

ILLUSTRATION FOR AN ARTICLE ON COMPUTER SOFTWARE ENTITLED "WHO NEEDS USER FRIENDLY?" BY BURTON L. ALPERSON IN *PC WORLD*, SEPTEMBER 1983.

Oil

199

ARTIST
David Wilcox

DESIGNER
Judy Garlan

ART DIRECTOR
Judy Garlan

PUBLICATION
The Atlantic Monthly

PUBLISHER
The Atlantic Monthly Co.

ILLUSTRATION FOR A SHORT STORY ENTITLED "THE BLINDING LIGHT OF THE MIND" BY JANE SMILEY IN *THE ATLANTIC MONTHLY*, DECEMBER 1983.

Acrylic on masonite

200

ARTIST
Mike Witte

DESIGNER
Marcia Wright

ART DIRECTOR
Marcia Wright

PUBLICATION
TWA Ambassador

PUBLISHER
Trans World Airlines

ILLUSTRATION FOR AN ESSAY ENTITLED "STORIES OF CHRISTMAS PAST: DOWN PENS" BY SAKI IN *TWA AMBASSADOR*, DECEMBER 1983.

Pen and ink

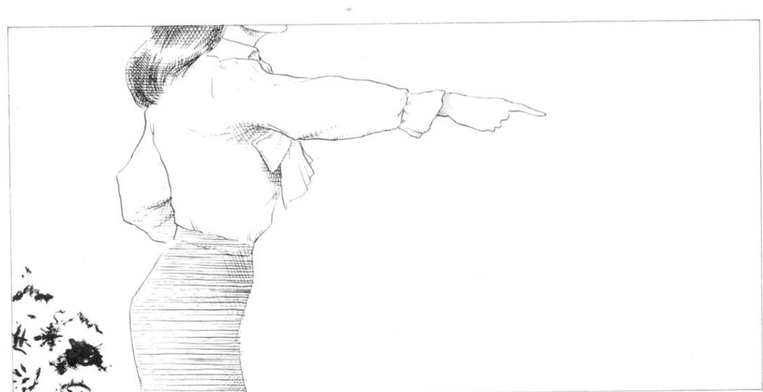

201

ARTIST
Mike Witte

DESIGNER
Judy Garlan

ART DIRECTOR
Judy Garlan

PUBLICATION
The Atlantic Monthly

PUBLISHER
The Atlantic Monthly Co.

SERIES OF ILLUSTRATIONS FOR A NON-FICTION PIECE ENTITLED "RAISING KIDS" BY JAMES Q. WILSON IN *THE ATLANTIC MONTHLY*, OCTOBER 1983.

Pen and ink

202

ARTIST
Thomas Woodruff

DESIGNER
Stephen Doyle

ART DIRECTOR
Derek W. Ungless

PUBLICATION
Rolling Stone

PUBLISHER
Straight Arrow Publishers, Inc.

ILLUSTRATION FOR AN ARTICLE ENTITLED "RANDY NEWMAN: SOURPUSS IN UTOPIA" BY CHRISTOPHER CONNELLY IN *ROLLING STONE*, FEBRUARY 1983.

Acrylic

203

ARTIST
Thomas Woodruff

DESIGNER
Gary Mele

ART DIRECTOR
Kati Korpijaakko

PUBLICATION
Ms

PUBLISHER
Ms Foundation for Education and Communication, Inc.

ILLUSTRATION FOR A STORY OF LOVE AND MURDER ENTITLED "THE ORCHARD WALLS" BY RUTH RENDELL IN *MS*, AUGUST 1983.

Acrylic

204

ARTIST
Thomas Woodruff

DESIGNER
Gary Mele

ART DIRECTOR
Phylis Schefer

PUBLISHER
Ms Foundation for Education and Communication, Inc.

PUBLISHER
Ms Magazine Corp.

ILLUSTRATION FOR AN ARTICLE ENTITLED "WEDLOCK" BY LYNNE SHARON SCHWARTZ IN *MS*, MARCH 1984.

Acrylic

205

ARTIST
Thomas Woodruff

DESIGNER
Kandy Littrell

ART DIRECTOR
Hans Teensma

PUBLICATION
New England Monthly

PUBLISHER
New England Monthly, Inc.

ILLUSTRATION FOR AN ARTICLE ENTITLED "NIGHT TRAIN" BY MARK KRAMER IN *NEW ENGLAND MONTHLY*, APRIL 1984.

Acrylic

206

ARTIST
Thomas Woodruff

DESIGNER
Derek W. Ungless

ART DIRECTOR
Derek W. Ungless

PUBLICATION
Rolling Stone

PUBLISHER
Straight Arrow Publishers, Inc.

ILLUSTRATION FOR AN ARTICLE ENTITLED "JACKSON BROWNE: NO MORE MR. L.A." BY CHRISTOPHER CONNELLY IN *ROLLING STONE*, SEPTEMBER 1983.

Acrylic

Books

This section includes work commissioned for book jackets, paperback covers, and all types of illustrated books, fiction and non-fiction

208

ARTIST
Stephen Alcorn

DESIGNER
R.D. Scudellari

ART DIRECTOR
R.D. Scudellari

AUTHORS
André Gide/Henry Miller/Joseph Conrad/Jerzy Kosinski

PUBLISHER
Modern Library

SERIES OF JACKET ILLUSTRATIONS FOR *THE IMMORALIST* BY ANDRÉ GIDE; *TROPIC OF CANCER* BY HENRY MILLER; *NOSTROMO* BY JOSEPH CONRAD; AND *STEPS* BY JERZY KOSINSKI, PUBLISHED 1983.

Woodcuts

209

ARTIST
Marshall Arisman

ART DIRECTOR
Rita Marshall

AUTHOR
Grimm

PUBLISHER
Creative Education Inc.

BOOK ILLUSTRATIONS FOR A GRIMM'S FAIRY TALE ENTITLED *FITCHER'S BIRD*, PUBLISHED 1983.

Oil on ragboard

210

ARTIST
Michael Aron

DESIGNER
Michael Aron

ART DIRECTOR
Seymour Chwast

PUBLISHER
American Showcase, Inc.

JACKET ILLUSTRATION FOR *THE ONE SHOW* ANNUAL, 1983.

Pastel and colored pencil

211

ARTIST
Bascove

DESIGNER
Louise Fili

ART DIRECTOR
Louise Fili

AUTHOR
Ariel Dorfman

PUBLISHER
Pantheon Books

JACKET ILLUSTRATION FOR A NOVEL ENTITLED *WIDOWS* BY ARIEL DORFMAN, PUBLISHED 1983.

Woodcut and watercolor

212

ARTIST
Guy Billout

DESIGNER
Louise Fili

ART DIRECTOR
Louise Fili

AUTHOR
C.L.R. James

PUBLISHER
Pantheon Books

COVER ILLUSTRATION FOR A BOOK ENTITLED *BEYOND A BOUNDARY* BY C.L.R. JAMES, PUBLISHED 1984.

Watercolor

213

ARTIST
Braldt Bralds

DESIGNER
Braldt Bralds

ART DIRECTOR
Lidia Ferrara

AUTHOR
Marion Zimmer Bradley

PUBLISHER
Alfred A. Knopf, Inc.

WRAPAROUND JACKET ILLUSTRATION FOR A BOOK ENTITLED *THE MISTS OF AVALON* BY MARION ZIMMER BRADLEY, PUBLISHED 1983.

Oil

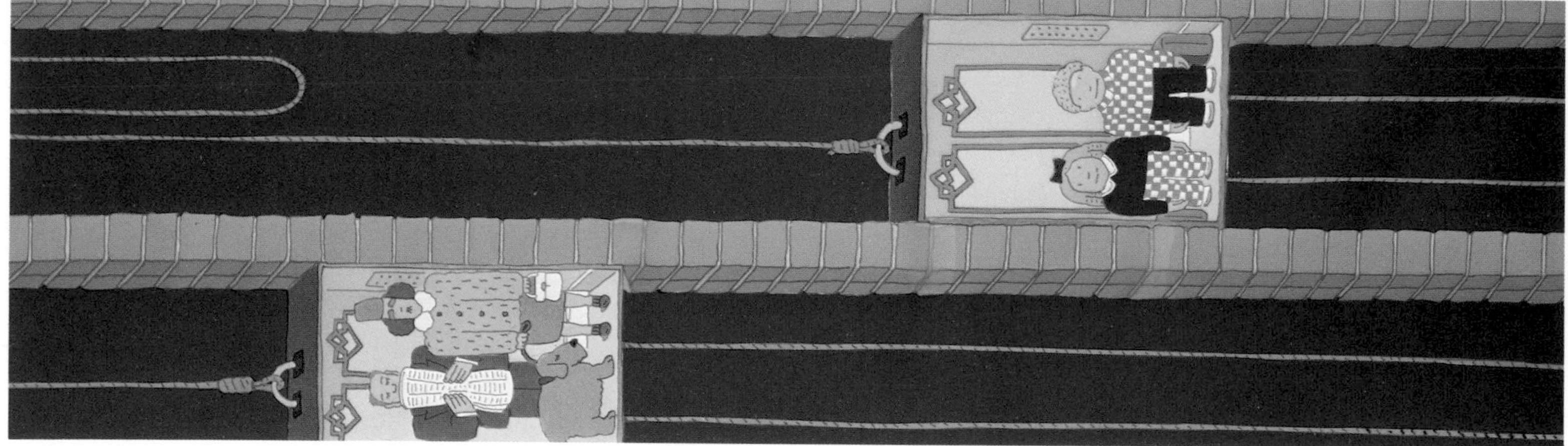

214

ARTIST
Seymour Chwast

DESIGNER
Seymour Chwast

ART DIRECTOR
Deborah Brody

AUTHOR
Seymour Chwast

PUBLISHER
Viking Press

SERIES OF ILLUSTRATIONS FOR A BOOK BY THE ARTIST ENTITLED *TALL CITY, WIDE COUNTRY* WHICH CAN BE READ FORWARD AND BACKWARD, PUBLISHED 1983.

Cello-tak

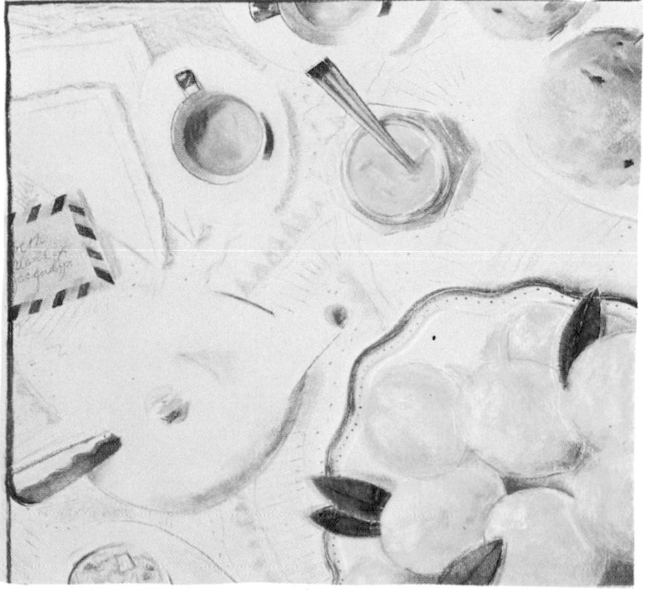

215

ARTIST
Vivienne Flesher

DESIGNER
Larry Kazal

ART DIRECTOR
Larry Kazal

AUTHOR
Emily Crumpker

PUBLISHER
William Morrow & Co., Inc.

ILLUSTRATIONS FOR A BOOK ENTITLED *SEASONAL GIFTS FROM THE KITCHEN* BY EMILY CRUMPKER, PUBLISHED 1983.

Watercolor

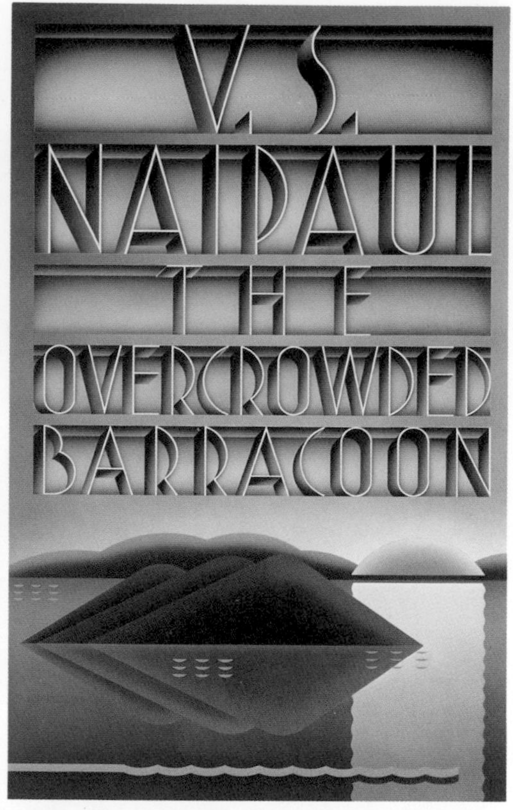

216

ARTIST
Nicholas Gaetano

DESIGNER
Nicholas Gaetano

ART DIRECTOR
Judy Loeser

AUTHOR
V.S. Naipaul

PUBLISHER
Random House/Vintage Books

COVER ILLUSTRATIONS FOR *THE MYSTIC MASSEUR*; *THE OVERCROWDED BARRACOON*; AND *IN A FREE STATE* BY V.S. NAIPAUL, PUBLISHED 1983.

Gouache

217

ARTISTS
Jean Michel Folon/ Milton Glaser

DESIGNERS
Jean Michel Folon/ Milton Glaser

PUBLISHER
Harmony Books

SERIES OF ILLUSTRATIONS FOR AN ACCORDION-FOLD BOOK ENTITLED *THE CONVERSATION*, PUBLISHED 1983.

Pen and ink, colored pencil, and colored ink

218

ARTIST
Frances Jetter

DESIGNER
Jennifer Dossin

ART DIRECTOR
Michael Mendelsohn

AUTHOR
Nikolai Gogol

PUBLISHER
The Franklin Library

SERIES OF ILLUSTRATIONS FOR A COLLECTION OF SHORT STORIES BY NIKOLAI GOGOL ENTITLED *TARAS BULBA AND OTHER TALES*, PUBLISHED 1984.

Woodcut

219

ARTIST
Pamela Lee

ART DIRECTOR
William K. Hartmann

AUTHOR
William K. Hartmann with Ron Miller/Pamela Lee

PUBLISHER
Workman Publishing Co., Inc.

SERIES OF ILLUSTRATIONS FOR A BOOK ABOUT THE EXPLORATION AND OCCUPATION OF SPACE ENTITLED *OUT OF THE CRADLE* BY WILLIAM K. HARTMANN WITH RON MILLER AND PAMELA LEE, PUBLISHED 1984.

Acrylic

220

ARTIST
Ed Lindlof

DESIGNER
Richard Hendel

ART DIRECTOR
Richard Hendel

AUTHOR
Anthony Boucher

PUBLISHER
Southern Illinois University Press

COVER ILLUSTRATION FOR A COLLECTION OF MYSTERY STORIES ENTITLED *EXEUNT MURDERERS* BY ANTHONY BOUCHER, PUBLISHED 1983.

Pen and ink

221

ARTIST
Mark Marek

DESIGNER
Manhattan Design

ART DIRECTOR
Manhattan Design

AUTHOR
Mark Marek

PUBLISHER
Manhattan Design

ILLUSTRATIONS FOR A BOOK BY THE ARTIST ENTITLED *MARK MAREK'S NEW WAVE COMICS*, PUBLISHED 1983.

Ink

222

ARTIST
John Martinez

DESIGNER
Louise Fili

ART DIRECTOR
Louise Fili

AUTHOR
Federal Writers Project

PUBLISHER
Pantheon Books

SERIES OF COVER ILLUSTRATIONS FOR THE REISSUE OF GUIDEBOOKS ORIGINALLY PUBLISHED IN THE '30s ENTITLED *THE WPA GUIDE TO NEW ORLEANS*, *MASSACHUSETTS*, AND *FLORIDA*, PUBLISHED 1983.

Ink

223

ARTIST
Wendell Minor

DESIGNER
Naomi Osnos

ART DIRECTOR
Sara Eisenman

AUTHOR
Henry Carlisle

PUBLISHER
Alfred A. Knopf, Inc.

JACKET ILLUSTRATION FOR A NINETEENTH CENTURY SEA-WHALING ADVENTURE ENTITLED *THE JONAH MAN* BY HENRY CARLISLE, PUBLISHED 1984.

Gouache

224

ARTIST
Yves Paquin

DESIGNER
Yves Paquin

ART DIRECTOR
Yves Paquin

AUTHOR
Yves Paquin

PUBLISHER
Les Éditions de Mortagne

TAROT CARD ILLUSTRATIONS FOR A BOOK BY THE ARTIST ENTITLED *LE TAROT IDÉOGRAPHIQUE DU KÉBÈK* (TAROT CARDS OF QUEBEC) PUBLISHED BY LES ÉDITIONS DE MORTAGNE, FEBRUARY 1983.

Black ink on acetate

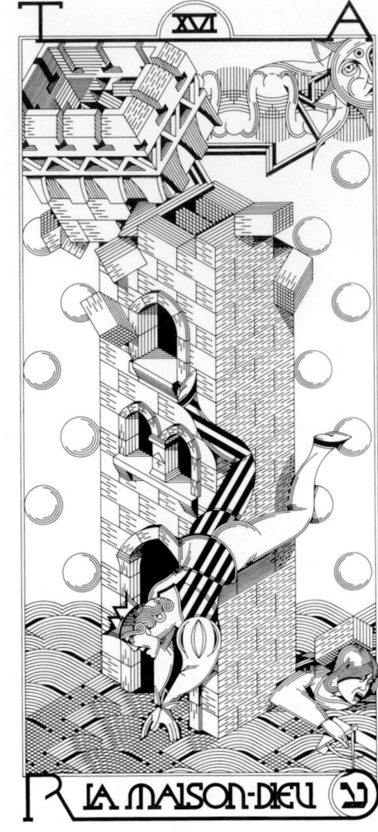

225

ARTIST
Judy Pedersen

DESIGNER
Bob Aulicino

ART DIRECTOR
Bob Aulicino

AUTHOR
Alfredo Viazzi

PUBLISHER
Random House, Inc.

JACKET ILLUSTRATION FOR A COOKBOOK ENTITLED *ALFREDO VIAZZI'S CUCINA E NOSTALGIA*, PUBLISHED 1983.

Pastel

226

ARTIST
Robert Rodriguez

DESIGNER
Roger Carpenter

ART DIRECTOR
Roger Carpenter

PUBLISHER
The Galliard Press

BOOK ILLUSTRATION TO INTERPRET THE SONG "WHAT A FOOL BELIEVES" IN *RADIO EYES: GREAT ROCK LYRICS SET TO ART* EDITED BY ED BOTT, PUBLISHED 1984.

Casein, acrylic, and pastel on paper

227

ARTIST
Michael Sell

ART DIRECTOR
Michael Sell

PUBLISHER
Galliard Press

BOOK ILLUSTRATION TO INTERPRET THE SONG "AT THE HOP" IN *RADIO EYES: GREAT ROCK LYRICS SET TO ART* EDITED BY ED BOTT, PUBLISHED 1984.

Watercolor and pastel

228

ARTIST
Edward Sorel

DESIGNER
Carin Goldberg

ART DIRECTOR
Lidia Ferrara

AUTHOR
Hugh Kenner

PUBLISHER
Alfred A. Knopf, Inc.

WRAPAROUND JACKET ILLUSTRATION FOR A BOOK ENTITLED *A COLDER EYE* BY HUGH KENNER, PUBLISHED 1983.

Pastel

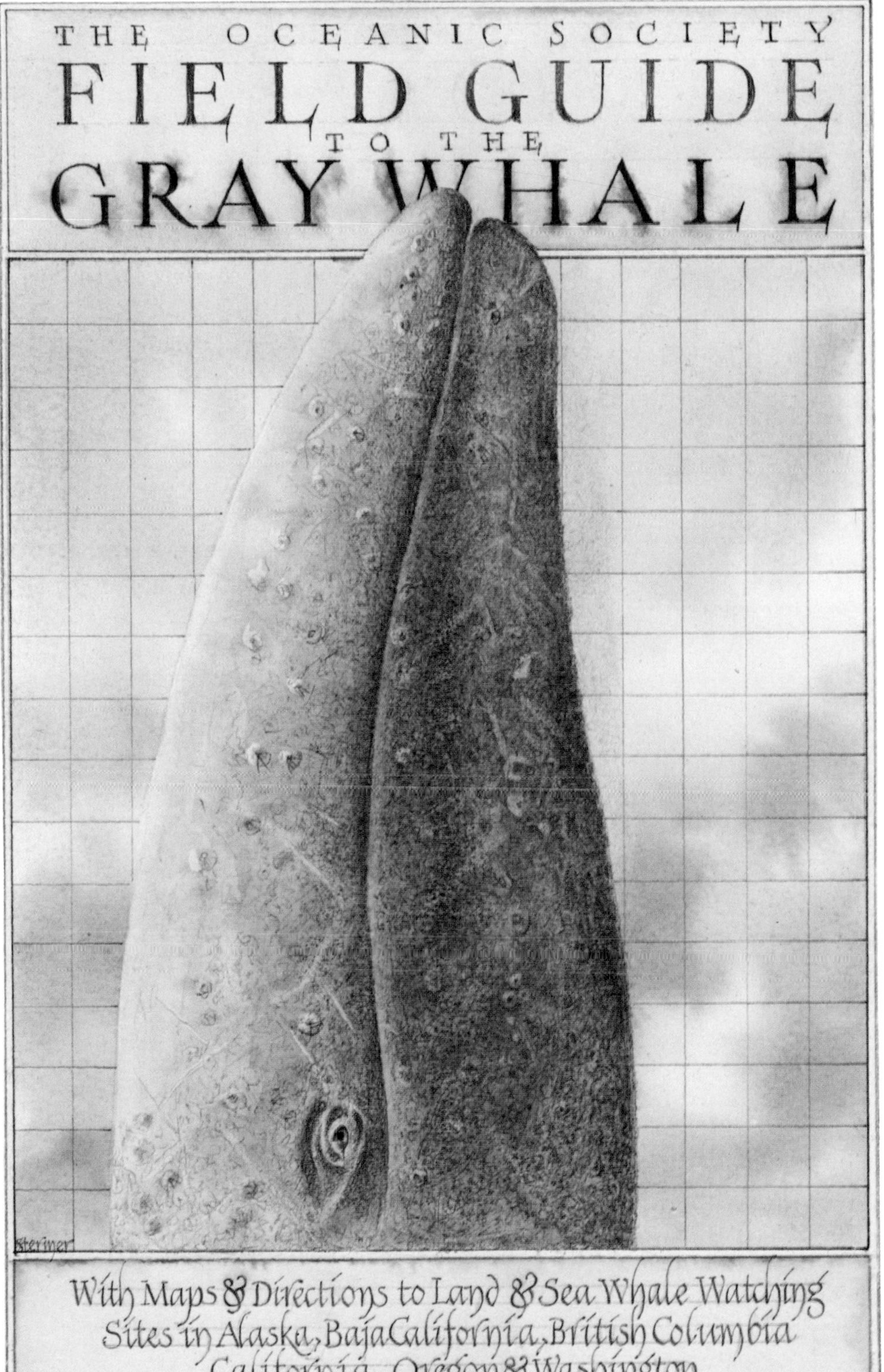

229

ARTIST
Dugald Stermer

DESIGNER
Dugald Stermer

ART DIRECTORS
Dugald Stermer/Dustin Kahn

AUTHOR
Ben Bennett

PUBLISHER
Legacy Publishing

COVER ILLUSTRATION FOR *FIELD GUIDE TO THE GRAY WHALE* BY BEN BENNETT, PUBLISHED SEPTEMBER 1983.

Pencil and watercolor

230

ARTIST
Bonnie Timmons

DESIGNER
Sheri Safran

ART DIRECTOR
Sheri Safran

AUTHOR
Bonnie Timmons

PUBLISHER
E.P. Dutton

ILLUSTRATIONS FOR A CHILDREN'S BOOK BY THE ARTIST ENTITLED *ORVILLE'S OUTING*, PUBLISHED 1983.

Ink and marker

231

ARTIST
Susan Walp

DESIGNER
Louise Fili

ART DIRECTOR
Louise Fili

AUTHOR
Francine Prose

PUBLISHER
Pantheon Books

JACKET ILLUSTRATION FOR A BOOK ENTITLED *HUNGRY HEARTS* BY FRANCINE PROSE, PUBLISHED 1983.

Oil

232

ARTIST
Michael Whelan

DESIGNER
Michael Whelan

ART DIRECTOR
Michael Whelan

AUTHOR
Poul Anderson/Gordon Dixon

PUBLISHER
TOR Books

COVER ILLUSTRATION FOR A SCIENCE FICTION BOOK ENTITLED *HOKA* BY POUL ANDERSON AND GORDON DIXON, PUBLISHED 1983.

Acrylic

Advertising

This section includes work commissioned for advertising in consumer, trade and professional magazines, and newspapers

234

ARTIST
Guy Billout

ART DIRECTORS
Rudy Hoglund/
John Borman

COPYWRITER
George Watts

AD AGENCY
Young & Rubicam

CLIENT
Time Inc.

ILLUSTRATION TO ADVERTISE *TIME* MAGAZINE WITH THE COPYLINE "HIRE EDUCATION," WHICH APPEARED IN *THE NEW YORK TIMES*, MARCH 1983.

Watercolor

235

ARTIST
R.O. Blechman

COPYWRITER
Francesca Blumenthal

AD AGENCY
Waring & LaRosa

CLIENT
Perrier

ILLUSTRATION TO ADVERTISE PERRIER WATER WITH THE COPYLINE "BORN SALT-FREE," WHICH APPEARED IN MAGAZINES, 1983.

Ink

236

ARTIST
Jeanne Fisher

CLIENT
Bloomingdale's

ILLUSTRATION FOR A CHRISTMAS SHOPPING BAG AND COVER ILLUSTRATION FOR A CHRISTMAS CATALOG, 1983.

Gouache

237

ARTIST
Dagmar Frinta

ART DIRECTOR
Barbara Loveland

COPYWRITER
Ralph Caplan

CLIENT
Herman Miller, Inc.

INTERPRETIVE ILLUSTRATION OF AN OCCASIONAL TABLE DESIGNED BY GEORGE NELSON, USED AS A POSTER AND CATALOG ADVERTISEMENT, JUNE 1984.

Oil

238

ARTIST
Steven Guarnaccia

COPYWRITER
Dan Altman

AD AGENCY
Altman & Manley

CLIENT
Multigroup

ILLUSTRATION TO ADVERTISE MULTIGROUP HEALTH PLAN WITH THE COPYLINE "THE MEDICAL LANDSCAPE. IT'S NO PLACE TO ACT LIKE A TOURIST," WHICH APPEARED IN *THE BOSTON GLOBE*, 1983.

Ink and screens

239

ARTIST
Jim Heimann

ART DIRECTOR
Jim Heimann

CLIENT
Heaven Contemporary Retail Store

ILLUSTRATION TO ADVERTISE HEAVEN, A RETAIL STORE, WITH THE COPYLINE "HEAVEN SALUTES POST-MODERN CLASSICISM," WHICH APPEARED IN *STUFF MAGAZINE*, FEBRUARY 1983.

Collage/mechanical

240

ARTIST
Tim C. Kilian

ART DIRECTOR
Candace Barnes

AD AGENCY
Floating Points Inc.

CLIENT
Floating Points Systems

ILLUSTRATION TO ADVERTISE ARRAY PROCESSORS WITH THE COPYLINE "THE 5000 SERIES FROM FLOATING POINTS SYSTEMS," 1983.

Wire, dental floss, paper, styrofoam, clay, and board

241

ARTIST
Dennis Luzak

ART DIRECTOR
Martha Anne Booth

AD AGENCY
Foote, Cone & Belding

CLIENT
Levi Strauss

ILLUSTRATION TO ADVERTISE LEVI'S JEANS WITH THE COPYLINE "WATER FANTASY," WHICH APPEARED IN CONSUMER MAGAZINES, SPRING-SUMMER 1983.

Oil

242

ARTIST
Marvin Mattelson

ART DIRECTOR
Ann Prochazka

AD AGENCY
Van Sant Dugdale

CLIENT
Westinghouse Defense

ADVERTISEMENT FOR WESTINGHOUSE DEFENSE WHICH APPEARED IN MAGAZINES, FALL 1983.

Acrylic on canvas

243

ARTIST
James McMullan

ART DIRECTOR
Seymour Chwast

DESIGN STUDIO
Pushpin, Lubalin, Peckolick

CLIENT
Biofitness Institute

ILLUSTRATION WITH THE COPYLINE "THE ENDLESS ACHER" FOR A BOOKLET PROMOTING BIOFITNESS HEALTH AND EXERCISE PROGRAM, FEBRUARY 1983.

Watercolor

244

ARTIST
Douglas Smith

COPYWRITER
Richard Binnell

AD AGENCY
Altman & Manley

CLIENT
BIG D Supermarkets

ILLUSTRATION FOR A SUPERMARKET CHAIN PROMOTION WITH THE COPYLINE "BIG D CONTINUES A THANKSGIVING TRADITION," APPEARING IN AREA NEWSPAPERS, 1983.

Scratchboard

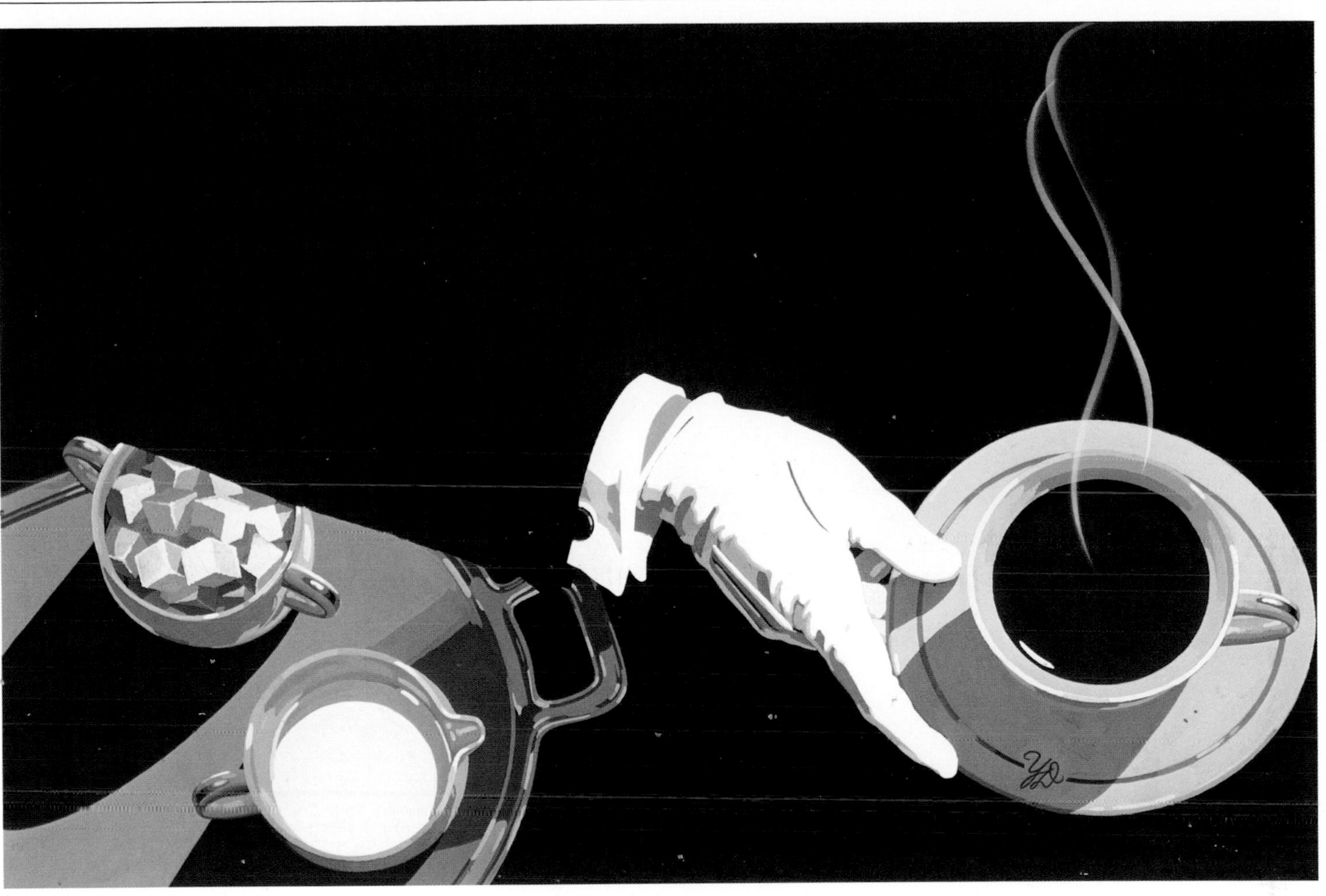

245

ARTIST
Nancy Stahl

COPYWRITER
Nan Haley Redmond

CLIENT
Maxwell House

ILLUSTRATION TO ADVERTISE COFFEE WITH THE COPYLINE "AND NOW, THE CRÈME DE LA DECAF: YUBAN-D" APPEARING IN *MAXWELL HOUSE MESSENGER*, FEBRUARY 1984.

Gouache

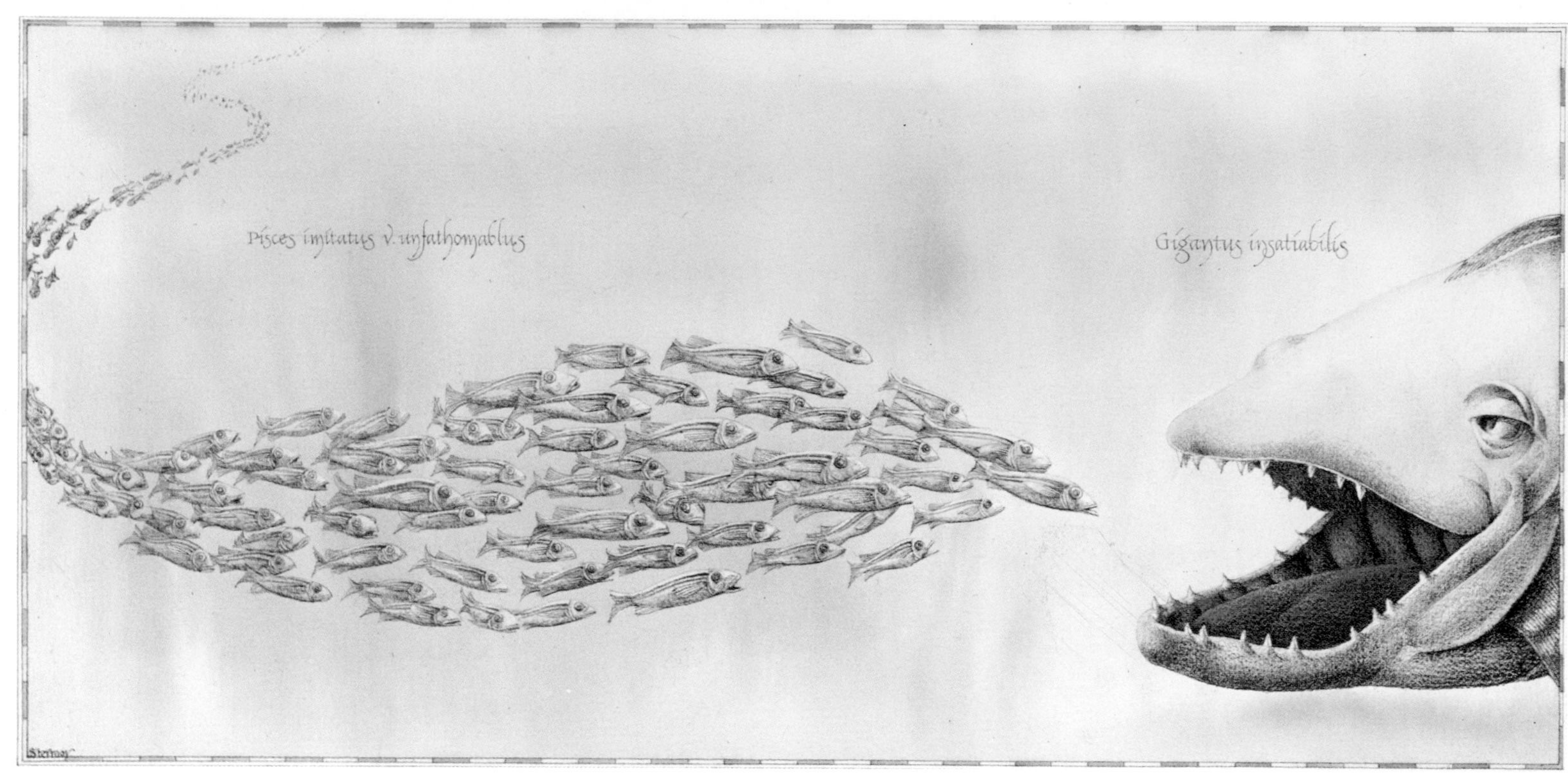

246

ARTIST
Dugald Stermer

COPYWRITER
Greg Karraker

AD AGENCY
D'Arcy MacManus & Masius

CLIENT
Wicat Systems

ILLUSTRATION TO ADVERTISE MICROCOMPUTERS WITH THE COPYLINE "THE MICROCOMPUTER SCHOOL OF THOUGHT" APPEARING IN TRADE AND CONSUMER MAGAZINES, 1983-84.

Watercolor and pencil

Posters

This section includes work commissioned for posters, including consumer products and institutional

248

ARTIST
Nina Berkson

ART DIRECTORS
Nina Berkson/Bob Russell

SELF-PROMOTION POSTER WITH THE COPYLINE "NINA BERKSON/ILLUSTRATION," MARCH 1983.

Chalk and pencil

249

ARTIST
Guy Billout

DESIGNER
Francis Brennan

CLIENT
China Seas, Inc.

ILLUSTRATION FOR A POSTER AND ADVERTISEMENT FOR CHINA SEAS TEXTILES AND WALLCOVERINGS, APPEARING IN NEWSPAPERS AND MAGAZINES, 1983.

Watercolor

250

ARTIST
Salvador Bru

ART DIRECTORS
Dan Pizer/Salvador Bru

AD AGENCY
Bru Associates, Inc.

CLIENT
U.S. International Communications Agency

POSTERS USED OVERSEAS TO PROMOTE THE 1984 OLYMPIC GAMES WITH THE COPYLINE "OLYMPICS '84 LOS ANGELES," 1984.

Gouache

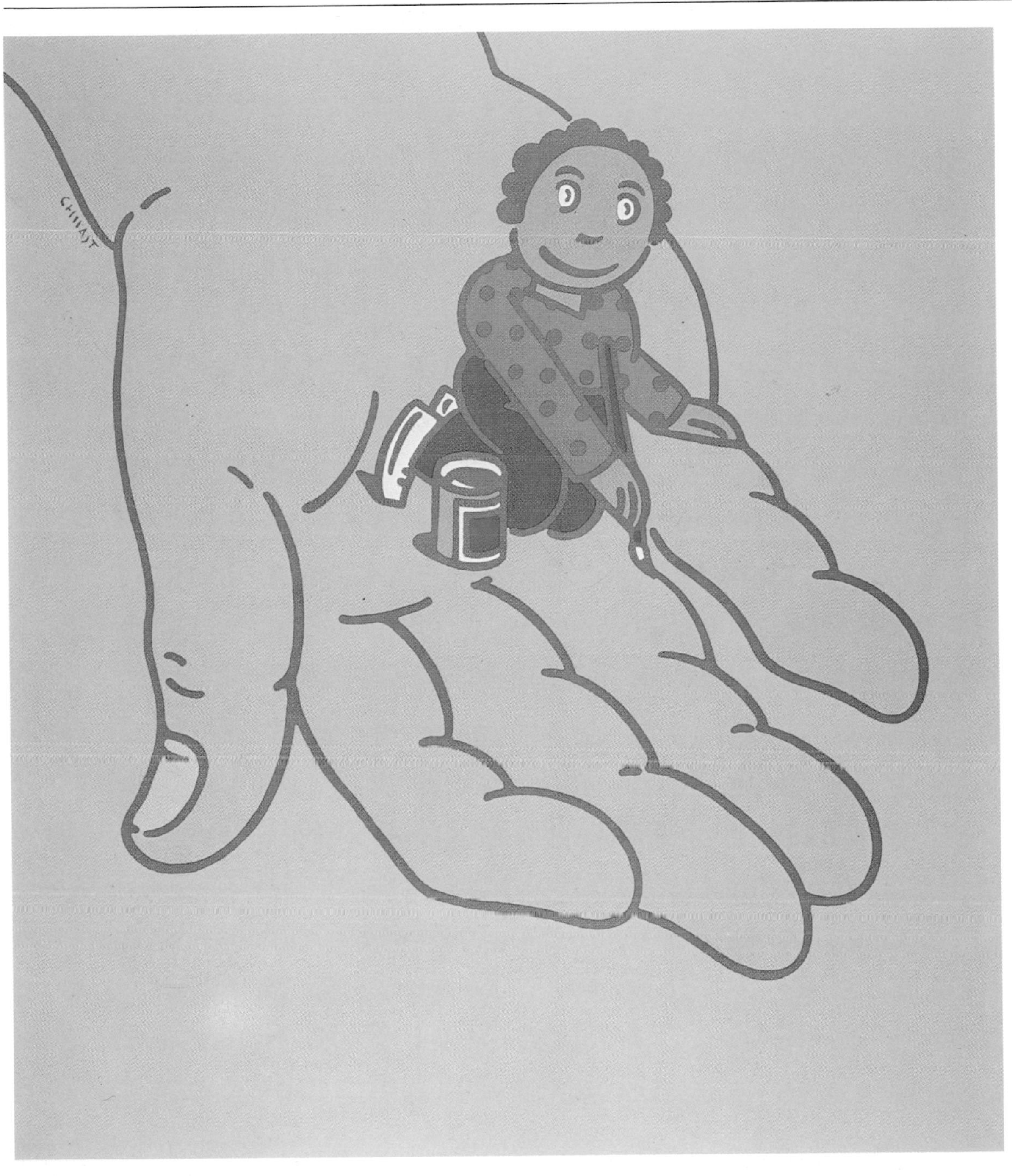

251

ARTIST
Seymour Chwast

ART DIRECTORS
Seymour Chwast/Kevin Gatta

COPYWRITER
Natalie Lieberman

DESIGN STUDIO
Pushpin Lubalin Peckolick

CLIENT
Learning to Read Through the Arts Programs Inc.

POSTER TO ADVERTISE A CHILDREN'S ART EXHIBITION AT THE GUGGENHEIM MUSEUM WITH THE COPYLINE "A YEAR WITH CHILDREN," 1983.

Pen and ink and Cello-tak

252

ARTIST
Nicholas Gaetano

ART DIRECTOR
Gary Alfredson

COPYWRITER
Lynn Dangel

CLIENT
Creative Access

PROMOTIONAL MAILER TO ADVERTISE CREATIVE INDEX BOOKS WITH THE COPYLINE "WHY CREATIVE PEOPLE WORK SO HARD," 1983-84.

Gouache

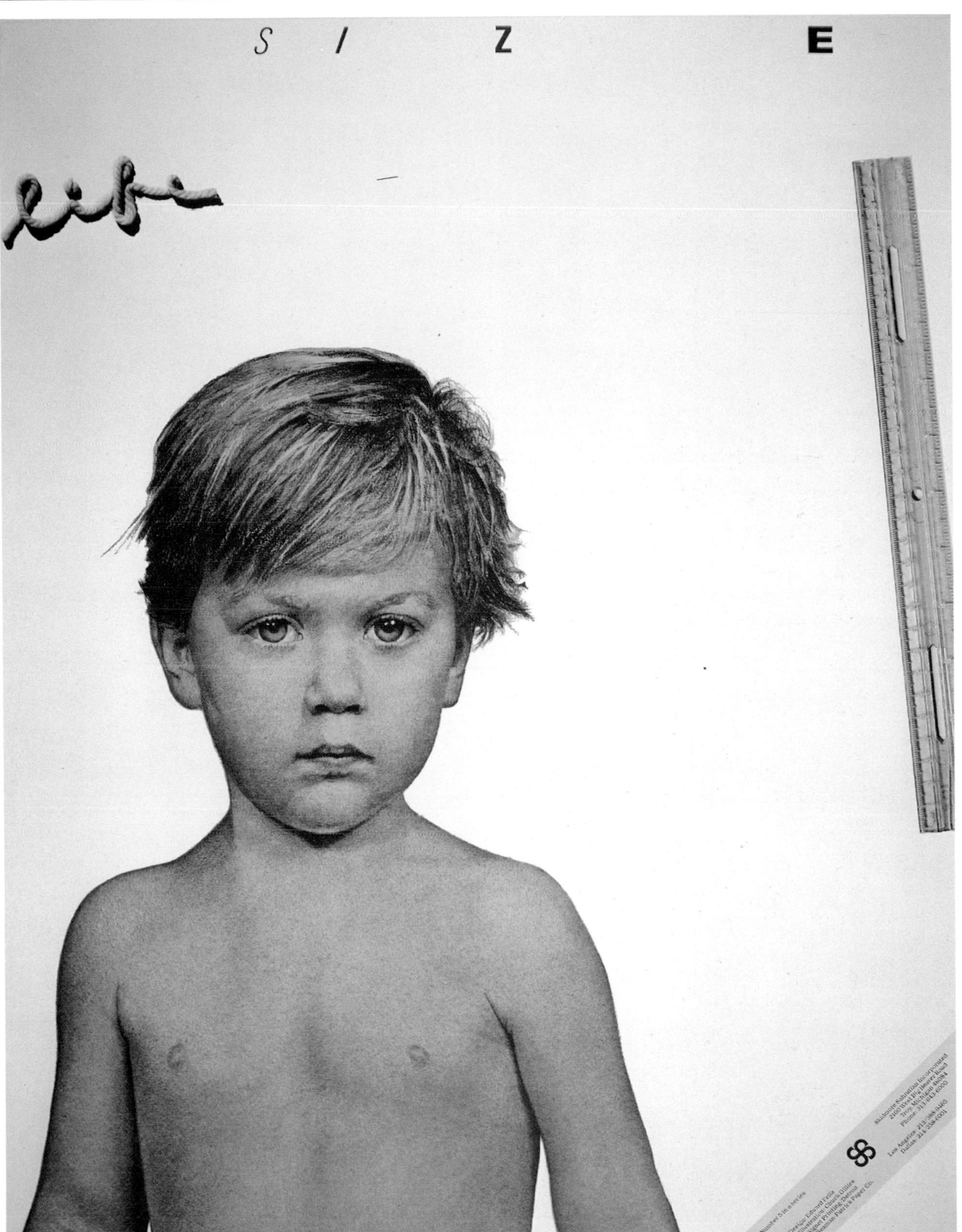

253

ARTIST
Chuck Gillies

ART DIRECTOR
Edward Fella

CLIENT
Skidmore Sahratian, Inc.

ONE OF A SERIES OF POSTERS PROMOTING A DESIGN AND ILLUSTRATION STUDIO, A PRINTER, AND A PAPER COMPANY, 1983.

Pencil and acrylic wash, printed with color varnishes

254

ARTIST
Milton Glaser

ART DIRECTOR
Milton Glaser

COPYWRITER
Milton Glaser

CLIENT
Zanders Feinpapiere, A.G.

ILLUSTRATIONS FROM A PROMOTIONAL CALENDAR ENTITLED "MASTERS OF COLOR" FOR A PAPER MANUFACTURING COMPANY, 1984.

Oil pastel, photostat, ink, cello-tak, colored pencil and tempera paint

255

ARTIST
Milton Glaser

ART DIRECTOR
Milton Glaser

COPYWRITER
Peter Matthiessen

CLIENT
New York Zoological Society

POSTER TO PUBLICIZE "THE NIGHT OF THE SNOW LEOPARD," A BENEFIT FOR THE NEW YORK ZOOLOGICAL SOCIETY, MAY 1983.

Ink and colored pencil

256

ARTIST
Lance Hidy

ART DIRECTOR
Lance Hidy

COPYWRITER
Lance Hidy

CLIENT
The Church of St. Luke in the Fields

LIMITED EDITION POSTER TO PUBLICIZE A FUND RAISING PROJECT FOR A CHURCH WITH THE COPYLINE "REBUILDING ST. LUKE IN THE FIELDS," DECEMBER 1983.

Hand silkscreen

257

ARTIST
Sandra Higashi

ART DIRECTOR
Marty Neumeier

COPYWRITER
Marty Neumeier

AD AGENCY
Neumeier Design Team

CLIENT
Zipatone, Inc.

POSTER TO PROMOTE THE USE OF TEXTURE SCREENS WITH THE COPYLINE "ZIPATONE—THE TEXTURE TOOL," JULY 1983.

Overlapping Zipatone screens assigned to three process colors

258

ARTIST
Fred Hilliard

ART DIRECTOR
Fred Hilliard

CLIENT
Seattle Repertory Theatre

POSTER FOR THE SEATTLE REPERTORY'S PRODUCTION OF THE PLAY "THE BALLAD OF SOAPY SMITH," OCTOBER 1983.

Gouache on paper

259

ARTIST
Lonni Sue Johnson

ART DIRECTOR
Michael Weymouth

CLIENT
Weymouth Design

ILLUSTRATION FOR POSTER/INVITATION TO ANNUAL PARTY AT WEYMOUTH DESIGN WITH THE COPYLINE "PARTY," APRIL 1983.

Watercolor and ink

260

ARTIST
Gary Kelley

ART DIRECTOR
Gary Kelley

CLIENT
Iowa Shakespeare Festival

POSTER TO PROMOTE THE IOWA SHAKESPEARE FESTIVAL WITH THE COPYLINE "LOVERS, LUNATICS AND POETS," SPRING 1984.

Pastel

261

ARTIST
Jean-Christian Knaff

ART DIRECTOR
Jean-Christian Knaff

PROMOTIONAL POSTER TO ANNOUNCE AN AUCTION SALE OF THE ARTIST'S WORKS IN MONTREAL, WINTER 1983-84.

Watercolor and mixed media

262

ARTIST
Anita Kunz

DESIGNER
Ann Ames

ART DIRECTOR
Ursula Kaiser

AD AGENCY
The Art Directors Club of Toronto

CLIENT
The Art Directors Club of Toronto

ILLUSTRATION FOR POSTER TO PROMOTE THE ART DIRECTORS CLUB OF TORONTO ANNUAL SHOW, FALL 1983.

Watercolor and gouache

263

ARTIST
Kam Mak

ART DIRECTORS
Bill Kobasz/Richard Wilde

CLIENT
School of Visual Arts

PROMOTIONAL POSTER ENTITLED "APARTMENTS FOR RENT" FOR A THEMATIC EXHIBITION AT THE MASTER EAGLE GALLERY, 1983.

Oil

264

ARTIST
Marvin Mattelson

DESIGNER
Wendell Minor

ART DIRECTOR
Marvin Mattelson

CLIENT
Society of Illustrators

CALL FOR ENTRIES/EXHIBITION POSTER FOR THE SOCIETY OF ILLUSTRATORS' ANNUAL SHOW, SUMMER 1983-WINTER 1984.

Acrylic on canvas

265

ARTIST
James McMullan

ART DIRECTOR
Silas Rhodes

COPYWRITER
Dee Ito

CLIENT
School of Visual Arts

PROMOTIONAL POSTER FOR THE SCHOOL OF VISUAL ARTS WITH THE COPYLINE "TO BE GOOD IS NOT ENOUGH WHEN YOU DREAM OF BEING GREAT," NOVEMBER 1983.

Watercolor

266

ARTIST
James McMullan

ART DIRECTOR
Carol Carson

CLIENT
Let's Find Out Magazine

POSTER FOR THE TEACHER'S EDITION OF *LET'S FIND OUT* WITH THE COPYLINE "IN THE JUNGLE," MAY 1983.

Watercolor

267

ARTIST
Alex Murawski

ART DIRECTOR
David Bartels

COPYWRITER
David Bartels

AD AGENCY
Bartels & Co. Inc.

CLIENT
Bruce Bendinger

PROMOTIONAL POSTER FOR THE APRIL FOOL FILM FESTIVAL CALL FOR ENTRIES, MARCH 1983.

Ink and acrylic

268

ARTIST
Bill Nelson

ART DIRECTOR
Randy Sherman

COPYWRITER
Don Pierce

AD AGENCY
Loucks Atelier, Inc.

CLIENT
Palmer Paper Company

POSTER TO ADVERTISE A NEW LINE OF HIGH QUALITY GERMAN PAPER WITH THE COPYLINE "GERMAN OPTICS/KEEPERS OF THE LIGHT," SPRING 1983.

Colored pencil and rubber stamps

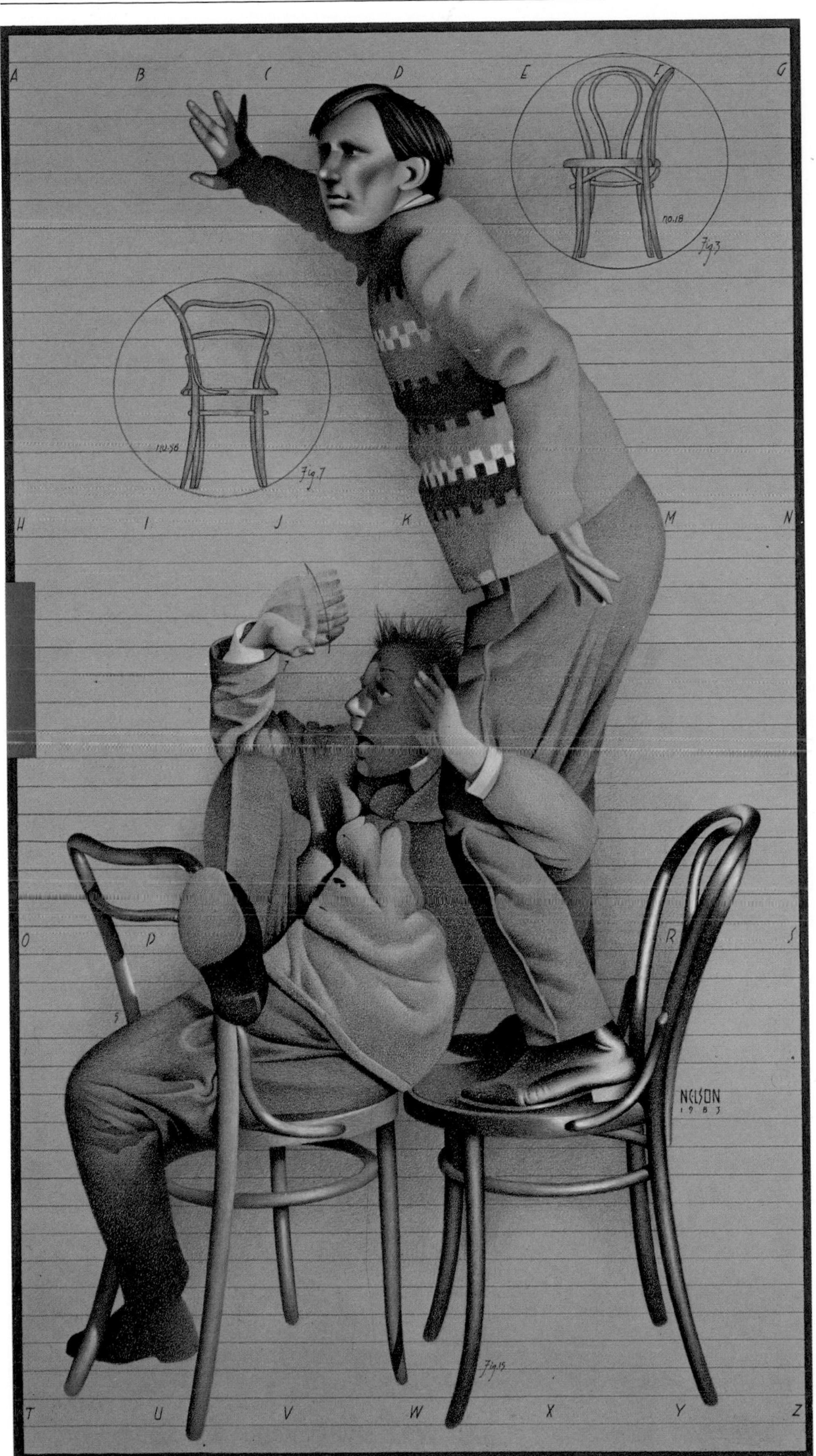

269

ARTIST
Bill Nelson

CLIENT
Tri Expo/Richmond Society for the Communicating Arts

POSTER
ILLUSTRATION FOR A TRADE SHOW INVITATION WITH THE COPYLINE "STANDING ROOM ONLY," SPRING 1984.

Colored pencil

270

ARTIST
Bill Nelson

ART DIRECTOR
Bill Nelson

CLIENT
Trinity Episcopal High School

POSTER FOR A FUND RAISING EVENT WITH THE COPYLINE "A CELEBRATION OF THE ARTS," MAY 1983.

Colored pencil

271

ARTIST
J. Rafal Olbinski

ART DIRECTOR
Jim Russek

COPYWRITER
Jim Russek

AD AGENCY
Laurence Charles & Free

POSTER DESIGN AND ILLUSTRATION FOR A MUSIC FESTIVAL IN NEW YORK CITY WITH THE COPYLINE "SUMMER MUSIC - 92ND. ST. Y," 1983.

Acrylic on canvas

272

ARTIST
Pamela Higgins Patrick

ART DIRECTOR
Pamela Higgins Patrick

AD AGENCY
Pamela Higgins Patrick Illustrations

CLIENT
The Art Store

ILLUSTRATION FOR A SELF-PROMOTION POSTER, 1983.

Pastel

273

ARTIST
Bradley O. Pomeroy

ART DIRECTOR
Judy Kirpich

AD AGENCY
Grafik Communications, Ltd.

CLIENT
VM Software, Inc.

PROMOTIONAL POSTER TO ADVERTISE SYSTEMS AND UTILITIES SOFTWARE WITH THE COPYLINE "VM, THE WAVE OF THE FUTURE" SENT AS A DIRECT MAIL PIECE, 1983.

Mixed media

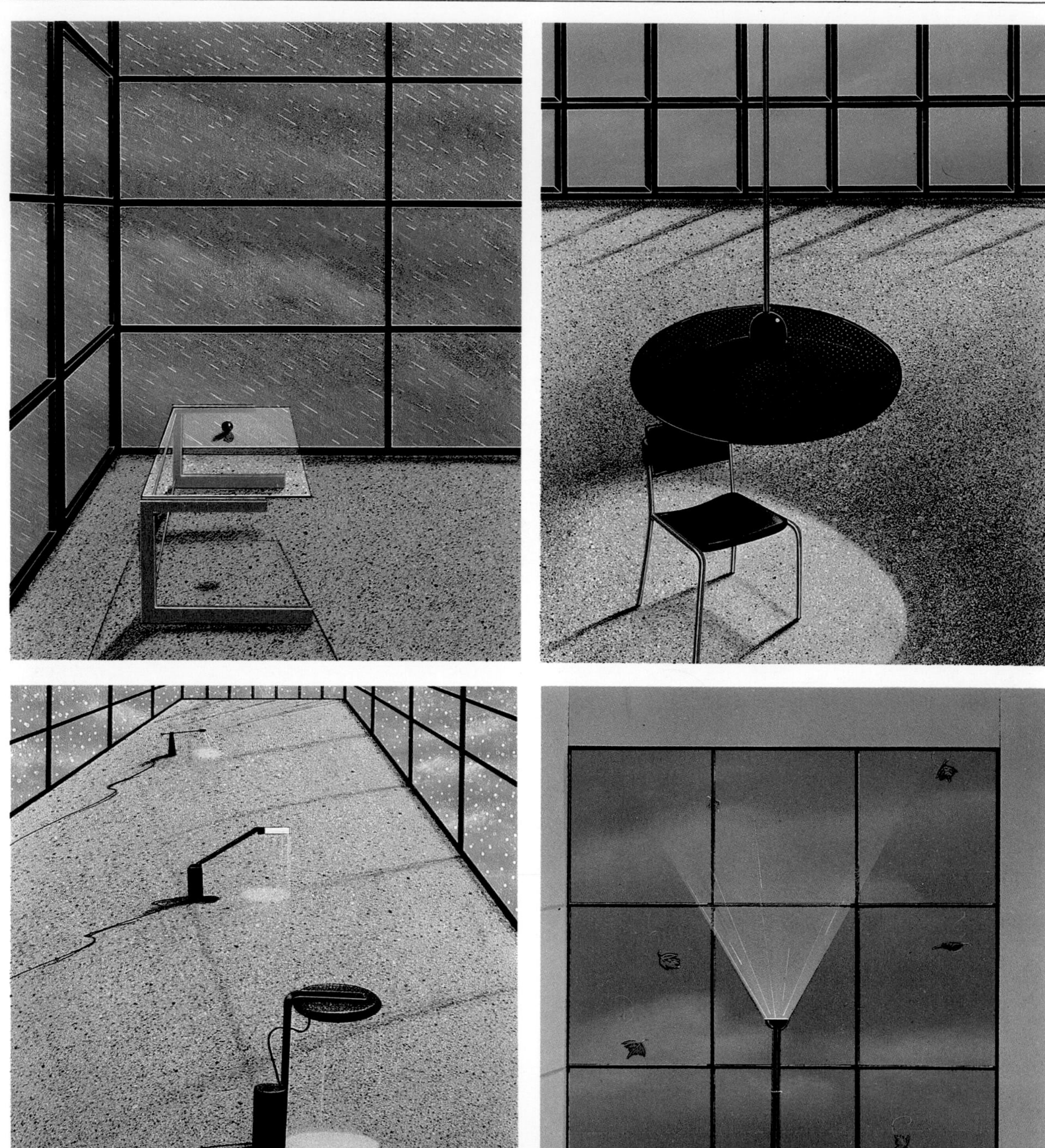

274

ARTIST
Greg Ragland

ART DIRECTOR
Greg Ragland

CLIENT
Ron Rezek Lighting and Furniture

LIMITED EDITION POSTER SERIES TO ADVERTISE RON REZEK LIGHTING AND FURNITURE, JANUARY 1984.

Acrylic

275

ARTIST
James Thorpe

ART DIRECTOR
James Thorpe

COPYWRITER
Joseph Ansell

CLIENT
College Art Association of America

ILLUSTRATION FOR A POSTER DESIGNED TO ADVERTISE A SERIES OF LECTURES BY ART HISTORIANS AND POSTER DESIGNERS WITH THE COPYLINE "THE POSTER—AN EXPRESSION OF ITS TIME," 1983.

Photo-montage, colored papers, and ink

276

ARTIST/DESIGNER
Cathleen Toelke

ART DIRECTOR/ DESIGNER
Jamie Mambro

COPYWRITERS
Gail Welch, Geoff Currier, Ray Welch, Cathleen Toelke

AD AGENCY
Welch, Currier, Smith, Inc.

CLIENT
Rand Typography

POSTER ILLUSTRATING THE HISTORY OF THE LETTER "B" FROM THE EGYPTIAN "CRANE" HIEROGLYPHIC WITH THE COPYLINE "HOW IT CAME TO B.," 1983.

Watercolor and gouache

277

ARTIST
Ken Vares

ART DIRECTOR
Ken Vares

AD AGENCY
Studio Bronze

SELF PROMOTIONAL POSTER ENTITLED "NICKEL FERRY, SAN FRANCISCO 1915," 1983.

Acrylic

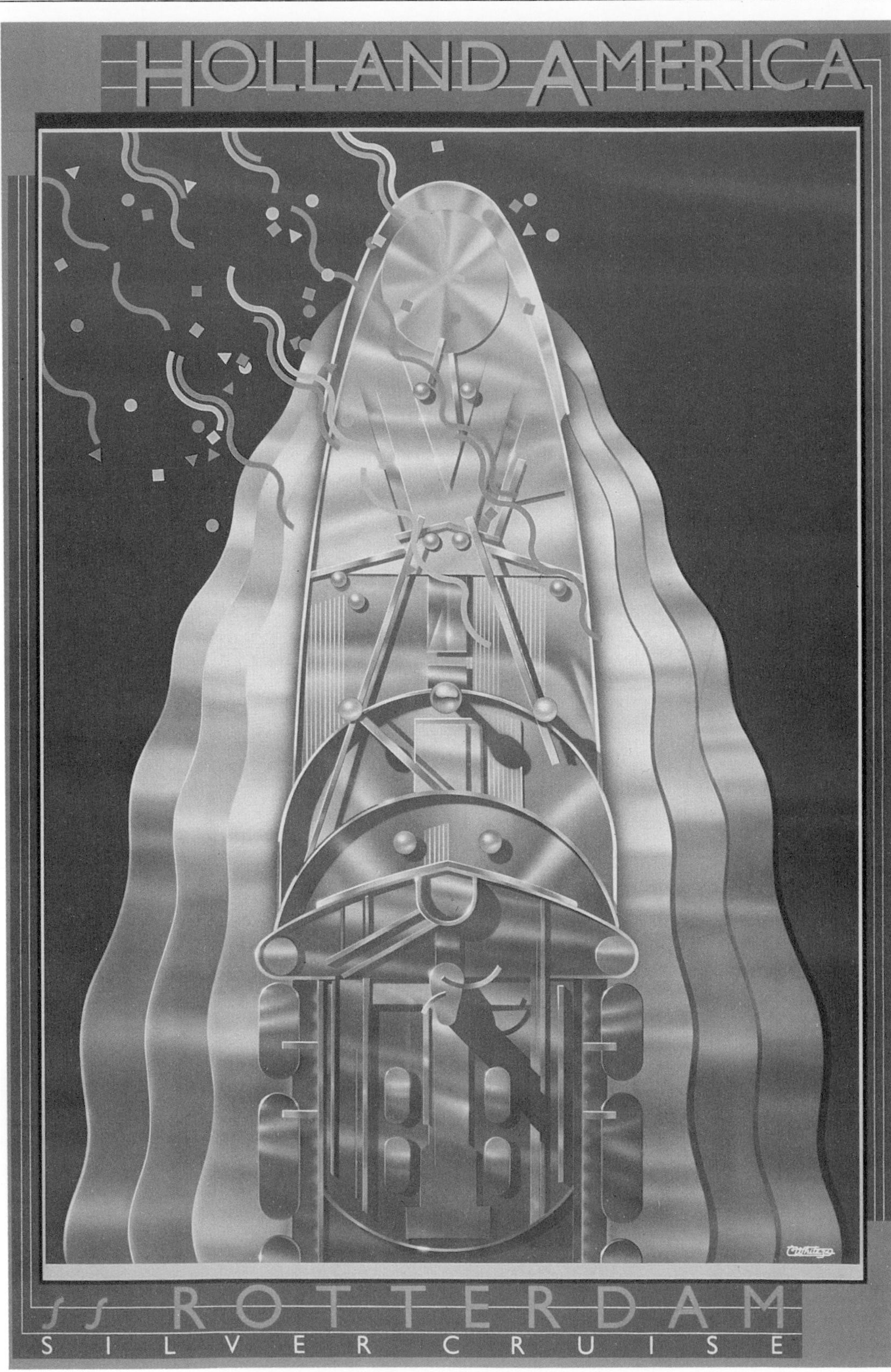

278

ARTIST
Charles White III

ART DIRECTOR
Keith Bright

AD AGENCY
Chiat-Day New York

CLIENT
Holland America Lines

POSTER FOR A CRUISE LINE WITH THE COPYLINE "SILVER CRUISE," SPRING 1983.

Acrylic

Promotion

This section includes work commissioned for calendars, direct mail announcements, greeting cards, promotional brochures and mailings, record album covers, technical and industrial catalogues

280

ARTIST
Braldt Bralds

DESIGNER
Braldt Bralds

ART DIRECTOR
Shinichiro Tora

PUBLISHER
Hotel & Bartender Association, Tokyo, Japan

ILLUSTRATION FOR A CALENDAR ENTITLED "CUBA LIBRE," 1983.

Oil on masonite

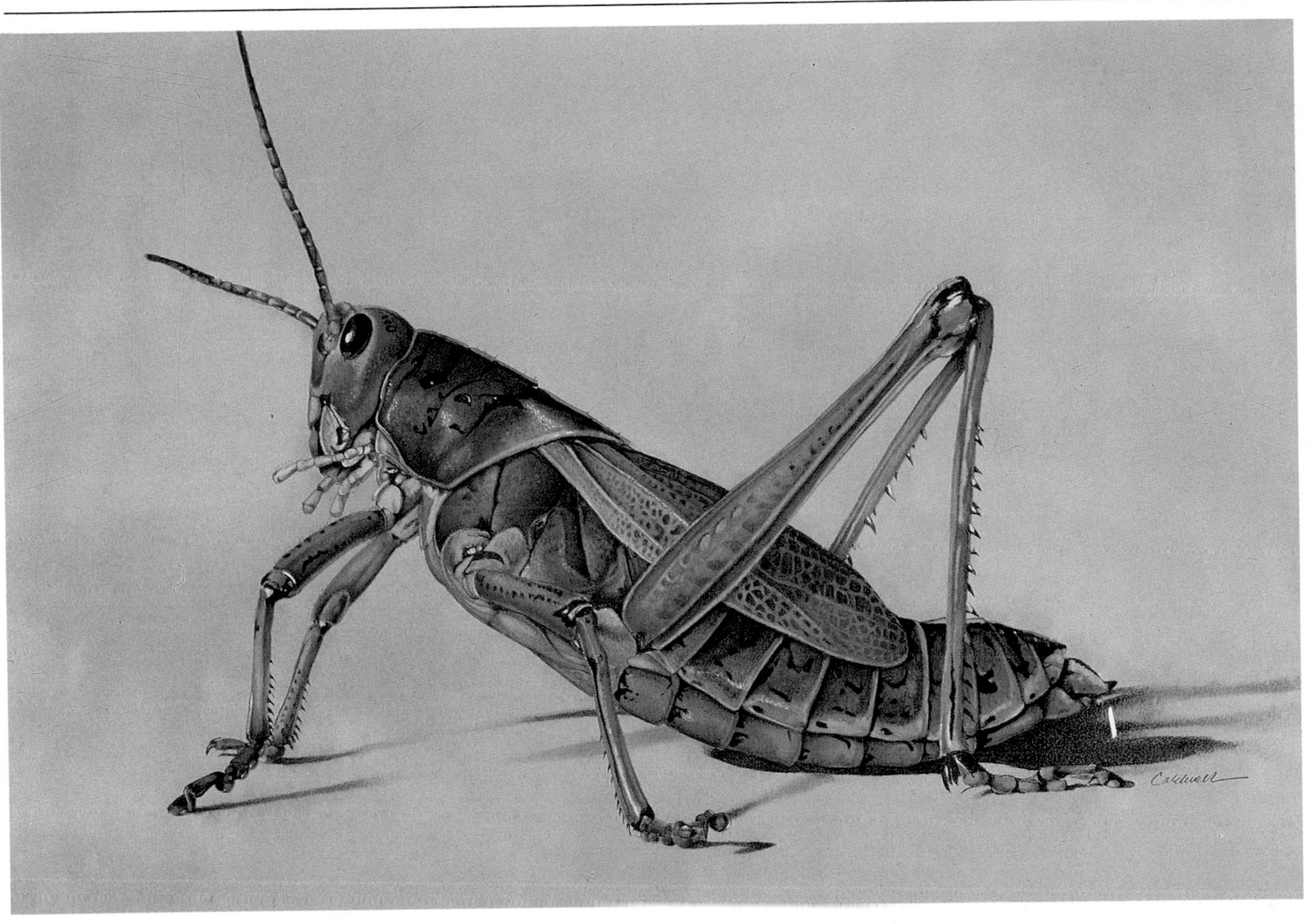

281

ARTIST
Kirk Caldwell

DESIGNER
Kirk Caldwell

ART DIRECTOR
Dugald Stermer

WRITER
Leslie Saul

PUBLISHER
San Francisco Zoological Society

ILLUSTRATION FOR A POSTER AND T-SHIRT FOR THE SAN FRANCISCO INSECT ZOO,
1983.

Graphite and dye

282

ARTIST
Ron Chan

DESIGNER
Dugald Stermer

ART DIRECTOR
Rich Silverstein

WRITER
Jeff Goodby

DESIGN GROUP
Goodby, Berlin & Silverstein

PUBLISHER
Electronic Arts

COVER ILLUSTRATION FOR SOFTWARE GAME PACKAGE, 1983.

Pen, ink, and Zipatone color film

283

ARTIST
Robert Giusti

DESIGNERS
Shinichiro Tora/Yasuhara Nakahara

ART DIRECTORS
Shinichiro Tora/Yasuhara Nakahara

DESIGN GROUP
Creative Design Center of Dai Nipon Printing

PUBLISHER
Japan Hotel Barman's Association

CALENDAR ILLUSTRATION FOR THE MONTH OF NOVEMBER ENTITLED "AMERICANO," 1984.

Acrylic on canvas

284

ARTIST
Gene Greif

DESIGNER
Gene Greif

ART DIRECTOR
Richard Hsu

ILLUSTRATION FOR A BLOOMINGDALE'S SHOPPING BAG USED IN STORES NATIONWIDE, JANUARY 1984.

Mixed media collage

285

ARTIST
Lonni Sue Johnson

DESIGNER
Dana Kasarsky

ART DIRECTOR
Dana Kasarsky

DESIGN GROUP
Dana Kasarsky Design

SELF-PROMOTIONAL PIECE USED AS A MAILER BY THE ARTIST,
1983.

Ink and watercolor

286

ARTIST
Barbara Klunder

DESIGNER
Barbara Klunder

ART DIRECTOR
Barbara Klunder

PUBLISHER
Creative Source/Wilcord Publications Ltd.

ILLUSTRATIONS FOR SELF-PROMOTION PAGES IN *CREATIVE SOURCE*, 1984.

Ink on illustration board

287

ARTIST
Jean-Christian Knaff

DESIGNER
Jean-Christian Knaff

ART DIRECTOR
Armand Deriaz

ILLUSTRATIONS FOR A SERIES OF CARDS DEPICTING THE HOLSTEIN COW ENTITLED "THANKS MR. GALLANT," 1983.

Watercolor and mixed media

288

ARTIST
Richard Mantel

DESIGNER
Ron Coro

ART DIRECTOR
Ron Coro

DESIGN GROUP
Mantel, Koppel & Scher

ILLUSTRATION FOR A RECORD ALBUM COVER,
JUNE 1983.

Acrylic

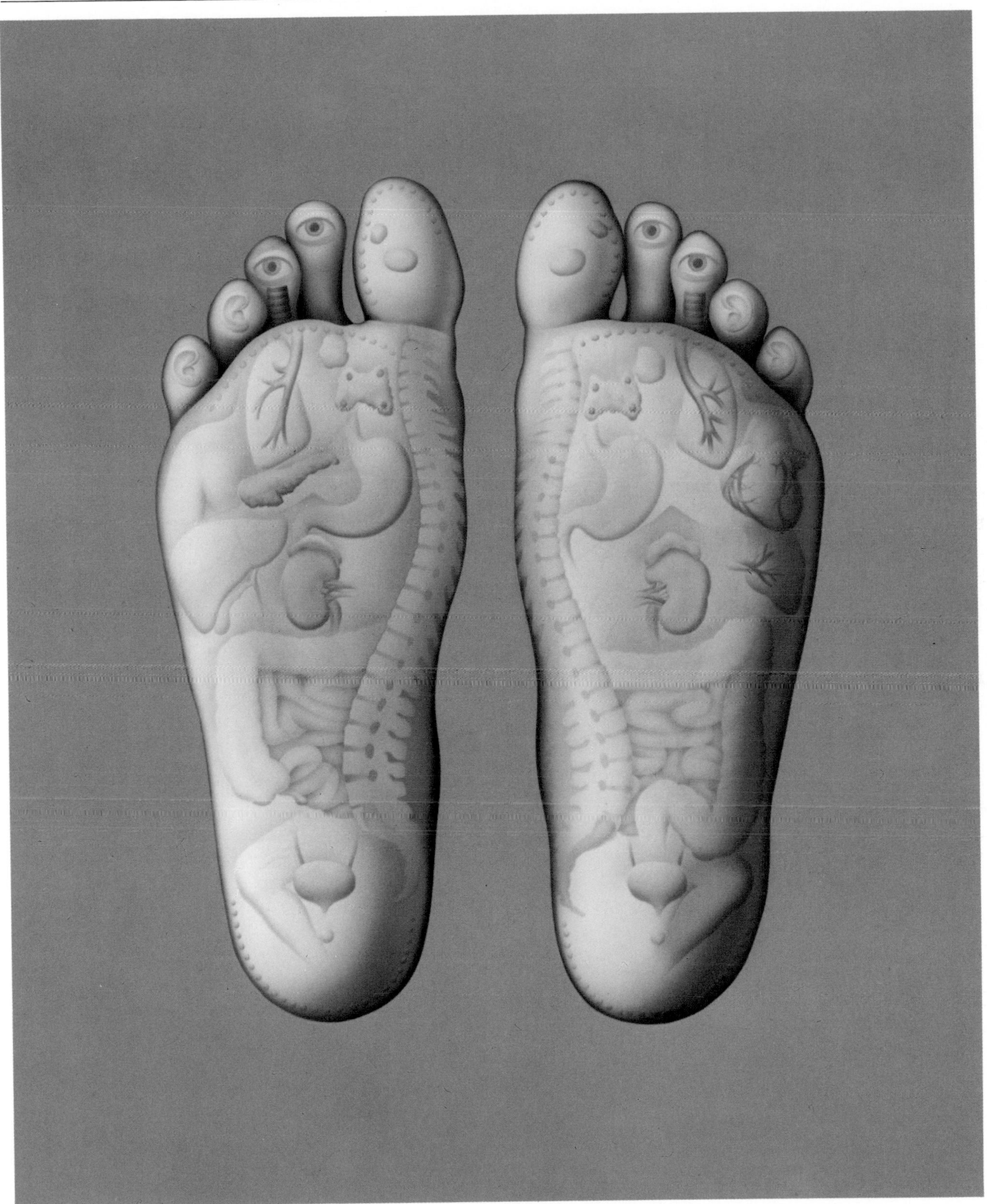

289

ARTIST
Leonard E. Morgan

DESIGNER
Michael V. Phillips

ART DIRECTOR
Michael V. Phillips

WRITER
Robert J. Kienle

ILLUSTRATION FOR A TWO-PAGE SALES AID IN USE BY WESTWOOD PHARMACEUTICAL SALES DEPARTMENT, 1984.

Gouache

290

ARTIST
Everett Peck

DESIGNER
Everett Peck

ART DIRECTOR
Everett Peck

CLIENT
Heaven Contemporary Retail Store

ILLUSTRATION FOR A GREETING CARD, 1984.

Graphite

291

ARTIST
Lane Smith

DESIGNER
Lane Smith

PUBLISHER
PVC Records/Jem

DESIGN FOR A RECORD ALBUM COVER FOR "STUKAS OVER DISNEYLAND" BY THE DICKIES,
1984.

Alkyd

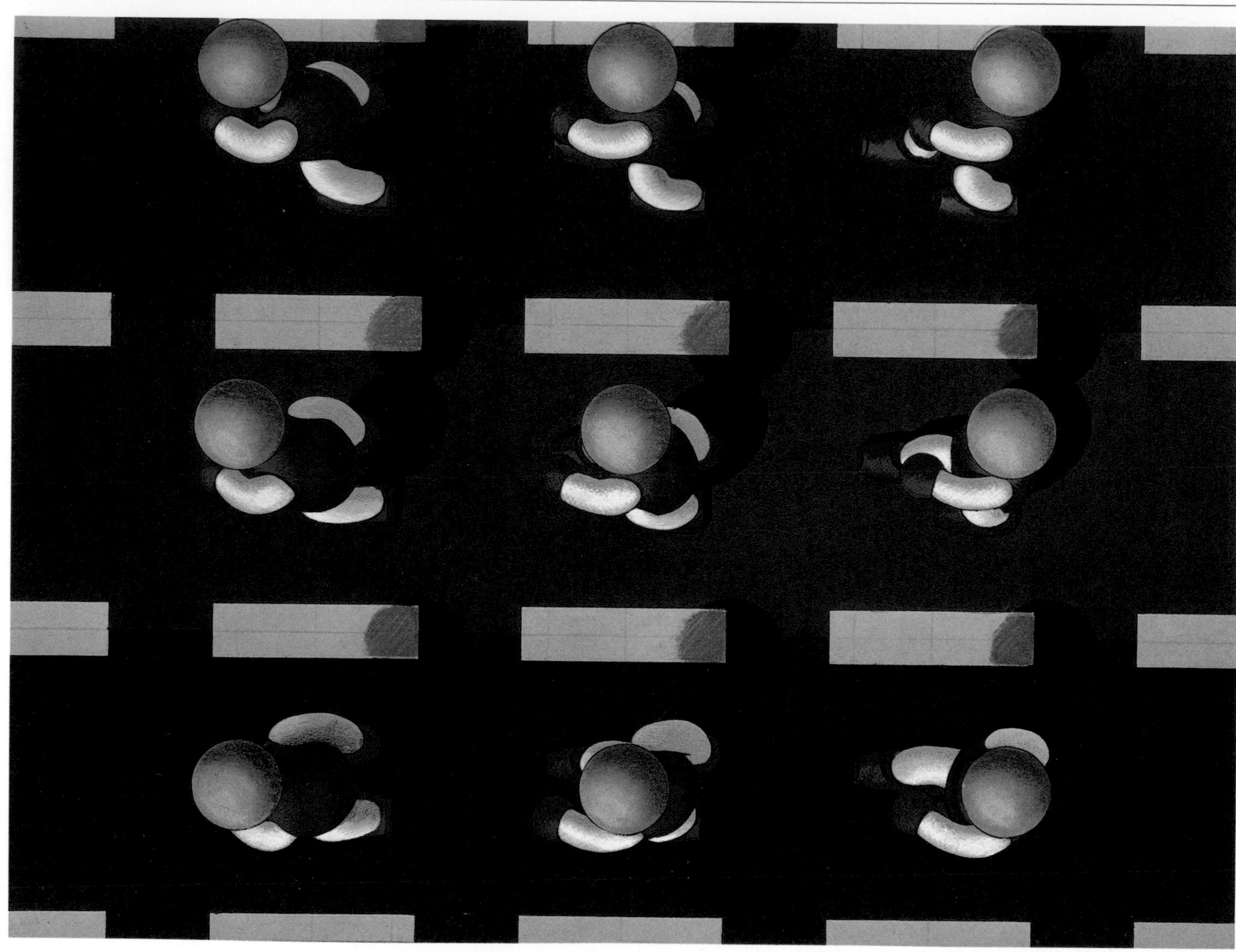

292

ARTIST
Barton E. Stabler

ART DIRECTOR
Barton E. Stabler

PROMOTIONAL PIECE FOR ROUNDHEAD FILM, 1983.

Acrylic, colored pencil, dye, and marker

293

ARTIST
Thomas Szumowski

ILLUSTRATION FOR A SELF-PROMOTION MAILER SENT TO ART DIRECTORS IN THE BOSTON AREA, JUNE 1983.

Acrylic

294

ARTIST
Rob Wood

DESIGNER
Rob Wood

ART DIRECTOR
Dan Snyder

WRITER
Dr. Paul R. Ehrlich

DESIGN GROUP
Porter, Novelli & Associates

PUBLISHER
Open Space Institute, Inc./The Center on the Consequences of Nuclear War

TWO IN A SERIES DEPICTING THE BIOLOGICAL CONSEQUENCES OF NUCLEAR WAR PRESENTED AT THE CONFERENCE ON THE WORLD AFTER NUCLEAR WAR IN WASHINGTON, OCTOBER 1983.

Airbrush and gouache

295

ARTIST
Rob Wood

DESIGNER
Rob Wood

ART DIRECTOR
Rob Wood

WRITER
Pamela Ronsaville

DESIGN GROUP
Stansbury, Ronsaville, Wood Inc.

PUBLISHER
Casio-Wolf, Inc.

ILLUSTRATION OF SATURN'S RINGS FOR THE JULY, AUGUST, AND SEPTEMBER SEGMENTS OF A CALENDAR SHOWING SOME OF THE NEW DISCOVERIES IN SPACE, 1983.

Airbrush, gouache

296

ARTIST
Paul Yalowitz

PUBLISHER
RSVP

ILLUSTRATION FOR A SELF-PROMOTION PIECE IN *RSVP-9*, 1984.

Pencil

Unpublished

This section includes commissioned but unpublished illustrations, personal work produced by professionals, and the work of students

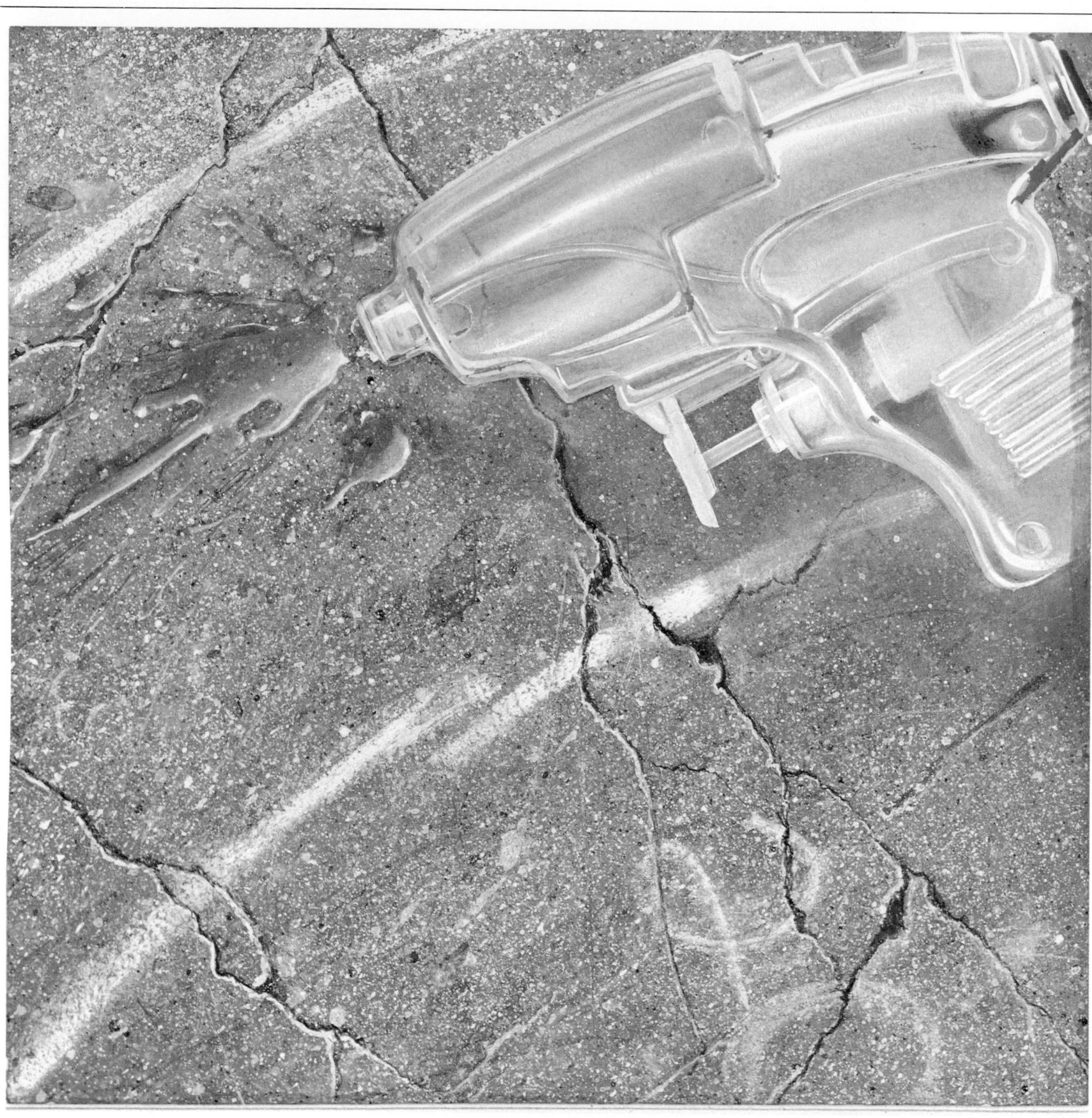

298

ARTIST

Jeffrey Adams

UNTITLED PERSONAL WORK.

Gouache

299

ARTIST
Brian Ajhar

ONE OF A SERIES OF SCENES DEPICTING NEW YORK CITY FOR THE ARTIST'S PORTFOLIO.

Oil base ink monoprint on rag paper

300

ARTIST
Karen Barbour

PERSONAL WORK BY THE ARTIST ENTITLED "PINK PALACE."

Watercolor and gouache

301

ARTIST
Deborah Barrett
ILLUSTRATION ENTITLED "CHILD ABUSE," PART OF THE ARTIST'S PORTFOLIO.
Acrylic on paper and canvas and plaster, then sewn

ARTIST
Deborah Barrett
ILLUSTRATION ENTITLED "FLYING MAN" EXECUTED FOR ARTIST'S PORTFOLIO.
Acrylic on torn paper with fabric and canvas, then sewn

302

ARTIST

Caty Bartholomew

ILLUSTRATION ENTITLED "ANIMAL CRACKERS," PART OF THE ARTIST'S PORTFOLIO.

Acrylic and pencil

303

ARTIST
Trent Burleson

PERSONAL WORK BY THE ARTIST ENTITLED "WHITE HOUSE."

Oil

304

ARTIST

Larry W. Carroll

ONE OF A SERIES OF ILLUSTRATIONS FROM THE ARTIST'S PORTFOLIO ENTITLED "JESUS."

Oil

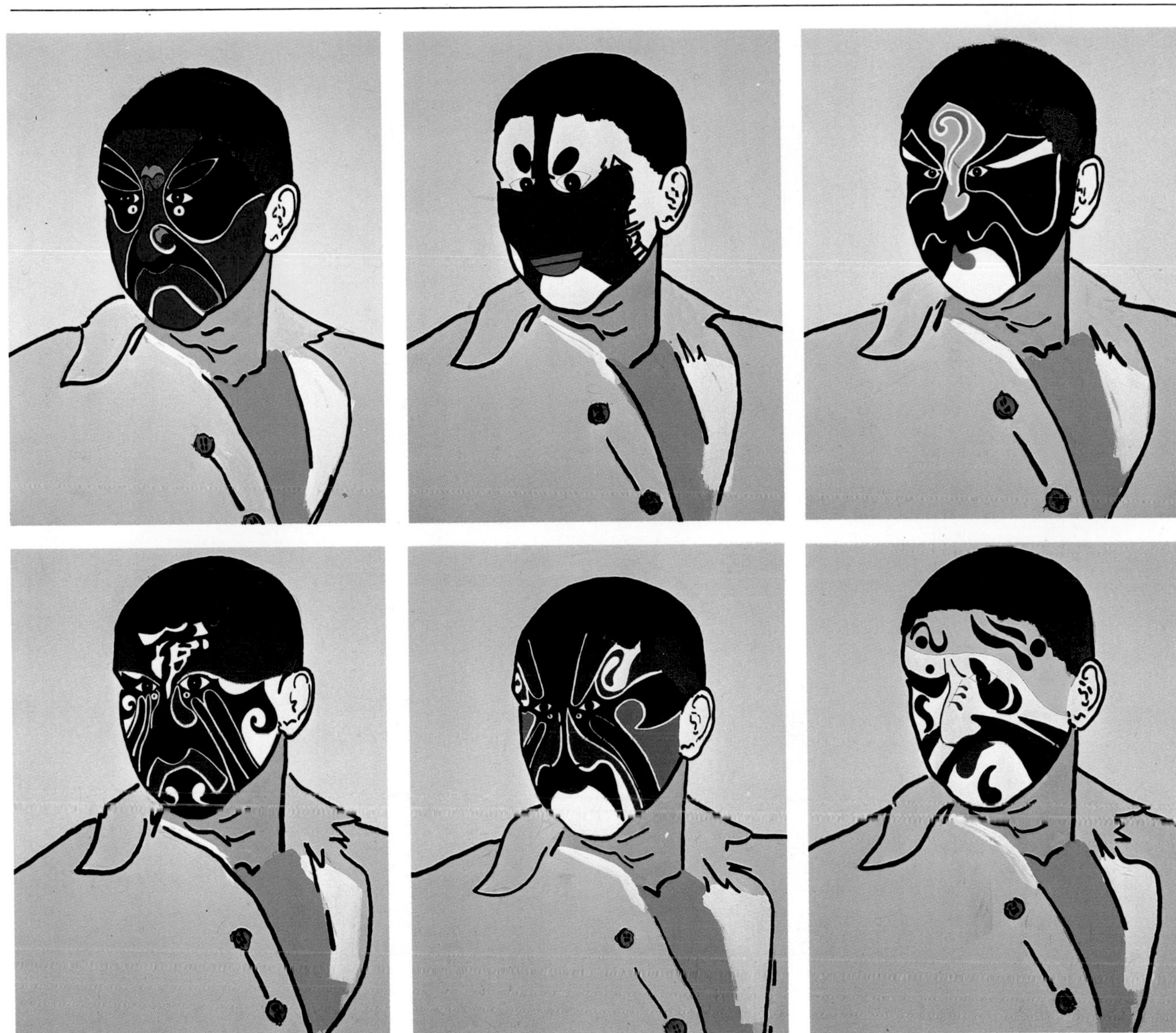

305

ARTIST

Michael Corris

SERIES OF PORTRAITS OF BRECHT AS CHINESE OPERA CHARACTERS.

Vinyl on foam core

306

ARTIST

Henrik Drescher

UNTITLED PERSONAL WORK.

Polaroid, acrylic, and ink

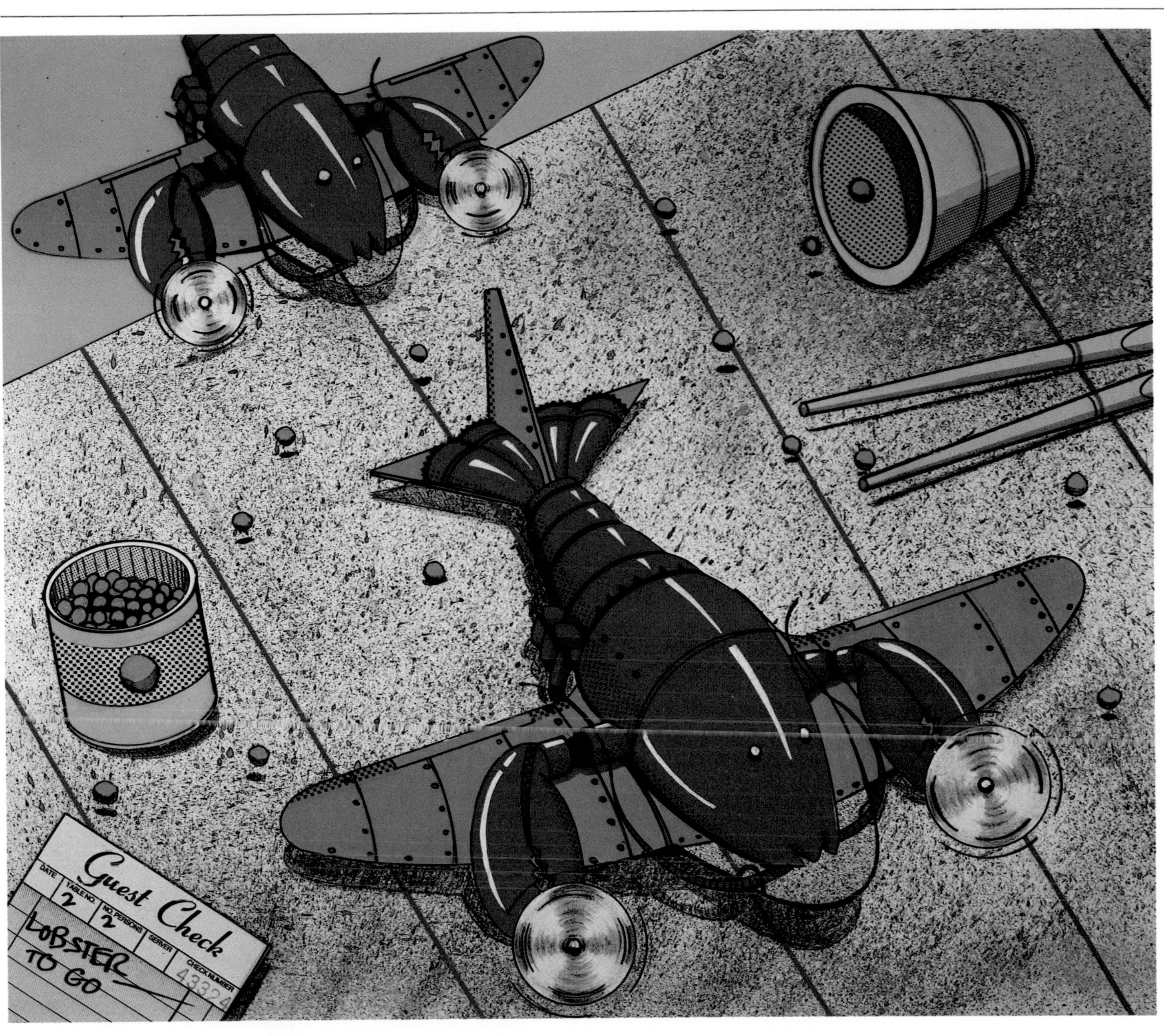

307

ARTIST
Cameron Eagle

ILLUSTRATION ENTITLED "LOBSTERS TO GO," PART OF THE ARTIST'S PORTFOLIO.

Mixed media

308

ARTIST
Randall Enos

ILLUSTRATION ENTITLED "WASHINGTON AND LINCOLN CUTTING DOWN CHERRY TREE" DONE AS A SELF-PROMOTION PIECE.

Linocut printed on colored paper

309

ARTIST
Mark S. Fisher

SKETCHBOOK DRAWING ENTITLED "40 YEARS LATER," A TAKE-OFF ON EDWARD HOPPER'S PAINTING "NIGHT HAWKS."

Ink, watercolor, and pencil

310

ARTIST

Bob Fortier

ILLUSTRATION COMMISSIONED BUT UNPUBLISHED BY *VANITY FAIR.*

Pencil and gouache

311

ARTIST

G. Allen Garns

PERSONAL WORK BY THE ARTIST ENTITLED "TICKET BOOTH."

Oil

312

ARTIST

Alexa Grace

SERIES OF ILLUSTRATIONS COMMISSIONED BUT UNPUBLISHED BY *SPORTS ILLUSTRATED.*

Watercolor and colored pencil

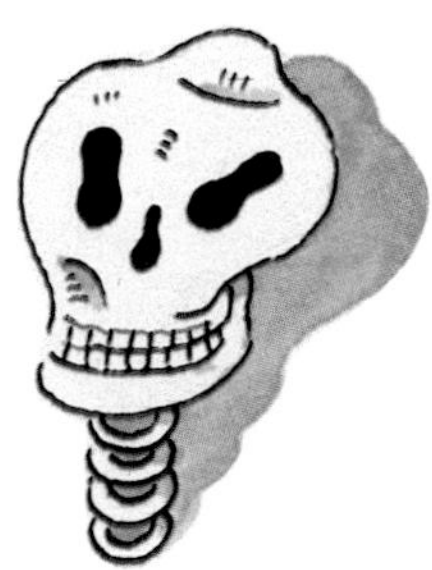

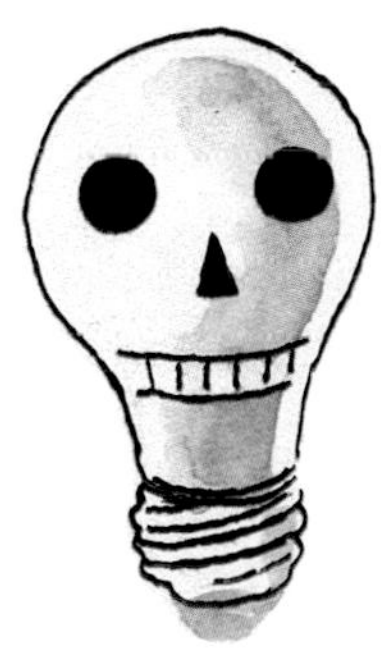

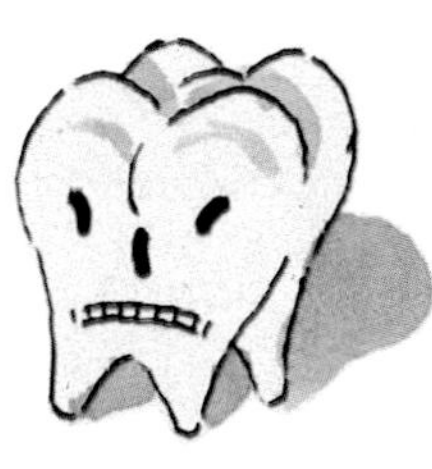

313

ARTIST
Steven Guarnaccia

ILLUSTRATION ENTITLED "SKULLS," PART OF THE ARTIST'S PORTFOLIO.

Ink and watercolor

314

ARTIST
John Hagen

SCHOOL
Rhode Island School of Design

ILLUSTRATION ENTITLED "PORTRAIT OF JOANNA" DONE AS PART OF A COLLEGE PROJECT TO DISTORT A PHOTOGRAPHIC IMAGE USING A GRID.

Graphite

315

ARTIST
Gary Head

PERSONAL WORK BY THE ARTIST ENTITLED "MAN WITH CAMERA."

Pastel

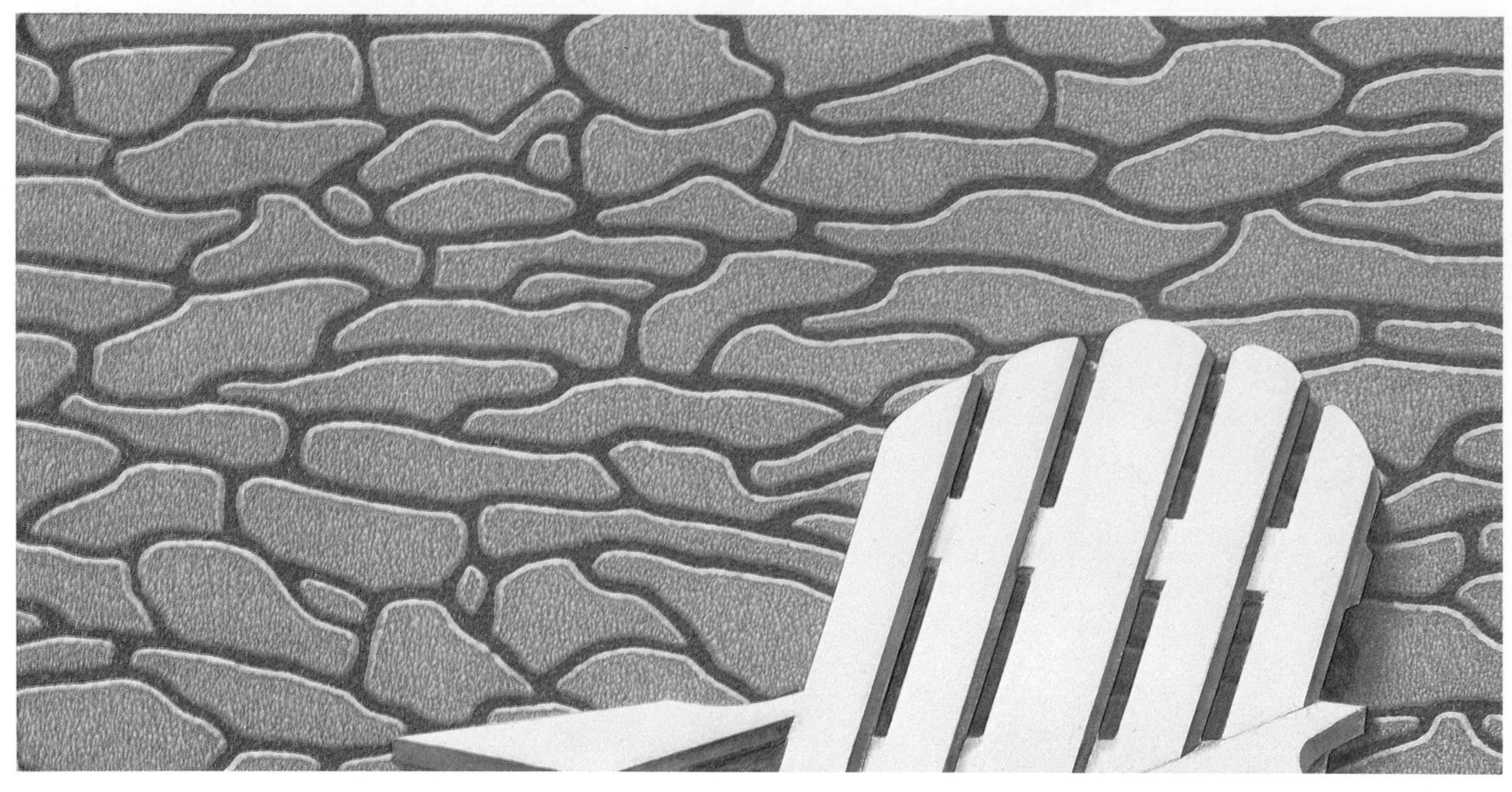

316

ARTIST

Laura Karp

ILLUSTRATION DEPICTING THE ARTIST'S MEMORY OF A BRONX GARDEN IN SUMMER.

Paper collage and pencil

317

ARTIST
Matt Mahurin

UNTITLED PERSONAL WORK.

Oil

318

ARTIST

Michael McGurl

UNTITLED PERSONAL WORK.

Gouache with airbrush

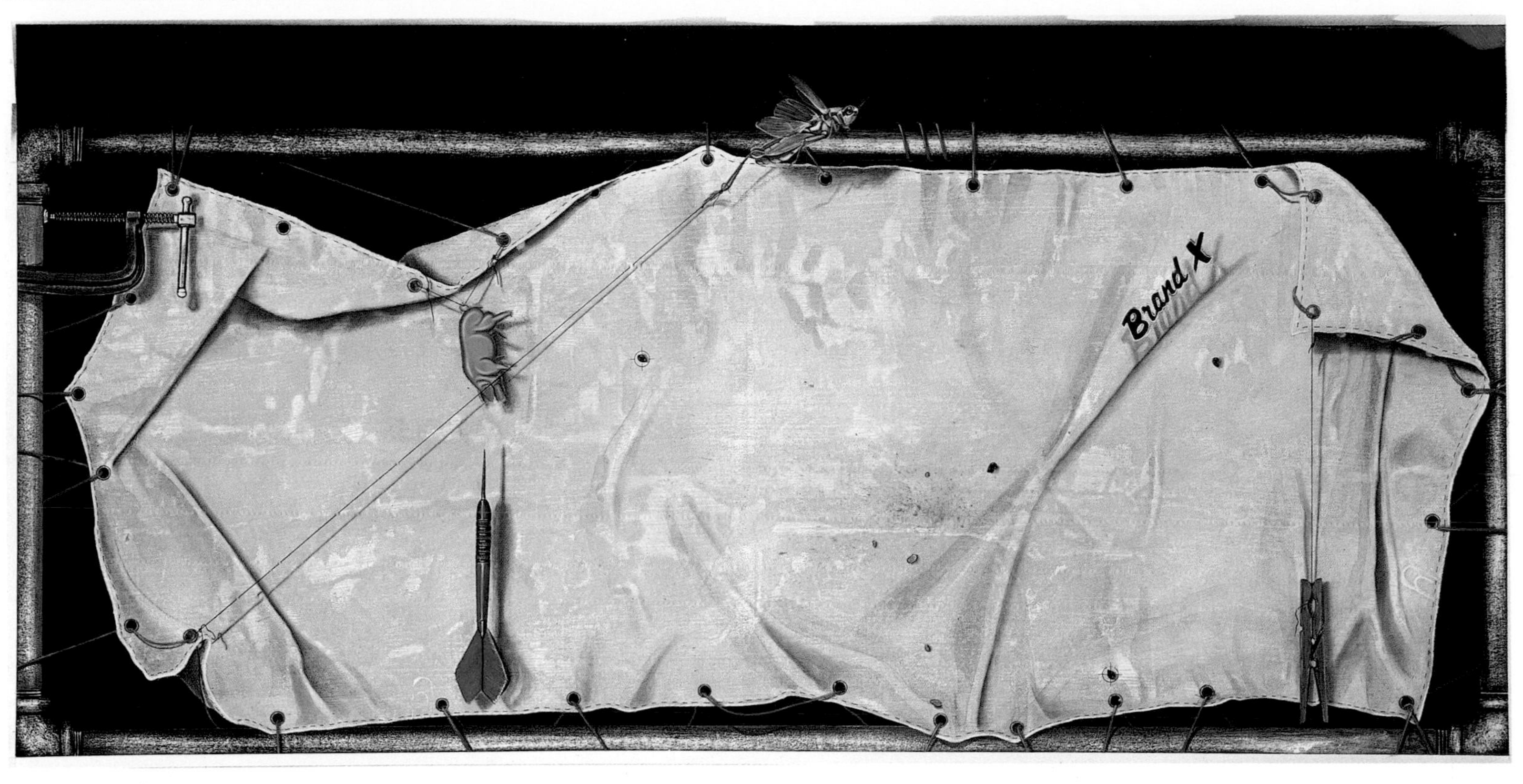

319

ARTIST

Joel Nakamura

RECORD COVER ILLUSTRATION FOR BRAND X, A PERSONAL WORK FOR THE ARTIST'S PORTFOLIO.

Acrylic and mixed media

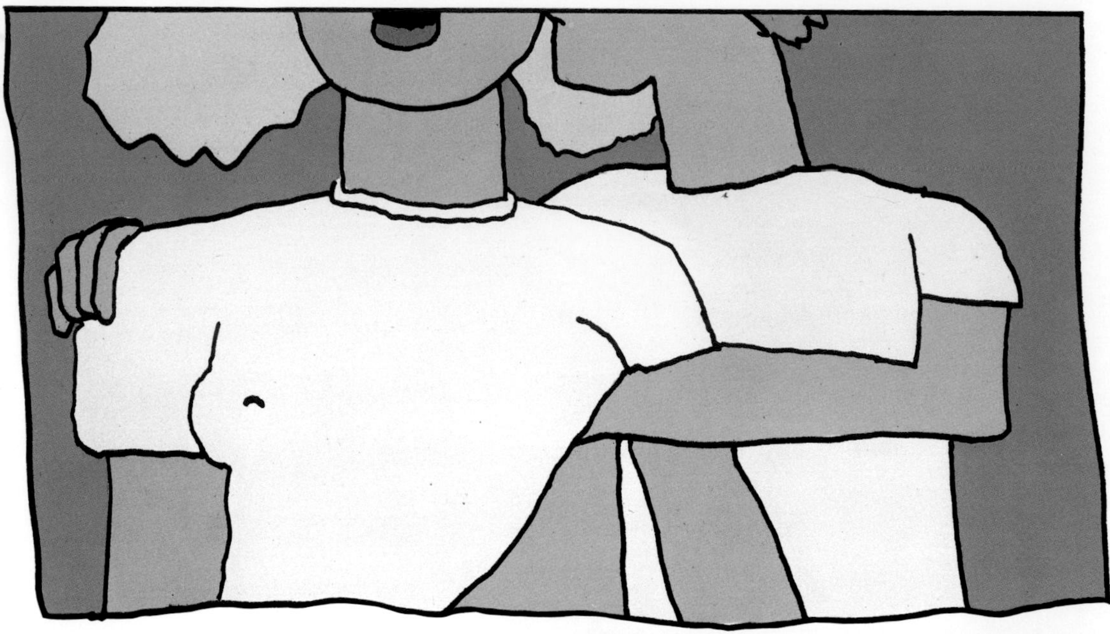

320

ARTIST
Frank Olinsky
UNTITLED PERSONAL WORK.
Pantone film

ARTIST
Frank Olinsky
PORTRAIT OF DAVID BYRNE DONE WITH THE INTENTION OF ILLUSTRATING A BOOK OF LYRICS BY THE GROUP 'TALKING HEADS.'
Pantone film

321

ARTIST
Bob Peters

UNTITLED PERSONAL WORK.

Acrylic on canvas

322

ARTIST
Rallé

PERSONAL WORK BY THE ARTIST.

Oil on board

323

ARTIST
Phil Rose

SELF-PROMOTION PIECE ENTITLED "ETERNAL SOLDIER."

Chinese brush and India ink

324

ARTISTS
Lee & Mary Sievers

PERSONAL WORK ILLUSTRATING MILITARY PARANOIA ENTITLED "HOODWINKER."

Paper mache, acrylic and fabric with props

325

ARTIST
Lane Smith

ILLUSTRATION ENTITLED "MAILMAN," PART OF AN EXHIBITION FEATURING SIX ARTISTS FROM LOS ANGELES HELD AT CALIFORNIA STATE UNIVERSITY.

Alkyd, collage, and colored pencil

ARTIST
Lane Smith

ILLUSTRATION SHOWING THE EFFECTS OF SPONTANEOUS COMBUSTION, PART OF THE ARTIST'S PORTFOLIO.

Alkyd

326

ARTIST

Greg Spalenka

ILLUSTRATIONS IN A CONTINUING SERIES ON YOUNG ILLUSTRATORS LIVING IN NEW YORK CITY.

Oil and acrylic

327

ARTIST
Robert Tuska

ILLUSTRATION ENTITLED "LAWN JOCKIES," PART OF THE ARTIST'S PORTFOLIO.

Gouache

328

ARTIST
Bill Vuksanovich

ILLUSTRATION ENTITLED "BARBER SHOP" DONE AS A SELF-PROMOTIONAL PIECE.

Oil on canvas

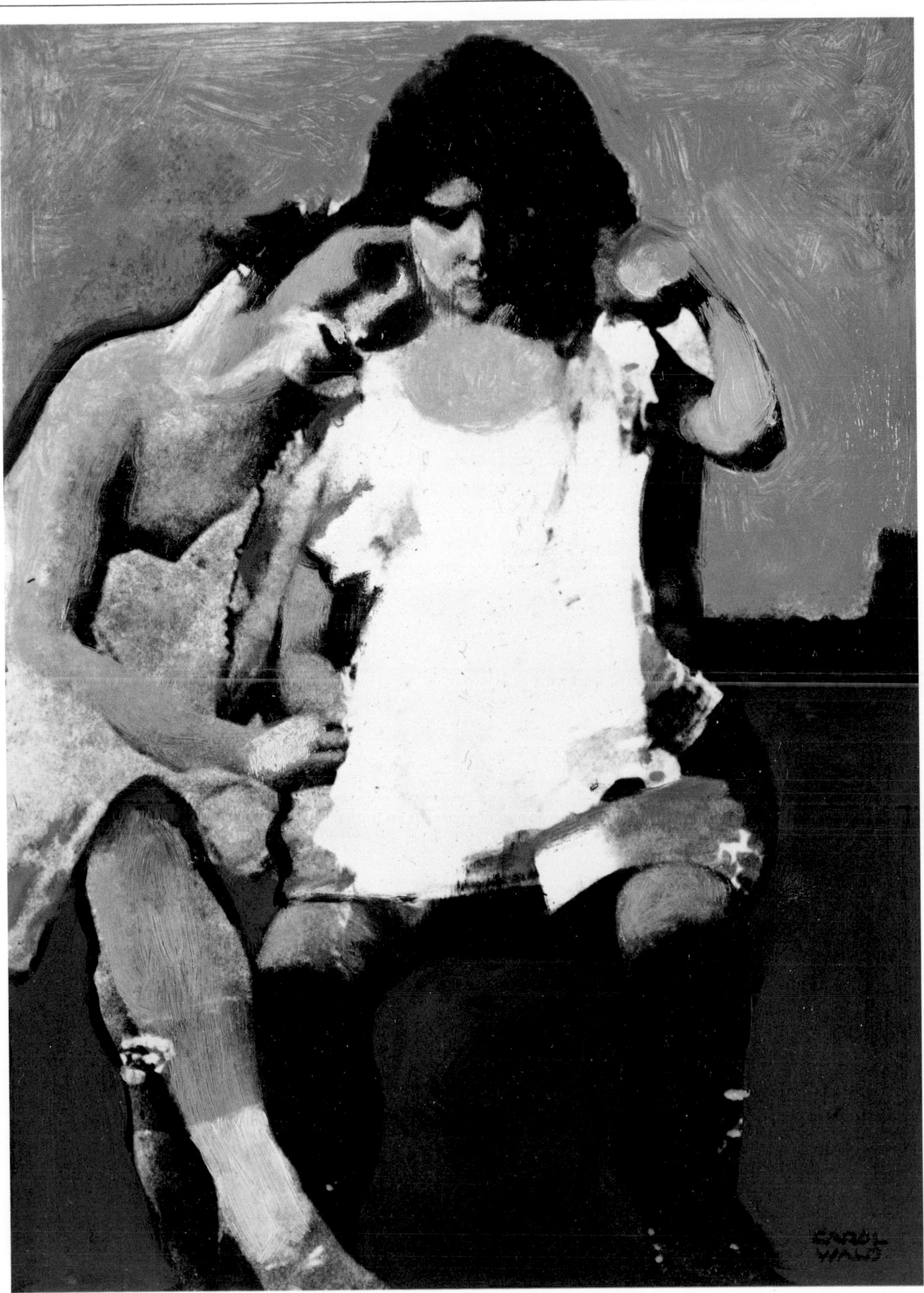

329

ARTIST
Carol Wald

ILLUSTRATION COMMISSIONED BUT UNPUBLISHED BY *TIME* FOR AN ARTICLE ON CHILD ABUSE.

Oil on photo-montage

330

ARTIST

Mick Wiggins

UNTITLED WORK DONE FOR SELF-PROMOTION.

Oil on canvas

331

ARTIST

Efram Wolff

ILLUSTRATION ENTITLED "YOUR TAX DOLLARS" PUBLISHED AND PRINTED BY THE ARTIST IN A LIMITED EDITION.

Multiple plate color intaglio print

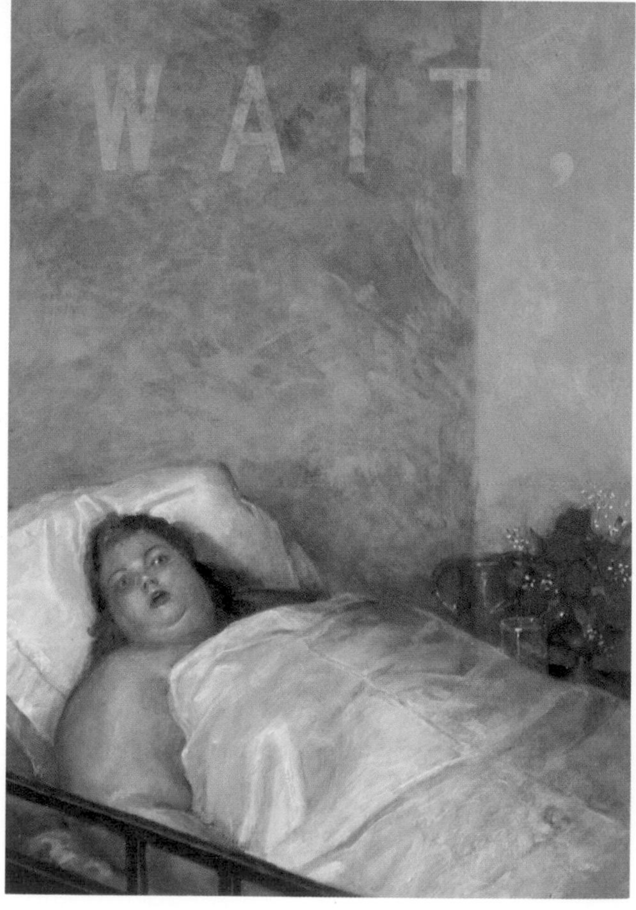

332

ARTIST
Thomas Woodruff
PERSONAL WORK BY THE ARTIST ENTITLED "APROPOS."
Acrylic

ARTIST
Thomas Woodruff
PERSONAL WORK BY THE ARTIST ENTITLED "WAIT."
Acrylic

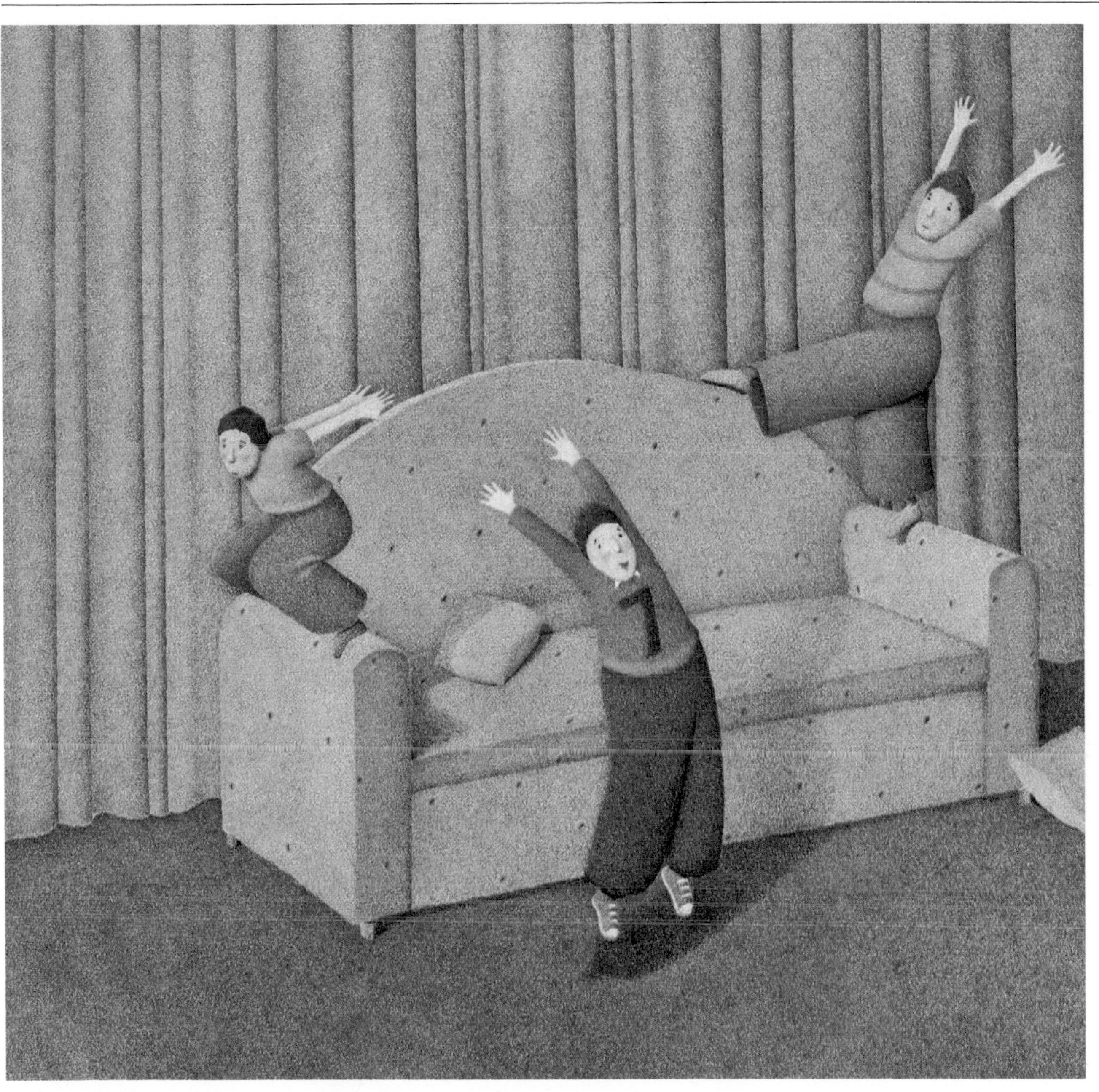

333

ARTIST
Paul Yalowitz

ILLUSTRATION ENTITLED "THE AMAZING PEPPERONI BROTHERS," PART OF THE ARTIST'S PORTFOLIO.

Colored pencil

334

ARTIST

Lisa Young

ILLUSTRATION ENTITLED "FOUR O'CLOCK," PART OF THE ARTIST'S PORTFOLIO.

Pastel

335

ARTIST
Paul Binkley

SCHOOL
Art Center College of Design

DESIGN FOR A POSTER BASED ON THE WORK OF MICHAEL GRAVES, DONE AS A COLLEGE PROJECT.

Acrylic, prisma, and pastel

336

ARTIST

Dave Calver

ALBUM COVER ILLUSTRATION COMMISSIONED BUT UNUSED BY THE BAND 'NEW MATH.'

Colored pencil

337

ARTIST
Mark Chiarello

SCHOOL
Pratt Institute

ILLUSTRATION ENTITLED "MAROONED," A COLLEGE PROJECT FOR A PAPERBACK BOOK COVER.

Gouache

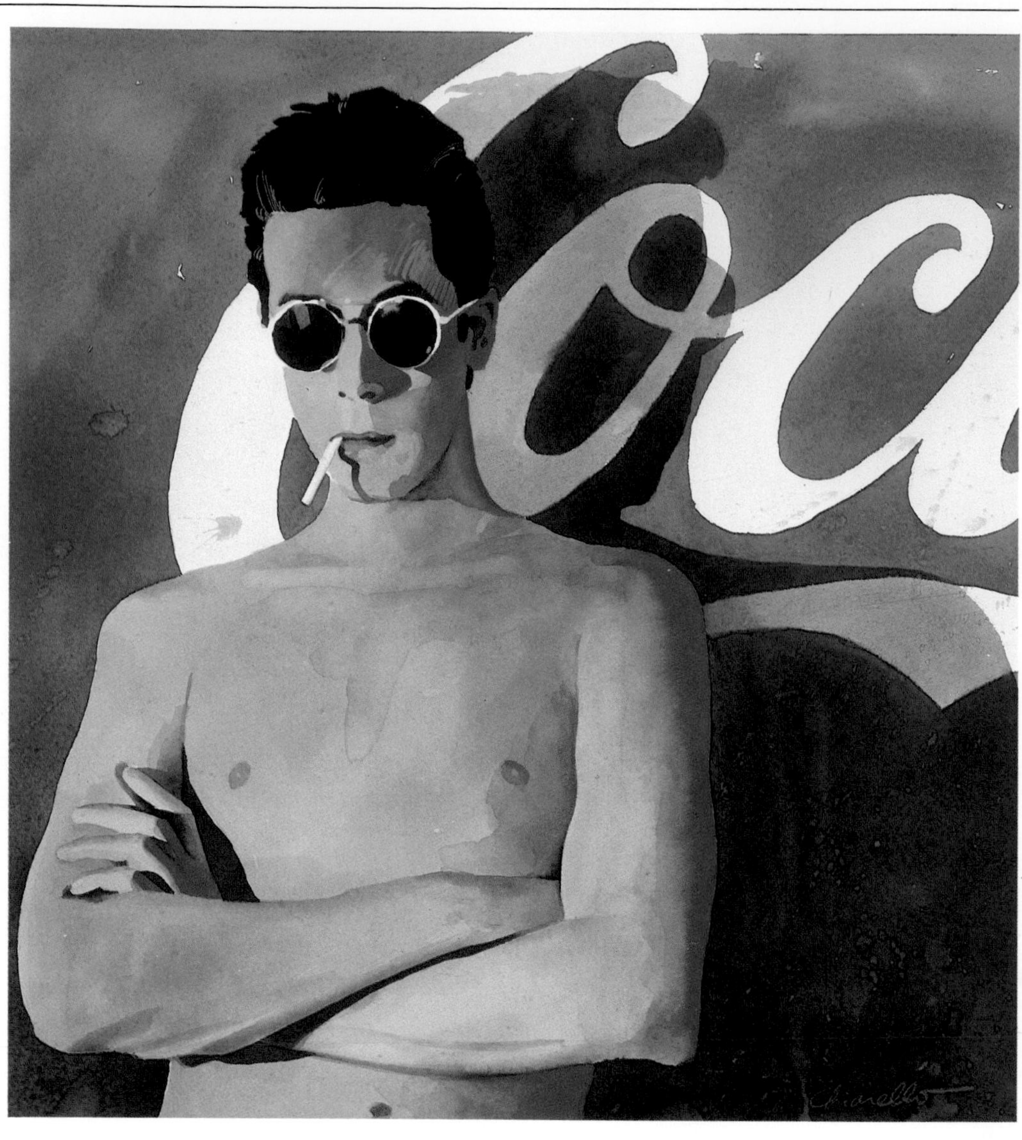

338

ARTIST
Mark Chiarello

SCHOOL
Pratt Institute

PERSONAL WORK ENTITLED "COCA COLA GUY."

Dye

339

ARTIST
James Costello

SCHOOL
Rhode Island School of Design

ILLUSTRATION ENTITLED "THE HOTEL UNDERGROUND," PART OF THE ARTIST'S PORTFOLIO.

Collage, neocolor, and pencil

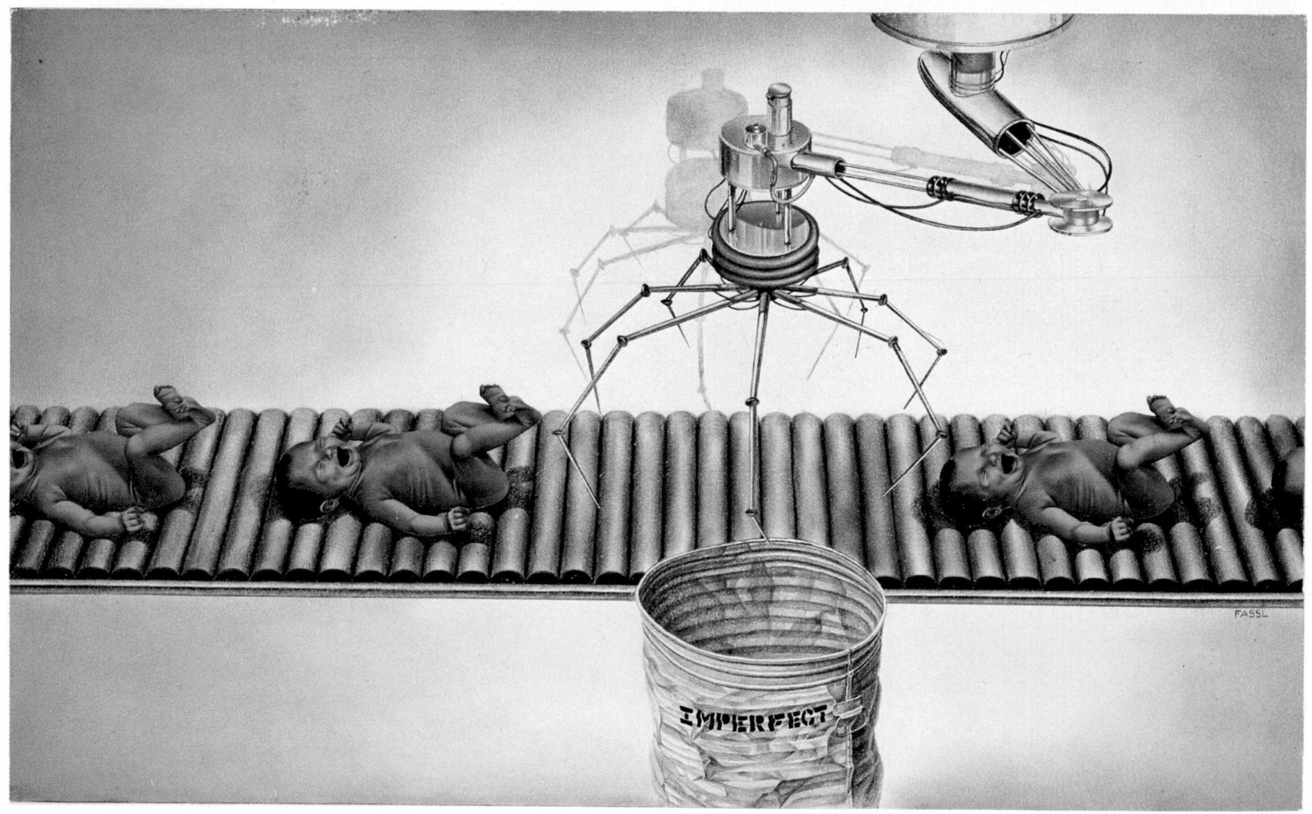

340

ARTIST
Robert F. Fassl

SCHOOL
Art Center College of Design

ILLUSTRATION ENTITLED "OLD WOMAN," A STUDENT ASSIGNMENT.

Acrylic and colored pencil

ARTIST
Robert F. Fassl

SCHOOL
Art Center College of Design

UNTITLED PERSONAL WORK.

Colored pencil

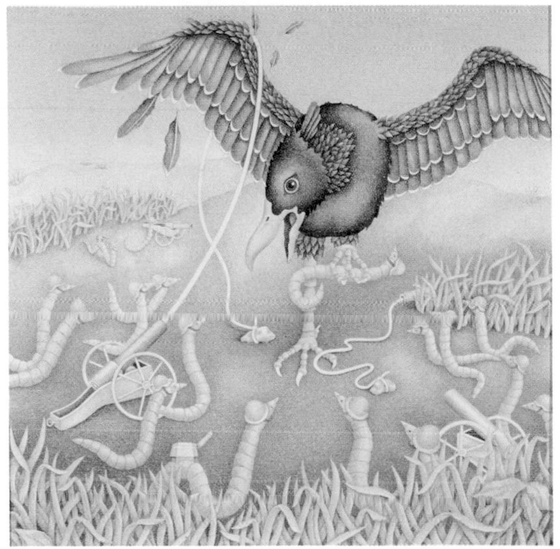

341

ARTIST
Gay W. Holland

SCHOOL
University of Arizona

SERIES ENTITLED "REVENGE OF THE WORMS" DONE AS A COLLEGE PROJECT TO ILLUSTRATE A NEW CONCEPT FOR A CHILDREN'S BOOK.

Prismacolor pencil

342

ARTIST
Christopher Jarrin

SCHOOL
Pratt Institute

PERSONAL WORK
ENTITLED "FACES."

Pastel

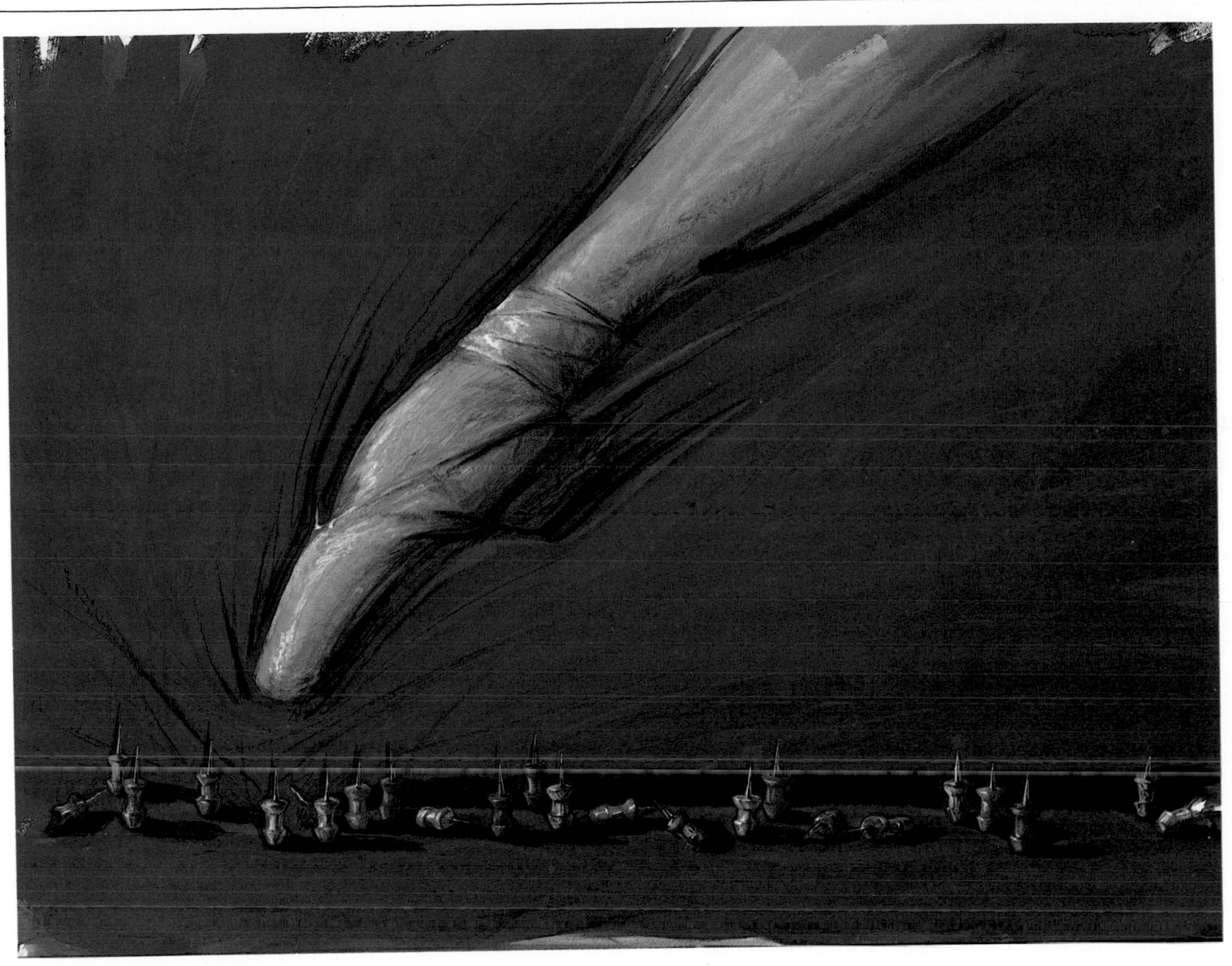

343

ARTIST
Shelly E. Johnson

SCHOOL
Art Center College of Design

ILLUSTRATION ENTITLED "DANCING THROUGH THE REAGAN YEARS..." DONE AS A COLLEGE PROJECT FOR A HYPOTHETICAL MAGAZINE ON CONTROVERSIAL SUBJECTS.

Gouache, prisma, pastel

344

ARTIST

Jeannette Louie

SCHOOL

Parsons School of Design

ILLUSTRATION ENTITLED "SUBWAY SCENE" DONE AS A COLLEGE PROJECT ON MASS TRANSIT.

Oil on paper

345

ARTIST
Mickey Paraskevas

SCHOOL
School of Visual Arts

ILLUSTRATION ENTITLED "PASS IT ON," PART OF THE ARTIST'S PORTFOLIO.

Oil on board

346

ARTIST
John Resi

SCHOOL
School of Visual Arts

ILLUSTRATION ENTITLED "GIRL IN A RED HAT (MODERN)."

Acrylic

347

ARTIST
Marla Tarbox
SCHOOL
Art Center College of Design
ILLUSTRATION ENTITLED "JOHN BELUSHI'S FINAL ACT" DONE AS A COLLEGE PROJECT FOR AN ARTICLE ON THE DEATH OF JOHN BELUSHI.
Acrylic

ARTIST
Marla Tarbox
SCHOOL
Art Center College of Design
ILLUSTRATION DONE AS A COLLEGE PROJECT FOR AN EDITORIAL PIECE ON HOW TO SELL ANYTHING TO ANYONE.
Acrylic

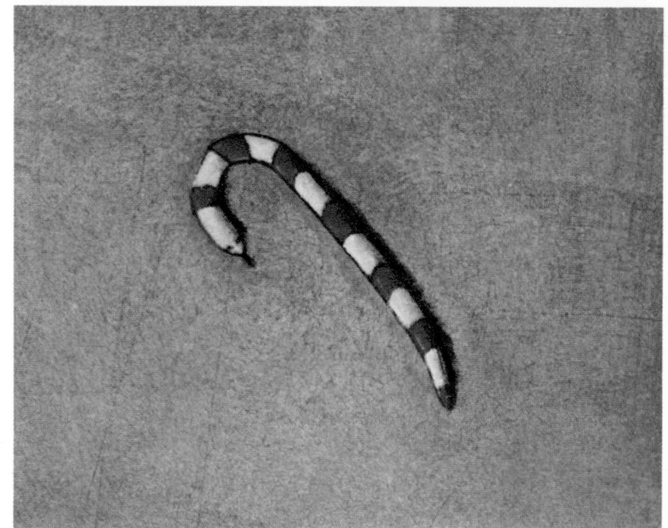

348

ARTIST
Roxana Villa

SCHOOL
Otis Art Institute of Parsons School of Design

SERIES OF ILLUSTRATIONS DONE AS A COLLEGE PROJECT.

Mixed media, collage, acrylic, and oil

Film

This section includes film animation for television, advertising, and short films

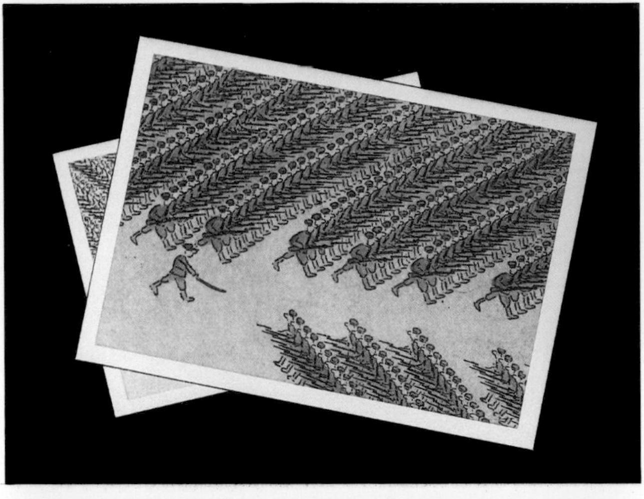

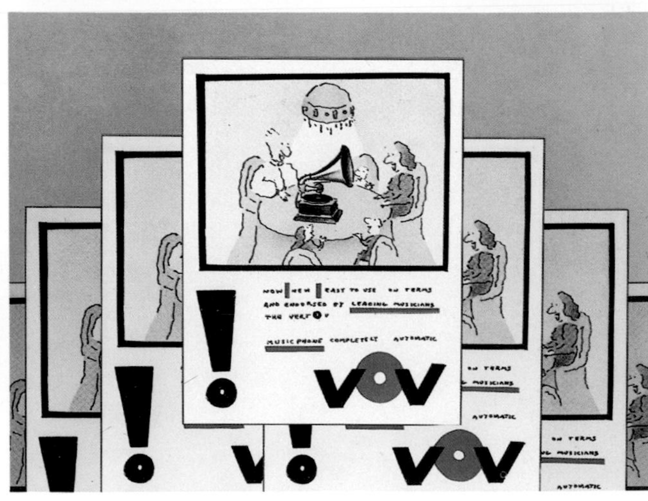

350

ANIMATORS
Tissa David, Ed Smith, Fred Mogubgub, Mary Szilagyi, Maciek Albrecht
ARTIST
R.O. Blechman
DIRECTOR
R.O. Blechman
WRITER
R.O. Blechman
ART DIRECTOR
R.O. Blechman
PRODUCTION COMPANY
The Ink Tank
CLIENT
Public Broadcasting System (PBS)

ANIMATED FEATURE FILM ENTITLED "THE SOLDIER'S TALE."
60 MINUTES

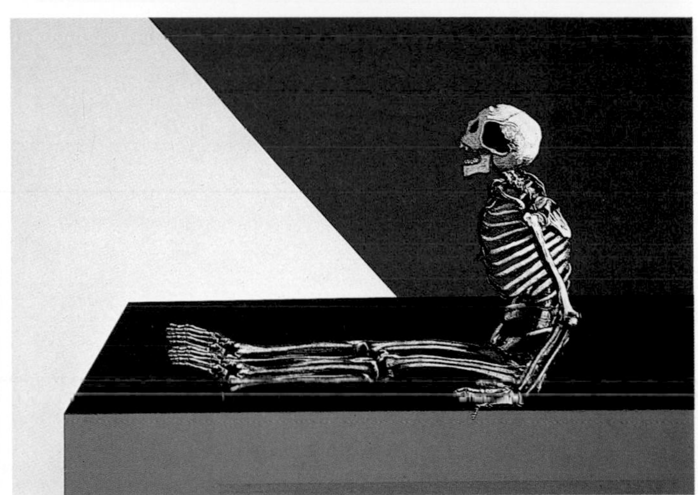

351

ANIMATOR
Gianni Caccia
ARTIST
Gianni Caccia
DIRECTOR
Laurent Gagliardi
WRITER
Laurent Gagliardi
ART DIRECTORS
Gianni Caccia/Laurent Gagliardi
PRODUCTION COMPANY
Les Films de l'Automne Ltd.
CLIENT
Radio-Quebec
A DOCUMENTARY FILM ENTITLED "MANUSCRITS: OCTAVE CREMAZIE" (OCTAVE CREMAZIE MANUSCRIPTS). 9 MINUTES 30 SECONDS

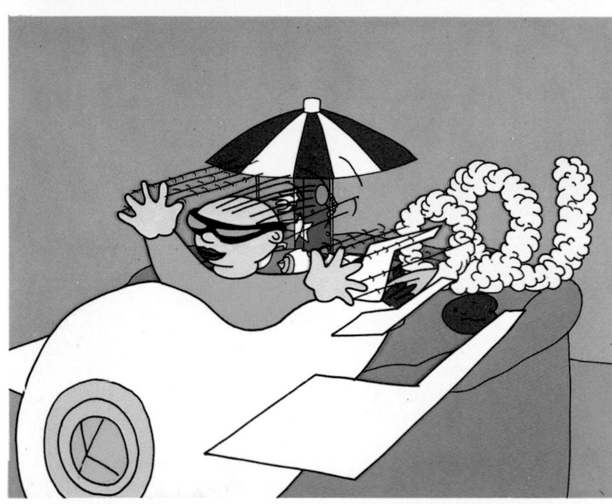

352

ANIMATORS
Howard Danelowitz/ Tracy Kirshenbaum
ARTIST
Howard Danelowitz
DIRECTOR
Howard Danelowitz
WRITER
Howard Danelowitz
ART DIRECTOR
Howard Danelowitz
PRODUCTION COMPANY
New York Animation
CLIENTS
American Film Institute/NYSCA in association with Community Environments

"LADY TREE," AN ANIMATED FILM PARABLE ABOUT NATURE VERSUS THE FORCES OF URBANIZATION. AN INDEPENDENT PRODUCTION.
6 MINUTES

353

ANIMATOR
Pam Cooke
ARTIST
Steven Guarnaccia
DIRECTOR
Bob Kurtz
WRITER
Dan Altman
ART DIRECTOR
Bob Manley
AGENCY PRODUCER
Dan Altman
AD AGENCY
Altman & Manley
PRODUCTION COMPANY
Kurtz & Friends
CLIENT
MultiGroup Insurance
COMMERCIAL ANIMATED FILM TO ADVERTISE MULTIGROUP INSURANCE ENTITLED "WAITING ROOM." 30 SECONDS

354

ANIMATORS
Pam Cooke/
Gary Mooney
ARTIST
Steven Guarnaccia
DIRECTOR
Bob Kurtz
WRITER
Dan Altman
ART DIRECTOR
Bob Manley
AGENCY PRODUCER
Dan Altman
AD AGENCY
Altman & Manley
PRODUCTION COMPANY
Kurtz & Friends
CLIENT
MultiGroup Insurance
COMMERCIAL ANIMATED FILM TO ADVERTISE MULTIGROUP INSURANCE ENTITLED "STREET CORNER." 30 SECONDS

Index

Names and addresses of contributing artists. Index of designers, art directors, publications, publishers, design groups, advertising agencies, copywriters, animators, film directors, production companies, and clients

ARTISTS

Jeffrey L. Adams 298
95 Horatio Street
New York, NY 10014

Brian Ajhar 299
321 East 12th Street #30
New York, NY 10003

Maciek Albrecht 10
251 West 102nd Street
New York, NY 10025

Stephen Alcorn 208
Hamburg Cove
RFD 2, Box 179
Lyme, CT 06371

Julian Allen 11, 12, 13
31 Walker Street
New York, NY 10013

Terry Allen 14
291 Carroll Street
Brooklyn, NY 11231

Thomas B. Allen 15, 16
300 Art & Design
The University of Kansas
Lawrence, KS 66045

Marshall Arisman 17, 18, 19, 209
314 West 100th Street
New York, NY 10025

Michael Aron 210
c/o Pushpin, Lubalin, Peckolick
67 Irving Place
New York, NY 10003

Karen Barbour 300
51 Warren Street, #5
New York, NY 10007

Deborah Barrett 301
5630 Snake Road
Oakland, CA 94611

Catherine Bartholomew 302
145 Prospect Park West, Apt. V
Brooklyn, NY 11215

Kent H. Barton 20
11021 Lakeview N. Drive
Pembroke Pines, FL 33026

Bascove 21, 211
319 East 52nd Street
New York, NY 10022

Philippe Beha 22
5182 Avenue du Parc
Montreal, Quebec H2U 4G6

Jamie Bennett 23
56 Glen Manor Drive
Toronto, Ontario M4E 2X2

Nina Berkson 248
680 Bathurst
Toronto, Ontario M5S 2R3

Guy Billout 24, 25, 26, 27, 212, 234, 249
222 West 15th Street
New York, NY 10011

Paul Binkley 335
3008 Tyburn Street
Los Angeles, CA 90039

Patrick Blackwell 28
Pond Road
North Truro, MA 02652

R.O. Blechman 235, 350
2 West 47th Street
New York, NY 10036

Cathie Bleck 29, 30
1019 N. Clinton
Dallas, TX 75208

Braldt Bralds 31, 213, 280
455 West 23rd Street, #14B
New York, NY 10011

Steve Brodner 32
446 West 58th Street
New York, NY 10019

Lou Brooks 33
415 West 55th Street
New York, NY 10019

Salvador Bru 250
5130 Bradley Blvd.
Chevy Chase, MD 20815

Christine Bunn 34, 35, 36
485 Huron Street, #506
Toronto, Ontario M5R 2RJ

Trent Burleson 303
87 Hope Street
Providence, RI 02906

Gianni Caccia 351
1677 rue Beaudry
Montreal, Quebec H2L 3E8

Kirk Caldwell 281
1844 Union Street
San Francisco, CA 94123

Dave Calver 37, 38, 336
271 Mulberry Street
Rochester, NY 14620

Larry W. Carroll 39, 304
219 Grant Avenue
Cliffside Park, NJ 07010

Steve Carver 40
125 Giles Street
Ithaca, NY 14850

Ron Chan 282
1717 Union Street
San Francisco, CA 94123

Denise Chapman 41
4737 Aftonshire, #5
Houston, TX 77027

Bill Charmatz 42
25 West 68th Street
New York, NY 10023

Mark Chiarello 337, 338
380 2nd Street, #2R
Brooklyn, NY 11215

Pete Christman 43
c/o The Savannah College of Art and Design
342 Bull Street
Savannah, GA 31401

Seymour Chwast 44, 45, 214, 251
Pushpin, Lubalin, Peckolick
67 Irving Place
New York, NY 10003

Judy Clifford 46
24 West 90th Street
New York, NY 10024

Alan E. Cober 47, 48, 49, 50
95 Croton Dam Road
Ossining, NY 10562

Sue Coe 51, 52
214 East 84th Street, #3C
New York, NY 10028

John Collier 53
2309 Willow Circle Lane
Lawrence, KS 66044

Ray-Mel Cornelius 54
4512 Swiss Avenue, #3
Dallas, TX 75204

Michael Corris 305
129 Front Street
New York, NY 10005

James Costello 339
c/o American Illustration
67 Irving Place
New York, NY 10003

Jerome Couelle 55
41A Glen Road
Toronto, Ontario M4W 2V2

Neverne K. Covington 56
2919 56th Street South
Gulfport, FL 33707

Kinuko Y. Craft 57
c/o Fran Seigel
515 Madison Avenue
New York, NY 10022

John Craig 58
Route 2, Box 81
Soldiers Grove, WI 54655

Robert Crawford 59
340 East 93rd Street, #9I
New York, NY 10128

José Cruz 60, 61, 62
Cruz Graphic Designs
4233 McKinney, #5
Dallas, TX 75205

Tom Curry 63, 64
1802 West Sixth
Austin, TX 78703

Howard Danelowitz 352
New York Animation
200 West 79th Street
Suite 2C
New York, NY 10024

Peter de Sève 65
321 East 12th Street
New York, NY 10003

Blair Drawson 66, 67, 68
156 Waverly Road
Toronto, Ontario M4L 3T3

Henrik Drescher 69, 70, 71, 72, 306
318 East 6th Street, #55
New York, NY 10003

Andrzej Dudzinski 73, 74
52 East 81st Street, #4
New York, NY 10028

Nina Duran 75
114 East 84th Street
New York, NY 10028

Cameron Eagle 307
440 Prospect Avenue, #3R
Brooklyn, NY 11215

Sean Earley 76, 77
349 West 17th Street
New York, NY 10011

James Endicott 78
Route 1, Box 27B
Newberg, OR 97132

Randall Enos 79, 308
11 Court of Oaks
Westport, CT 06880

Robert Fassl 340
30961 Agoura Road
Westlake Village, CA 91361

Jeanne Fisher 236
235 East 10th Street
New York, NY 10003

Mark S. Fisher 309
233 Rindge Avenue
Cambridge, MA 02140

Vivienne Flesher 80, 81, 215
23 East 10th Street
New York, NY 10003

Jean Michel Folon 217
c/o Baumont du Gatinais
Burcy 77890 France

Bob Fortier 310
c/o Reactor Art & Design
51 Camden Street
Toronto, Ontario M5V 1V2

Dagmar Frinta 82, 83, 84, 85, 237
87 Hope Street
Providence, RI 02906

Nicholas Gaetano 216, 252
51 East 12th Street
New York, NY 10003

G. Allen Garns 311
3314 East El Moro
Mesa, AZ 85204

Audra Geras 86
44 Charles Street W.
Suite 4911
Toronto, Ontario M4Y 1R8

Chuck Gillies 253
c/o Skidmore Sahratian Inc.
2100 Big Beaver
Troy, MI 48084

Robert Giusti 87, 283
350 East 52nd Street
New York, NY 10022

Milton Glaser 217, 254, 255
Milton Glaser Inc.
207 East 32nd Street
New York, NY 10016

Bob Goldstrom 88
471 5th Street
Brooklyn, NY 11215

Scott Gordley 89
610 Cedar Swamp Road
Glen Head, NY 11545

Dale Gottleib 90
487 4th Street
Brooklyn, NY 11215

Alexa Grace 91, 92, 93, 312
70 University Place
New York, NY 10003

Gene Greif 284
215 West 10th Street
New York, NY 10014

Melissa Grimes 94
1904 Bremen
Austin, TX 78703

Steven Guarnaccia 95, 238, 313, 353, 354
89 Bleecker Street, #6B
New York, NY 10012

John Hagen 314
51 Manning Street
Providence, RI 02906

Michael Hampshire 96
2844 Wisconsin Ave. N.W.
Washington, D.C. 20007

Greg Harlin 97
c/o Stansbury, Ronsaville, Wood Inc.
1993 Moreland Parkway
Annapolis, MD 21401

Ron Hauge 98
221 Avenue B, #4
New York, NY 10009

Philip Hayes 99
5218 Pacific Avenue
Marina del Rey, CA 90292

Gary Head 315
3432 Gillham, #13
Kansas City, MO 64111

Jim Heimann 239
618 S. Western, #205
Los Angeles, CA 90005

Sandra Hendler 100
1823 Spruce Street
Philadelphia, PA 19103

John Hersey 101
1930 Hyde Street, #1
San Francisco, CA 94109

Lance Hidy 256
55 Boardman Street
Newburyport, MA 01950

Sandra Higashi 257
Neumeier Design Team
1421 Chapala Street
Santa Barbara, CA 93101

Fred Hilliard 258
c/o Sam Brody
230 E. 44th Street, #2F
New York, NY 10017

Brad Holland 102, 103, 104, 105, 106, 107, 108
96 Greene Street
New York, NY 10012

Gay W. Holland 341
1620 N. Wilmot, #L-206
Tucson, AZ 85712

Nigel Holmes 109
137 East 36th Street
New York, NY 10016

Thomas Hunt 110
c/o Reactor Art & Design
51 Camden Street
Toronto, Ontario M5V 1V2

Jeff Jackson 111, 112
c/o Bill Grigsby
Reactor Art & Design
51 Camden Street
Toronto, Ontario M5V 1V2

Christopher Jarrin 342
1474 Third Avenue
New York, NY 10028

Frances Jetter 113, 114, 218
390 West End Avenue
New York, NY 10024

David A. Johnson 115, 116
299 South Avenue
New Canaan, CT 06840

Lonni Sue Johnson 259, 285
2109 Broadway, #13-159
New York, NY 10023

Shelly E. Johnson 343
229 West 78th Street, #84
New York, NY 10024

Laura Karp 316
462 Greenwich Street
New York, NY 10013

Gary Kelley 117, 118, 260
Hellman Design Associates
1225 W. Fourth Street
Waterloo, IA 50702

Tim C. Kilian 240
3403 SW Corbett Avenue
Portland, OR 97201

Julia King 119
5502 Bonita
Dallas, TX 75206

Renee Klein 120
291 Carroll Street
Brooklyn, NY 11231

Barbara Klunder 286
c/o Stan Olthuis
Sharpshooter Studio
1179A King Street W.
Toronto, Ontario

Jean-Christian Knaff
121, 122, 261, 287
c/o Elvira Rychlak
3953 Avenue Laval
Montreal, Quebec H2W
2H9

George F. Kocar 123
2141 West 98
Cleveland, OH 44102

Jerzy Kolacz 124
c/o Reactor Art & Design
51 Camden Street
Toronto, Ontario M5V
1V2

Edward Koren 125
New York Magazine
25 West 43rd Street
New York, NY 10036

Stephen Kroninger
126, 127
250 West 10th Street,
GF3
New York, NY 10014

Mark Kseniak 128
219 East 81st Street, #4H
New York, NY 10028

Kuniyasu 129
339 East 9th Street, #4C
New York, NY 10003

Anita Kunz 130, 131,
132, 133, 262
230 Ontario Street
Toronto, Ontario M5A
2V3

Pamela Lee 219
2801 Keller Street
Modesto, CA 95355

David Lesh 134
6021 Rosslyn Avenue
Indianapolis, IN 46220

Birney Lettick 135
121 East 35th Street
New York, NY 10016

David Levine 136
c/o Forum Gallery
1018 Madison Avenue
New York, NY 10021

Ron Lightburn 137
401-270 Simcoe Street
Victoria, BC V8V 1K7

Ed Lindlof 220
603 Carolyn Avenue
Austin, TX 78705

John C. Long 138
P.O. Box 6311
Lincoln Park, MI 48146

Jeannette Louie 344
395 Broadway, #13C
New York, NY 10013

Dennis Luzak 241
Box 342
Redding Ridge, CT
06876

Matt Mahurin 139,
140, 141, 142, 143, 317
95 Horatio Street, #316
New York, NY 10014

Kam Mak 263
388 Pearl Street, #4B
New York, NY 10038

Richard Mantel 288
40 West 27th Street
New York, NY 10001

Mark Marek 144, 145,
146, 147, 148, 221
508 East 5th Street Apt. B
New York, NY 10009

John Martinez 222
55 Hudson Street
New York, NY 10013

Marvin Mattelson
242, 264
88 Lexington Avenue,
#12G
New York, NY 10016

Michael McGurl 318
83 8th Avenue
Brooklyn, NY 11215

James McMullan 243,
265, 266
Visible Studio Inc.
99 Lexington Avenue
New York, NY 10016

Eugene Mihaesco 149,
150, 151
25 Tudor City Place
New York, NY 10017

Wendell Minor 223
277 West 4th Street
New York, NY 10014

David Montiel 152
115 West 16th Street,
#211
New York, NY 10011

Leonard E. Morgan
289
1163 E. Ogden Avenue
Suite 705, Room 130
Naperville, IL 60540

Geoffrey Moss 153
315 East 68th Street
New York, NY 10021

San Murata 154
489 Parliament Street
Toronto, Ontario M5A
3A3

Alex Murawski 267
4900 Rowena
Austin, TX 78751

Joel Nakamura 319
622 Stratford Avenue
South Pasadena, CA
91030

Bill Nelson 155, 268,
269, 270
1402 Wilmington Avenue
Richmond, VA 23227

Barbara Nessim 156
240 East 15th Street
New York, NY 10003

Mel Odom 157
252 West 76th Street
New York, NY 10023

J. Rafal Olbinski 271
c/o Tania Kimche
470 West 23rd Street
New York, NY 10001

Frank Olinsky 320
Manhattan Design
47 West 13th Street
New York, NY 10011

Yves Paquin 224
4321 de Bordeaux
Montreal, Quebec H2H
1Z4

Mickey Paraskevas
345
228 Charlotte Terrace
Roselle Park, NJ 07204

**Robert Andrew
Parker** 158
c/o Ted Riley
215 East 31st Street
New York, NY 10016

**Pamela Higgins
Patrick** 272
410 S. Union Street
Kennett Square, PA 19348

Everett Peck 290
1915 Mill Road
South Pasadena, CA
91030

Judy Pedersen 159,
160, 225
96 Greene Street
New York, NY 10012

Mark Penberthy 161,
162
185 East 85th Street,
#35E
New York, NY 10028

Bob Peters 321
P.O. Box 7014
Phoenix, AZ 85011

Paola Piglia 163
100 West 87th Street,
#3A
New York, NY 10024

Bradley O. Pomeroy
273
2616 Redcoat Drive, #2C
Alexandria, VA 22303

Glenn Priestley 164
c/o Saturday Night
Magazine
70 Bond Street
Toronto, Ontario M5B 2J3

Greg Ragland 274
2497 Ridgeway Road
San Marino, CA 91108

Rallé 165, 166, 167, 322
35 Trudelle Street, #406
Scarborough, Ontario
M1T 1Z5

John Resi 346
Jaycox Road
Box 308
Cold Spring, NY 10516

Scott Reynolds 168
308 West 30th Street,
#9B
New York, NY 10001

Robert Rodriguez 226
618 S. Western, #203
Los Angeles, CA 90005

Phil Rose 323
Artery Graphic
1133 Broadway
New York, NY 10010

Richard Schlecht 169
2724 South June Street
Arlington, VA 22202

Michael Sell 227
253 West 72nd Street
#1014
New York, NY 10023

Lee & Mary Sievers
324
5516 Queen Avenue S.
Minneapolis, MN 55410

Collette Slade 170
99 Golden Hinde
Boulevard
San Rafael, CA 94903

Douglas Smith 171,
172, 244
405 Washington Street,
#2
Brookline, MA 02146

Elwood H. Smith 173,
174, 175
2 Locust Grove Road
Rhinebeck, NY 12572

Jeff Smith 176
255 E. Prospect Avenue,
#1B
Mt. Vernon, NY 10550

Lane Smith 177, 291,
325
355 South End Avenue,
#31C
New York, NY 10280

Edward Sorel 178, 228
156 Franklin Street
New York, NY 10013

Greg Spalenka 179,
180, 326
95 Horatio Street, #203
New York, NY 10014

Barton E. Stabler 292
407 East 77th Street, #1A
New York, NY 10021

Nancy Stahl 245
470 West End Avenue
New York, NY 10024

Dugald Stermer 181,
182, 183, 184, 229, 246
1844 Union Street
San Francisco, CA 94123

Randy Stevens 185
25 Edinboro Road
Boston, MA 02111

Barron Storey 186
852 Union Street
San Francisco, CA 94133

Mark Strathy 187
1438 Ocean Avenue
Brooklyn, NY 11230

Thomas Szumowski
293
17-1 Hammond Street
Waltham, MA 02154

Marla Tarbox 347
228 Beech Road
Newbury Park, CA 91320

James Thorpe 275
6503 Queens Chapel
Road
University Park, MD
20782

Bonnie Timmons 188,
189, 230
4085 West Floyd
Denver, CO 80236

Cathleen Toelke 276
c/o Katherine Tise
200 East 78th Street
New York, NY 10021

James Tughan 190,
191, 192
1179A King Street W.
Suite 310
Toronto, Ontario M6K
3C5

Paul D. Turnbaugh
193
7 N. Melrose Avenue
Elgin, IL 60120

Jean Tuttle 194, 195
220 East 29th Street, #3B
New York, NY 10016

Robert Tuska 327
127 First Avenue
New York, NY 10003

Ken Vares 277
208 Goodwin Street
Hayward, CA 94544

Roxana Villa 348
16771 Addison Street
Encino, CA 91436

Bill Vuksanovich 328
3224 N. Nordica
Chicago, IL 60634

Carol Wald 329
57 East 78th Street
New York, NY 10021

Susan Walp 231
57 Greene Street
New York, NY 10012

Andy Warhol 196
860 Broadway
New York, NY 10003

Philippe Weisbecker
197
21 West 86th Street,
#1606
New York, NY 10024

Michael Whelan 232
172 Candlewood Lake
Road
Brookfield, CT 06804

Charles White III 278
8383 Grandview Drive
Los Angeles, CA 90046

Mick Wiggins 198, 330
1051 Merced
Berkeley, CA 94707

David Wilcox 199
P.O. Box 232
Califon, NJ 07830

Michael Witte 200, 201
Voorhis Point
South Nyack, NY 10960

Efram Wolff 331
14535 Arminta Street "E"
Van Nuys, CA 91402

Rob Wood 294, 295
Stansbury, Ronsaville,
Wood Inc.
1993 Moreland Parkway,
Suite 201
Annapolis, MD 21401

Thomas Woodruff 202,
203, 204, 205, 206, 332
29 Cornelia Street, #17
New York, NY 10014

Paul Yalowitz 296, 333
598 Freeman Avenue
Brentwood, NY 11717

Lisa Young 334
545 West 111th Street
New York, NY 10025

DESIGNERS

Riki Allred 168
Ann Ames 262
Michael Aron 210
Bob Aulicino 225
Kent H. Barton 20
Tom Bentkowski 150
Gary Bernloehr 117
Robert Best 81
Patricia Bradbury 26, 37
Braldt Bralds 213, 280
Francis Brennan 249
Nancy Butkus 99
Kirk Caldwell 281
Ronn Campisi 18, 28, 73,
79, 83, 92, 113, 172
Sam Capuano 123
Roger Carpenter 226
Larry W. Carroll 39
Mary Challinor 84, 107
Charles Churchward 91
Seymour Chwast 214
John Cohoe 69
Alice Cook 72
Ron Coro 288
Neverne K. Covington 56
José Cruz 62
Tom Curry 64
Jolene Cuyler 11, 55, 124,
164
Wynn Dan 156
Jennifer Dossin 218
Stephen Doyle 120, 202
Nancy Duckworth 125
Louise Fili 211, 212, 222,
231
Louis Fishauf 110, 130,
175
Wayne Fitzpatrick 85
Patrick JB Flynn 70, 127

ART DIRECTORS

PUBLICATIONS

PUBLISHERS

DESIGN GROUPS

ADVERTISING AGENCIES

COPYWRITERS

ANIMATORS

FILM DIRECTORS

PRODUCTION COMPANIES

CLIENTS

AMERICAN ILLUSTRATION®

Every fall American Illustration, Inc. has a symposium on creativity which attracts people from all over the world. It is held in New York and one of the aspects on the agenda is the "Studio Visits" whereby students and professionals in the graphic arts field visit with illustrators, film animators, art directors, and designers in their studios.

If you would like to know more about this and other American Illustration® activities, or if you are a practicing illustrator, artist, or student and want to submit work to the annual competition, write to:

American Illustration, Inc.
67 Irving Place
New York, New York 10003
(212) 460-5558

Edward Booth-Clibborn
President

Lita Telerico
Managing Editor

THE COMMITTEE